Kevin Ray

How to Change Your Church Without Killing It

How to Change Your Church Without Killing It

By

ALAN NELSON AND GENE APPEL

WORD PUBLISHING

NASHVILLE

A Thomas Nelson Company

ISBN 0-8499-1660-7

Printed in the United States of America

00 01 02 03 04 05 06 BVG 6 5 4 3 2 1

CONTENTS

ACKNOWLEDGMENTS

Alan Nelson:

This book is dedicated to the Joshuas and Calebs of the world, faith-filled men and women who are unafraid to call things as they see them, who let us peek into promised lands of God's leading:

My creative wife, Nancy, who has been with me through so many of life's changes already and has been a spiritual model and mentor like no one else.

Our innovative team at Scottsdale Family Church, who put up with an innovative leader.

My friends Brad Smith, Sue Mallory, Greg Ligon, Bob Buford, and Dave Travis and the staff and clientele of Leadership Network and Leadership Training Network.

My friends Paul Allen, John Fanella, and Dave Thornton and the staff at Group Publishing.

My friends Jim Mellado, Cathy Burnett, Gary Schwemlein, Wendy Seidman, Kristen Gough, Joe Sherman, and Doug Yonamine and the staff at the Willow Creek Association.

My friends George and Nancy Barna and the staff at Barna Research.

Special thanks to my friend and teaching buddy Gene Appel, who is one of the most humble leaders I know (at least that's what he keeps telling me) and who partnered with me on this book while moving Nevada's largest congregation onto its new property.

Special thanks to the Beskinds and Ingrams, whose mountainside house and cabin are a writer's paradise.

Thanks to Shawn Bichler for graphics work and Jennifer Sturkie, who consulted on the conflict chapter.

Thanks also to Mark Sweeney, who patiently worked with three parties—us, Willow Creek Association, and Word—to make this project a reality.

Jeff, Josh, Jesse . . . *I love ya, men.*

Gene Appel:

I find it rather amusing that my name even appears on the cover of this book. God must get a good chuckle out of it too, because he and I both know this book is really the result of an incredible team of people.

You would not be holding this book in your hands were it not for my friend and coauthor Alan Nelson. Alan was the one who first approached me about a book on the hot-potato topic of church change. He took our experience at Central Christian Church, coupled it with his vast knowledge on leading change, and created the skeleton for this work. He contacted publishers, met deadlines, and was patient with me when I didn't. Plus, he did it all with grace, class, and Christlikeness. He's a passionate Christ follower, a courageous leader, and a writing machine. I'm so thankful our paths have crossed.

I would have no story to tell were it not for the courageous elders and staff of Central Christian Church in Las Vegas, Nevada. They have been consistently willing to dream, step out of their comfort zone, absorb criticism, and be open to the fresh breezes of change blown by the Holy Spirit. To know these change agents and their passion to advance the kingdom of God is to understand why God has honored their efforts. Every pastor should be blessed with a leadership team that is so easy to love.

It's hard to imagine what my life and ministry would be like without the mentoring, example, and friendship of Bill Hybels. His willingness to follow the Spirit's leading, think outside of the box, and create new paradigms to share an unchanging message in a rapidly changing culture have consistently taken me out of my own comfort zone. I know Christ better and see God's dream for his church with more clarity because of Bill's ministry in my life.

Next to Jesus Christ, the most gracious gift God has given me is my wife, Barbara. She makes our home a paradise and me a better person. When you're leading through difficult eras of change, it's great to be able to walk into a house of love, laughter, warmth, and support. She, along with our children, Jeremy, Alayna, and Jenna, are definitely *the Appels* of my eye.

It's impossible to write a book about church improvement without bursting with praise and thanksgiving for the heavenly Father, who is continually doing his transformational work of change in my own heart. While I serve a church that has navigated lots of changes, the more significant changes are the ones God has done inside of me. I'm well aware he has much more to do and am so grateful that his mercies are new every day.

Finally, I want to dedicate my contribution in this book to the people of Central Christian Church, who have allowed me the privilege of being a part of their family for nearly fifteen years. Thank you for being more concerned about advancing the kingdom of God than holding tightly to your own traditions and personal preferences. Thank you for not just saying you love lost people, but for moving in dramatic ways to reach them. Truly you are not just hearers of the Word, but doers also.

FOREWORD

I just love the local church. If I could express that thought more poetically I would, but words seem to fail me. After giving twenty-five years of my life to Willow Creek, I still find myself choking back tears at a baptism service or shaking my head in quiet wonderment as ever-increasing numbers of people gather around the Communion table. And I believe more strongly than ever that the local church is the hope of the world. What other institution stewards a message with eternity-altering power?

Sadly, most local churches are functioning at only a fraction of their redemptive potential. Too often, visions are fuzzy, values are undefined, and volunteers are unmotivated. Revitalizing defeated churches is a huge challenge. Turning around a Fortune 500 corporation would likely extract less blood from a leader. That's why this book is so terribly important. As we move into the twenty-first century, massive changes must be made in how we do church. Yesterday's approaches will not work tomorrow. We must learn not only what to improve, but how to make the transitions manageable. In other words, how can we remedy the flock's illness without making it sicker? God is going to have to raise up a whole new generation of church leaders who see themselves more as change agents than maintainers; pioneers instead of pacifiers. Alan, Gene, and Jim are such leaders. In their individual areas of influence, they have adapted their followers to new wineskins without confusing or compromising the timeless truths of the gospel message. They lived this book before they sat down to write it.

My prayer is that God will use this book to help you become the kind of leader who can lift your church to its full redemptive potential.

—BILL HYBELS
Senior Pastor, Willow Creek Community Church

PREFACE
A Word to the Leery and Those Who Lead Them

We uncover a great paradoxical truth. Change is hell. Yet not to change,
to stay on the path of slow death, is also hell. The difference is that the
hell of deep change is the hero's journey. The journey puts us on a path
of exhilaration, growth, and progress.

—ROBERT QUINN

I (Alan) admit it: My little boy, Jesse, is incredibly cute. In fact, he's been that way for nearly ten years now. You see, when Jesse was four, he mispronounced and used words in such a way that even the roughest person would grin at his adorability. He was compliant and the talk of the church. "What a cute boy," people would say. So, we began treating him in such a way to preserve that stage. Believe it or not, Jesse stopped growing. His vocabulary froze at the four-year-old level. He did not learn the alphabet or how to read. Now, when people ask how old our cute little boy is, they look queerly at us when we tell them fifteen.

Perhaps it is because other fifteen-year-olds are in ninth grade, getting ready to drive cars, and studying algebra. Maybe we have gone too far as parents, trying to preserve that cute phase, not wanting him to become something else. Who could fault us as parents? We're only trying to do what seems natural to us, to save him from the loss of freshness that often comes with growth and maturity.

Obviously, that kind of sordid tale is just that—a tale. Our little four-year-old is actually now six, and he's zooming in height, knowledge, and emotional development. We love our memories of Jesse's preschool years, but we don't want to hold him back. It's not about us; it's about him and what's right. We want him to develop, to grow and mature as any healthy person does.

If we agree that this is the appropriate course of action, why do we treat our churches differently from the way we do our children? Why do we try to preserve our memories and keep things the way they always have been for decade after decade? Like people, organizations need to grow and develop. To remain the same for long periods of time is unhealthy. To develop means that change will occur, that we will not be the same as we were the year before.

CHANGE IS INEVITABLE

The word *change* means to cause to turn or pass from one state to another; to vary in form or essence; to alter or make different. Do you realize that you cannot *not* change? You and I are not the same today as we were yesterday. We are a bit wiser, perhaps have less hair, are a day closer to eternity, and are deeper in a relationship or two. A church that is at one time in tune with its community, changes even when it stays the same; as the community evolves, the church is no longer in tune with its community.

Whether we realize it or not, pure status quo is a myth. Unfortunately, if everything but the church is changing, we are changing too, because we lose our grip of service and influence on society. Yet many people strive to perpetuate the myth, supposing that doing what we've always done somehow maintains the good old days.

Admittedly, change is difficult. While perpetual change is a part of Christian maturation, even those of us wired for continual progress still feel overwhelmed at times with the stress of adjustment. Whether it is a new character trait, a ministry project, or the transformation of a congregation, we all know that change can be a scary, perplexing, and sometimes negative experience. On the other hand, transitions can bring about the most exciting, liberating experiences in life.

If the word *change* seems negative to you because of fear or unfortunate experiences, we suggest that whenever you see the word in this book, you substitute the word *improvement*. Ultimately, our goal is to help churches and congregational leaders pursue betterment, or greater fruitfulness. We want to give you tools for making church improvement doable, effective, and lasting—with as little pain as possible.

THIS BOOK IS FOR

- People in plateaued or declining churches who already are convinced they want to change for the better.
- People in churches that are growing who know that they cannot continue with the same structure for effectiveness in an ever-changing culture.
- Pastors, staff, and congregational members who want to go about ministry improvement as a team and in a healthy format.
- Church change/improvement team members who may need some ideas as to what they want to improve and how to go about it.
- People in general who want a tool to bring about healthy organizational change and improvement.
- Those who are perfectly comfortable where they are in their church.
- People who want to understand the improvement process in order to sabotage it in their specific situation.

HOW TO USE THIS BOOK

This book is a synthesis of organizational and church change concepts and best practices. We have researched nearly forty books, read countless articles, and conducted numerous interviews to find ideas for implementing change in the local church. This book is designed specifically as a tool for leadership groups. Unlike most ministerial books, we are not writing specifically to pastors or priests. We are considering potential members of ministry improvement teams, which may include pastors, staff members, elected lay leaders, and informal influencers within a local congregation.

The content includes these ingredients:

- Real-life stories of churches that successfully navigated change and some that didn't; and lessons you can learn from each. Gene shares specific highlights (and low-lights) from his eventful and informative tenure at Central Christian Church in Las Vegas, Nevada.
- An array of exercises to put your new knowledge to work. Each chapter contains at least one wrench for your Application Toolbox, invaluable instruments that allow you to work through the improvement process in depth and at your own pace. A motivated leader can take an improvement team through this book, focusing on the application principles. This resource alone makes this book unique among most organizational change books and nearly all church change books.

- Instructions for developing a "Dream Team" of improvement-minded folks.
- Questions and Answers: Sometimes common issues arise from the content that can be answered best via a synthesized dialogue. Here we respond to questions you may have after absorbing and considering each chapter's content.
- Discussion Starters: Near the end of each chapter, we provide discussion questions that can be used to debrief teams, develop subsequent exercises, and stimulate further thought. Some questions may relate to you; others may not. Pick and choose the ones that are beneficial and use them as launch pads for deeper discussion.
- Contemplation: We want this book to be more than just a mental endeavor into organizational change in the local church. We as a faith community consider spiritual growth and guidance from Scripture and the Holy Spirit vital to our very existence. In order to help facilitate soul growth as a tool for improved ministry change, we provide a devotional centered on a Scripture and change issue.

USE THIS BOOK AS A TEAM TOOL

1. Give this book to formal and informal influencers in the church, people who have a heart for the ministry and who have at least a minimal sense that they want to improve as a church.
2. Designate a specific improvement team, whether it be a formally elected group or an informally selected team. Our recommendation is to avoid messy elections. Strive for selective invitations. Create an ad hoc Dream Team task force.
3. Establish regular meeting times to discuss and implement the ideas and tools in each chapter. Let the book become a low-cost consultant that can lead you through a process of introspection and reflection. This may begin with a focused retreat or weekly/monthly meetings or both.

SPARE SOME CHANGE?

Our prayers are that you and your leadership team will experience God in a new and powerful way as a result of working through these change issues together.

The local church is the primary vehicle entrusted with the saving and discipling grace of God's love. It is up to us to do whatever is necessary to become more effective and fruitful. The future of Christianity is in the hands of every generation, to promote the gospel or to drive it to extinction. Because our culture is so fluid, forcing us to reexamine and change our methods for reaching the lost, these are times of great opportunity.

Whatever you do, do not let church change become a divisive tool for the enemy to damage God's family. History shows us that God can salvage good things from even the worst scenarios we throw at him, but he is far from pleased with our fights and arguments. Keeping peace at all costs seldom results in change and progress, but if we can minimize the pain while pursuing the gain, we can see God's kingdom expanded.

The purpose of this book is to help you and your team develop a very constructive approach to what is often quite destructive: change and transitions. There is no need to fear the future or the changes it brings. The God we serve today is the very same God that Moses, David, the prophets, Jesus, and the apostles served. To the prophets, Calebs and Joshuas, and even the timid but obedient believers reading this book we say: *Go for it! Be strong. Dream new dreams. Honor the past, but do not live there. God has too much in store for us in the promised lands he has prepared for our churches!*

INTRODUCTION

I will build my church, and the gates of Hades will not overcome it" (Matt. 16:18). These words of Christ, spoken almost two thousand years ago, still ring true today. The transformed lives of millions of Christians stand as testimony to that end. The work of Christ through his body, the church, truly has prevailed and will continue to do so.

Jesus also said, "Go and make disciples of all nations, baptizing them in the name of the Father and of the Son and of the Holy Spirit, and teaching them to obey everything I have commanded you" (Matt. 28:19–20). This was the ultimate challenge Jesus left his followers. How is the church in the United States living up to that challenge today?

On the average—not so well. Apparently the gates of hell often do overcome local churches. Each year, estimates are that as many as 2,700 churches in the United States alone hold their last service, close their doors, and put up the "For Sale" sign.[1] Scores of others exist in a holding pattern, going through the motions of church, void of vitality, hoping only to keep the bills paid and attendees pacified. Why does this happen? How is it that a flame of passion for God and his purposes gets extinguished in a church over time? Looking at church history, why is it that there are so few examples of churches that indeed prevailed from one generation to the next?

During the last ten years, the combined membership of all Protestant denominations has declined 9.5 percent while the national population has increased 11.4 percent.[2] Average attendance in churches has declined from 104 persons in 1992 to ninety in 1999.[3] Half of all churches last year did not add even one new member through conversion growth.[4] And even though nearly four out of every ten adults attend a church on a typical Sunday, Baby Busters (those aged eighteen to thirty-four) are considerably less likely than older adults to attend services (28 percent compared to 51 percent of adults fifty-five or older).[5] The numbers don't lie: The younger the adult, the less likely he or she is to attend church. This does not bode well for the church of the next generation.

Secularization has to do with living life without the idea that God is alive and well in everyday life. Secularized people, for the most part, are completely insulated from church influences. In the fifties, the degree of secularization in our country was measured at 6 percent.[6] Today that figure has grown to about a third of our adult population.[7] That represents more than a 500 percent increase in that time period. The impact of the church on society is decreasing as well. Today, many churches remain open simply because the resources are there to keep the bills paid, even though they have no relevant connection or ministry to the people who appear on their membership rosters, much less to those in their communities. I can't imagine that was the initial vision of each church's founders.

WHAT HAS GONE WRONG?

I remember the sad history of a church I was part of that started out with vision and passion to reach lost people for Christ. To do that, the leaders of the church felt that "business as usual," in terms of approach, would not work well in that community. When the leaders put forth this challenge, the bickering, infighting, and division that ensued were nothing short of an embarrassment to the church. That church no longer exists today.

I believe that story is repeated over and over. What baffles me about the story is that the process involved well-meaning Christians. Why does this happen so often? How could a well-intended church with wonderful dreams end up closing its doors? The answer is painful but true: The leaders of that church, including myself, didn't know *how* to lead change in the church. We had the right hearts, but we didn't have the right strategy or expertise.

Where does your church stand today? How are things going? Is change needed? Has your church developed the right skills and abilities to follow God-inspired change if that were required? Is your church positioned to be even stronger in the next generation than in this one? When was the last time your church introduced a new pattern of church life to better reflect God's purpose for your ministry?

These are tough questions, but they are necessary. Change is not an option for churches. All churches either change to continue prevailing or they change by becoming irrelevant to people and eventually disappear. The passion behind this book is to help pastors, staff, and lay leaders, intentionally and with God's direction, lead their churches through positive change. Far too many church leaders unintentionally abdicate that responsibility because they are caught up in the current week-to-week activities of the church, which are challenging in and of themselves. Others feel overwhelmed by the daunting task of leading change in their church. The tragic result is that the life-and-death task of leading the church into the future does not happen and by default, natural drift occurs. And the church loses its effectiveness.

CHANGE IS MORE THAN A GOOD IDEA

I've participated as a member in eleven Bible-believing churches. I never remember a time when local church involvement was not a significant part of my life. I have great memories of people who discipled me along the way, from a small church in the poorest section of Managua, Nicaragua, to medium-sized churches of a few hundred and even thousands in the States, to Willow Creek Community Church, which is averaging about seventeen thousand in weekend attendance. Overall, my church experience has worked for me. I will always be indebted to those along the way who invested in me.

Most of the churches I was a part of were growing churches where God's Word was preached diligently, so I'm intrigued as to why I am so compelled to help churches learn how to improve. Maybe I should be trying to help churches maintain what they have. But I'm not, because the methods God used to reach me are ineffective to reach today's culture. History reflects that the church as a whole has prevailed in large part because leaders followed God-inspired change and implemented new biblical patterns of church life.

Too often what I see happening is that churches fall in love with their methods at the expense of their purpose. When the methods are no longer effective to accomplish their purpose, they can't change them because they are attached to the wrong thing (the method, not the purpose).

I have a lot of friends, neighbors, and community associates who don't know Christ. To one extent or another, that's true of every believer. My prayer is that someday it would be normal for churches to partner with their congregations to help them reach their lost friends and family members who need Christ. Those of us who have kids don't want to see our children grow up in the context of an increasingly anemic church. We want our kids to see the work of God through the local church as the most exciting place for them to invest their gifts and abilities for the glory of God. That won't happen if leaders refuse to lead appropriate improvement in their churches.

WHAT KIND OF CHURCH DO YOU LEAD?

Before you dive into this book, I want to invite you to make a quick, intuitive assessment of where your church stands right now. Hopefully this will give you a sense of the areas of church life on which you could focus initial improvement efforts as you go through this book.

The following diagram will serve as our guide in this exercise. The horizontal line represents different stages of spiritual development, starting with a cynic on the left and ending with a mature believer on the right. The graph reveals the kinds of people your church engages in its ministries regularly.

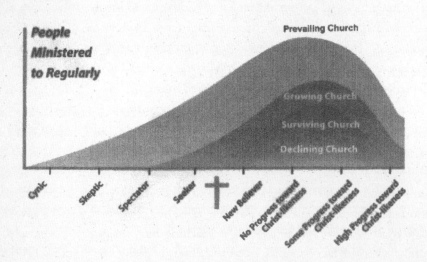

On this graph are the profiles of four kinds of churches. I've been actively involved in each kind. The first is the *Declining Church,* where hardly any new believers come to Christ. The Declining Church could go years without adding even one new unchurched person to its membership through conversion. Members rarely desire to come into meaningful contact with the world. Non-Christians seem more like the enemy than the object of God's love. These churches tend to be inwardly focused. Largely, church services offer more spiritual hygiene than life transformation. The average age of attendees in this kind of church is likely to increase over time.

The *Surviving Church* has some life. Its leaders preach the Word diligently and carefully. It has some good ministries that have developed over the years. This kind of church may be fairly good at reaching people for Christ after they have become a part of the church; that is, it is quite effective at evangelizing the kids of the parents who attend the church. At best, this church could grow at the rate of population increase. The Surviving Church is filled with people who have a sense that they should do better but just don't know how.

The *Growing Church* can be a really exciting place. It is lively, appeals to younger adults, and seems to be attracting new members at a fast pace. Preaching and teaching are likely strong. This church has many more ministries and programs that would be attractive to Christian families than does the Surviving Church. Its growth comes mostly from Christians moving their memberships from other congregations because of what this church provides.

In addition to transfer growth, this church has some evangelistic fires burning. A small number of gifted evangelists are being empowered to reach people for Christ because of visitation programs and evangelism training. Unfortunately, most members are more concerned with what the church can provide for them than what it can provide through them to their lost friends.

The Growing Church is usually investing in missions programs that have impact in various parts of the world. Some of the Growing Churches I was a part of as I grew up invested up to a fifth of their yearly budget to help bring seekers to Christ—but they were always seekers "over there," on the other side of the world. One Growing Church planted dozens of churches elsewhere that were also intended to lead seekers to Christ. All these projects were wonderful and important efforts. The problem was that all of our projects seemed to give us a false sense of satisfaction that we were reaching our evangelistic potential as a church, when in fact we were not even close to doing that locally. We were investing in missionaries to be trained in the language, traditions, and cultural norms of people on the other side of the world, but we were not effectively doing the same to reach the people we encountered routinely. This is the main distinction between the Growing Church and the *Prevailing Church*.

Prevailing Churches partner with their believers in a significant way to provide ministries that actively and regularly engage seekers on their spiritual journeys that lead them to Christ, in addition to spurring on believers in their spiritual journeys toward Christlikeness. The effect of doing both, actively and regularly, produces synergy, excitement, and energy as more believers get in the game and start viewing the church as the hope of the world. Something happens in a church when people see a known atheist come to Christ and grow up in him.

The most unique thing about this church is that its leadership has mobilized not only the few gifted evangelists, but also the average member to do the work of an evangelist—as the Bible instructs. Nonevangelist types are getting involved in evangelism. In *Becoming a Contagious Christian*, Bill Hybels and Mark Mittelberg describe this kind of church:

> These are churches where evangelism is a basic value held by most not just a few. Relationships with unchurched people are prioritized. Lost people are prioritized and their seeking process respected. Outreach is a part of the church's overall strategy. Seekers' questions are valued and addressed. Leaders model reaching lost people. Members are equipped to spread their faith. Various approaches to evangelism are celebrated. The efforts of individuals are supplemented by multiple church outreach events. . . . The relevancy of the Bible is emphasized and the Gospel never compromised.[8]

MAKING IT PERSONAL: DRAW YOUR OWN CHURCH

With each of these profiles in mind, intuitively draw a profile of your church and label it "Present State." Draw a curved line that reflects whom you are currently attracting and in what percentages. Remember to keep it at a local level. This is a profile of the people you think your church connects with directly in ministry on a regular basis. What does it look like?

Look at the profile you drew and let me ask you some questions. Are you satisfied with where you drew that line? How wide are the boundaries of your church? The Great Commission compels us all to build churches that are effective at reaching people wherever they are spiritually—even those who are secularized and very far from the cross. For many churches, improvement initiatives are needed to expand the reach of its boundaries, usually by starting new ministries that reach whole new people groups.

Let me ask: In your church, as it is now, are people on a journey toward Christ and maturity in him? To what extent is there spiritual activity in the right direction? It's not enough for your church to merely engage different people groups—you must see them come to Christ and get integrated in the community life of the church. Can you regularly tell stories of different people who started their journey to Christ at all points on the spiritual spectrum and who experience life change through God's work in your church? How many people who came to Christ through your church were cynics when they first visited? Skeptics? Spectators? Seekers? A Prevailing Church includes former members of all of these groups.

The Barna Research Group recently revealed this staggering fact: "Most people who come to Christ in American churches leave within the first eight weeks."[9] For some churches, the improvements needed are about developing and implementing better strategies and processes that attract all kinds of people to the local church.

But we can't stop there. The point is not just to have seekers in your church, but to bring them to Christ. And the more secularized the people are, the longer a process that's usually going to involve. The point is not to engage in ministry that keeps people where they are, but to challenge them with the claims of Christ, which leads to positive spiritual action. Consider the testimonials of those who have come to Christ in your church; see where their starting points were when they first came into your church. That will give you an indication of how far the reach of your church extends into the culture.

Is your church's profile dynamic or static? Is the boundary of your church expanding or shrinking? Is the ability of your church to relate to and connect with people, wherever they are spiritually, blossoming or shriveling? We all should be striving to continually grow the boundaries of our church ministries to include more and more different kinds of people, on both the evangelistic side and the disciple-making side.

Sometimes leaders recognize that their church needs to improve on the evangelism side, thinking their church is doing a great job on the disciple-making side. Yet Gallup's collective statistics on the state of the church do not back this up. In his book *The Saints Among Us,* Gallup documents that in spite of church attendance being fairly constant at 40 percent, he could detect a behavioral and attitudinal difference in only 13 percent of the people. That research, along with other data, compelled him to conclude that the faith of most people in the United States who claim to be Christians is shallow and not very significant in terms of impacting their behaviors.[10]

I know it's hard to manage the tension between reaching people for Christ and helping people become like Christ. At Willow Creek Community Church, the evangelistic fervor is running high. My commitment to personal evangelism has been rekindled. But right in the middle of all that, we are trying to grow our profile on the disciple-making side. John Ortberg, one of our teaching pastors, is leading that cause. He's asking such questions as, "I know that a lot of people have come to Christ here, but are we more loving than we were five years ago? Are we more joyful, patient, and kind? Do we have more peace in our lives? What does it mean to do something the way Jesus would if he were in our place? In short, are we truly becoming Christlike as people?" A Prevailing Church is one that is stretching to invite both the secularized seeker and the growing believer.

Take another inward look at your own church graph. Draw a second curve representing where you want your church to be in approximately five years. The distance between the two lines, the present and the future, is the issue to resolve. The challenge for your church is to discover how God wants you to close the gap. This book is about helping you transition your church to realize its potential as you envision it.

Jesus said that the gates of hell would not prevail against the church. For his words to remain true with each new generation, God calls people to be on the solution side of connecting his love to a changing world. He inspires church leaders to innovate new, biblical patterns of church life to better connect God's solutions to the needs of seekers and believers. From my vantage point as president of the Willow Creek Association, I'm encouraged to see a growing number of churches making these courageous adjustments to better reach people for Jesus and to grow them up in Christ. Some are making small changes, such as adjusting their church name and times of services. Others are making much more significant moves, such as changing worship patterns completely or adding other weekly services for evangelistic reasons, all in an effort to better realize their redemptive potential.

In the church, we don't change just for the sake of being on the cutting edge.

We change only because God would have us improve to better accomplish his purposes. Remember that something dies every time change happens. Sometimes the thing that dies was once vibrant, effective, and loved by many. At one time it may have been used to facilitate God's working in someone's life. It's hard to let something like that go—even if it's lost its usefulness. Along the way, you'll need to give honor to many things that don't fit in the new vision but that served everyone well in the past.

Improvement and change in the church, as in life, are serious and often painful processes. I remember my grandfather, who copastored a church in Mexico the last ten years of his life. Three years ago, he went to be with the Lord at the age of ninety-eight. As it became clear that illness was overtaking him, I resisted the change—the thought of losing him. I'll never forget my final encounter with him. I asked him about his life. He said that he wished I could have known him when he was strong and when his eyes and ears worked. He said, "We would have been friends—we would have liked each other, done ministry better together." And then he prayed for me and blessed my future ministry as the sun was setting on his. It was the last time I saw him. At the funeral, as difficult as it was, I could let his body go and watch them bury it because I knew he wasn't residing in that broken-down body anymore. He was in heaven.

In the same way that it wouldn't be right for me to cling to my grandfather's lifeless body, *it's not right for churches to cling to ineffective ways of doing things that are void of life.* Let them go. It may not be easy, but for Christ's sake, for the sake of lost people with broken lives who need healing, for the sake of believers who would love to be excited about what God is doing in their church, you have to do it. This book is intended to help in that change process. It comes at a critical time in the life of the American church. Everyone knows that our culture is changing at an alarming rate. The church must adjust to continue connecting the unchanging message of God's love with changing people.

I'm not sure where you are coming from as you pick up this book. Maybe you're a pastor in a thriving church but you sense in your spirit that improvement needs to happen. Your church needs to ratchet up to the next level. Perhaps you are pastoring a church where things aren't going very well and there is little doubt in your mind and heart that change is essential. You might be a passionate lay leader who is concerned that your church is heading in the wrong direction or even dying.

Whatever the case may be, my prayer for you as you read this book is three-fold. I ask that God grant you courage to ask tough questions and initiate God-directed improvement in your church; that he give you wisdom to know what and how to improve; and that he inspire you with perseverance to stay the course. May God's blessings and protection be on you and your congregation as you collectively strive to realize your church's redemptive potential.

—JIM MELLADO
President, Willow Creek Association

CHAPTER 1
Honest to God: Getting Real with Ourselves

I know that most people, including those at ease with problems of the greatest complexity, can seldom accept even the simplest and most obvious truth if it be such as would obligate them to admit the falsity of conclusions which they have delighted in explaining to colleagues, which they have proudly taught to others, and which they have woven, thread by thread, into the fabric of their lives.

—LEO TOLSTOY

LET US MAKE SOMETHING CLEAR RIGHT AWAY. We, the authors, don't have a beef with the traditional, institutional church. The reality is that each of us is a satisfied participant and product of the local church. We grew up in Christian families where our lives centered around church and its many activities. We're all grateful for the congregations of our youth—these faith communities introduced us to the love and grace of God. Our churches taught us how to pray, to be transformed by the Holy Spirit, to worship, to give, and to put our spiritual gifts into play. We experienced God and tasted Christian community and felt a part of his family. In our childhood churches, we caught a vision for investing our lives in the advancement of his kingdom. We know these were not perfect churches, but for the most part, they did things right.

We feel it is important that you understand we do not have an axe to grind with the churches of our youth. In fact, it's precisely because they did so many things right that we're writing this book. Our passion is to see these same churches, possibly similar to the one you attend, continue to be kingdom-advancing churches for many years to come. Our dream is to see these same churches be effective and responsive to the needs of people in an ever-changing world. Our hearts' desire is that for decades to come, these congregations will prevail, lives will change, hearts will be transformed, and believers will grow in devotion.

While we appreciate the way our churches introduced us to Christ, we also know that the world is teeming with millions who do not have the luxury or compulsion to know him as we do. We realize that the churches we grew up in will need to change to be effective and to express the gospel in the twenty-first century, to postmodern society. While we heard about Christ early in life because of our families and churches, millions of people today do not have that opportunity. Depending on the research you read, the United States is between the third and fifth largest mission field in the world, with more than 150 million not knowing Christ.[1] We know that the churches like the ones we grew up in will have to change and adapt in order to be effective in Great Commission duties. For many, it is more an issue of surviving, let alone thriving.

COMING TO TERMS WITH REALITY

So how is your church doing? Surveys show that the average American believes he/she is above average. What goes for individuals is true for churches. Most congregations of believers think of themselves as above average, but based on what criteria? Let's take that question to the North American church at large. The most recent data show some alarming trends in recent years, in spite of the typical churchgoer's belief that all is well.

Between 1997 and 1998, average adult church attendance dropped 10 percent. Giving to the average church annual operating budget decreased 15 percent from 1997 to 1998. Most pastors (67 percent) agree that their churches are committed to doing as much as possible to bring about spiritual revival, and 54 percent believe that revival is taking place, but less than 1 percent have revival as an objective. Perhaps the most disturbing trend of all is that the younger the age group of Americans, the less they attend church. As many as 85 percent of churches are plateaued or declining. Only 1 percent are growing primarily because of reaching the lost, which means that 14 to 19 percent are growing because of transfer growth from the declining congregations.[2]

Here are some other trend bullets noted by Christian researcher George Barna:

- Fifty percent who attend church on any given Sunday are not Christians but have been attending that church for ten years.

- Sixty-five percent of Christians will die without ever sharing their faith.
- Half a trillion dollars spent in domestic ministry has resulted in no increase in percentage of adult believers.
- Only 10 to 15 percent of churches are highly effective (meaning that they competently complete strategic tasks, challenge people spiritually so that they become more Christlike, and address intentional spiritual development, faith sharing, resource management, worship, relationship building, and community service).[3]

The sad reality is that with each generation, the American church is becoming less effective. If the church is unable to navigate change and communicate the gospel to a changing world, our grandchildren and great-grandchildren may have little chance of attending a vibrant congregation. We must stop the denial and face the facts.

CENTRAL CHRISTIAN CHURCH: OUR STORY

Identifying the Need for Change

Let me set the scene for you. It was 1985. I (Gene) was a twenty-five-year-old, newly hired senior pastor from Illinois, where I had served as a youth pastor. Central Christian Church was a solid, biblical, conservative church of about 450 in the growing desert city of Las Vegas. The only thing I was certain of in those days was my calling; no doubt, God sent me to Central Christian Church. I feel confident of this because I know the church leaders turned down several more experienced, educated, proven, and logical candidates. Three of them were Bible college presidents! I didn't think I had a chance. When I got the job, I knew God had spoken.

After landing in Las Vegas and getting oriented, I took stock. From most outward appearances, Central Church seemed to be a healthy, thriving, vibrant congregation. For many, our church had become a sort of fortress from the renowned worldliness of "Sin City." A spirit of enthusiasm exuded from the people. By most measuring sticks, we looked successful. Settling in for a season of complacency would have been an easy thing to do. But then we began asking that irritating question—a question that forced us to look behind the growing attendance in our services, an expanding church staff, and the numerous programs that necessitated additional expansion of our facilities. It's hard to believe that one simple question can lead to so many sleepless nights, agonizing prayer sessions, and difficult conversations. Who would have thought such an innocently asked question would be the catalyst for a transformational change in the life of a church and its leaders?

In the midst of our busy, expanding ministry, we took time to ask, "How does our local church measure up against the biblical purpose of Christ's body?" Ouch! The answer surprised and stung us. As we looked closer at our church's growth, it became evident that although Central was enlarging, the kingdom of God was not expanding in our corner of the world. The majority of our increasing numbers were already convinced believers. They were joining our ranks because they appreciated the Bible teaching, the music, and the ministry to our children and youth. Most of the conversions taking place at Central were among the children of the existing members. The data could not be ignored: Our ministry did not seem to reflect God's heartbeat for seeking the lost and helping the unchurched develop a personal relationship with Christ.

What an eye-opening, sobering experience for church leaders who could have easily patted themselves on the back for having a church that was growing in numbers. We were making sacrifices, giving money, and praying, and the sum total amounted to very little profit in terms of kingdom growth. Our numbers increased, but as we say in Las Vegas, we were just reshuffling the deck.

Something needed to change, but what? Obviously, our methods for advancing God's work were not as effective as we thought. Perhaps the most painful discovery of all was what we learned about ourselves. The temptation existed to feel good about achieving what so few do in church life—a growing congregation of several hundred. The natural tendency was to flatter ourselves, not to think we were missing the mark. After all, by effectively growing existing Christians, at least we were accomplishing half of the Great Commission (Matt. 28:19–20). An increasing number of believers were deepening in their faith toward maturity in Jesus Christ, weren't they?

But we began to realize that if our spiritual maturity did not foster a sincere passion and ministry for lost people, then maybe we were not as mature as we thought. Another big ouch! The time had come to repent of our self-centeredness and complacency. The winds of change began blowing in our hearts. We humbled ourselves and asked God to make us more like the church that Jesus envisioned us to be. The adventure of change and improvement was about to begin.

BLACK SHEEP AND HOW TO REACH THEM

One Sunday morning during a summer vacation, my family and I (Gene) were seated in the back of a church in a small Midwest town. A couple sitting in front of us got our attention. They were twenty-something bikers. He was wearing a Harley Davidson T-shirt and jeans. His long hair hadn't had time to dry from his morning shower. She had a number of tattoos and long black hair in dreadlocks. They not only looked out of place in this conservatively dressed church; you could tell they felt out of place. It was obvious that they were not there because they wanted to be. They seemed bored stiff.

A family reunion evidently was the occasion behind the visit. You could tell the biker's mom and dad felt good to have all their children in church. There sat the other brothers and sisters with their spouses and children. The biker appeared to be the black sheep in the family.

I started hoping and praying that there would be something in the service that would connect with the bikers, something that would help them discover how much they mattered to God and to what extent Jesus had sacrificed for them. But everything about the service seemed wrong. We sang all five verses of an eighteenth-century hymn. I watched them trying to follow in the hymnal, but the lyrics were full of strange words. (In fact, I didn't understand them either.) The musical style must have seemed foreign to them. A women's trio then sang a bouncy, harmonized gospel song, but the biker couple did not seem to have listened to much trio music.

My heart was breaking. Here were people who desperately needed to hear biblical truth and the message of a cross, but they needed it to be presented in a way that they could understand. The theology was accurate and biblical, but the methodology prevented effective communication.

I don't know the parents of that biker I sat behind in church. My guess is that they personally would not have favored the church using more contemporary styles of music and communication such as drama or video. But if that kind of service could reach their family members, I know they would have eagerly embraced it. Wouldn't you? Wouldn't you be willing to change and adapt so the message of the saving grace of Jesus Christ could reach your own family?

The apostle Paul said that he would "become all things to all people" in order to reach folks from different backgrounds and beliefs. Shouldn't we do the same? We can stick our heads in the sand and deny there is a problem, but it won't change the fact that the average church is in crisis and is unprepared to do ministry in a rapidly changing world.

George Barna warns, "The church in America is losing influence and adherents faster than any other major institution in the nation. Having devoted the last eighteen years of my life to studying the American people, their churches, and the prevailing culture, I've concluded that within the next few years America will experience one of two outcomes: either massive spiritual revival or total moral anarchy."[4]

Like Barna, Mike Regele examines cultural trends and social demographics. In his book *Death of the Church,* he writes:

> What about the literally thousands of churches across America in which no progressive strategies are attempted? Let's be frank. In reality, many of them will not see the dawn of the twenty-first century. Many more will pass away by the end of the first decade. We have looked at the demographics. There is no future for most. Let's stop the denial!
>
> No one wants to close a church. There is something fundamentally wrong about it. We feel as if we have failed. Making matters worse, those remaining in churches that need to close are inevitably dear old saints. The prospect of "taking their church away from them" doesn't make any of us feel particularly heroic! So we . . . tell ourselves a little tale that goes like this: "When people get older, they come back to church. We just need to wait for the young people to come and care for all these little churches."
>
> But the changes transforming our world reflect more than the fact that the young have temporarily wandered away to "sow their oats." They are not coming back. . . . The place and role of the church in America has changed. . . . We just haven't accepted our death yet.[5]

The churches in which we grew up ministered in communities where many of the basic life and spiritual issues had already been settled. Most people had a fundamental awareness of and belief in God. They possessed an appreciation and respect for the Bible as a sacred book and a source of absolute truth. They even had an understanding that Jesus was the Son of God. It was not uncommon for nonbelieving people in these communities to come into our churches, hear a gospel sermon, and respond immediately like folks did on the day of Pentecost.

But today, our communities more closely resemble the religious texture and atmosphere of cities like Athens and Corinth. The apostle Paul didn't just stand up and preach one sermon to draw in all the unsaved; evangelism was more of a process. Bridges had to be built. Lack of an appreciation of the Scriptures as a divinely inspired source had to be overcome. Paul had to present the one way, one truth, and one life that come only through Jesus to a culture that believed in many gods and many ways to heaven. Evangelism was not impossible. But the style and technique that had been used in Jerusalem would not be effective in places like Athens and Corinth.

At the dawn of a new millennium, the church is facing a similar communication challenge. Our communities reflect Athens and Corinth. Our methodologies for ministry reflect Jerusalem. The result is a huge disconnect between thousands of churches and the people who live in the communities where we minister. The implications are that unless we learn to communicate more effectively with people, a whole generation may be unable to understand the gospel.

Improvement Story: Crossings Community Church, Oklahoma City

In the fall of 1985, Crossings (then called Belle Isle) Community Church called associate pastor Marty Grubbs to lead their church. The twenty-two-year-old congregation averaged 143 in Sunday morning worship when Marty took the helm. This traditionally-styled church seemed open to making changes: "We've never had any significant fallout or real power struggle as we have tried to bring about improvements over the years," Marty reports. Some of the changes included replacing the Sunday evening service with home Bible studies, which helped make Christianity more relational and less event oriented. They also added Bible study and discipleship class electives to Wednesday evening prayer meeting as well as a dinner option so that people could come right from work to church. They did not do anything drastically or quickly, but they relied heavily upon gradual education and dialogue. They made sure the leaders were pretty much united before embarking in a new direction.

Marty says, "I didn't change the worship style a lot, but I did change my preaching toward a more seeker-sensitive style. But one of the biggest breakthroughs happened because of a personal event. My parents divorced after thirty years of marriage and ministry. This was very painful for the two of them as well as all who loved them.

"One day, a parishioner invited me to attend a twelve-step program with him. I thought, I'm not an alcoholic. Why would I need to go there? But I went and heard a group of people bare their souls, share their stories, and accept each other, even without the mention of the Bible or Jesus. I realized that our church did not offer that. I knew that I wanted to pastor a congregation where that kind of love and acceptance were part of our everyday culture. I soon did a Sunday morning series based on the twelve steps, and the people responded very well."

The congregation also responded well to the leadership's improvements in quality and attitude. Crossings' resultant growth has been gradual but consistent: Today services minister to 2,500 and the congregation has moved into new facilities on a seventy-seven-acre campus.

Improvement Lessons:

- Personal experiences and brokenness in leaders can be great tools to bring about change and improvement in congregations. Make the most of what God places in your path and does in your heart.
- Consensus building is vital. If you expect an idea to work, develop it with others' input. Don't spring surprises on people.

A SIMPLE VISION—WITH UNCOMFORTABLE IMPLICATIONS

What would happen if thousands of churches had a love for lost people so great that they would be willing to obey whatever God led them to do to communicate his love in ways that people could grasp, accept, and grow in? Imagine what would happen in your church if you and other key leaders were willing to change anything except the unchanging message of the gospel in order to build bridges to your community.

That's what your missionaries do, isn't it? Your church probably supports missionaries who serve in faraway places. These servants understand that they must build a bridge of communication and earn respect if they are to share the greatest story ever told. These missionaries no longer dress the way they used to before entering the foreign culture. They no longer speak the same dialect they grew up with. They no longer practice the same cultural customs and eat the same foods. Their love for Christ and the people of these cultures compels them to adapt. It's exciting to hear the stories of how lives change once the missionaries learn to communicate in the language and customs of the culture.

Trying to communicate to a foreign culture is a challenge. The Dairy Association's huge success with the campaign "Got milk?" prompted its leaders to expand advertising to Mexico. It was soon brought to their attention that the Spanish translation read, "Are you lactating?" In another advertising faux pas, Clairol introduced the "mist stick," a curling iron, into Germany, only to find out that "mist" is slang for manure.[6] The application is clear: In order to communicate the gospel effectively in our changing Western culture, churches must begin to think of themselves as strategic missions in foreign territories. Church leadership teams must begin to think of themselves as missionaries learning the language and customs of a vastly different culture.

And—this is important—we must not assume that people are less interested in the gospel than they once were. Their perceived lack of receptivity is actually an indication that we are not communicating effectively. The postmodern community is not resistant or maliciously silent. They just can't understand our lingo. We must adjust to them, not expect them to adjust to us, to get our message across.

While Jesus Christ is the same yesterday and today and forever (Heb. 13:8), the message endures but the methods must adapt. While the apostle Paul wrote his books with a quill and papyrus, we are using laptop computers with e-mail and laser printers. Paul shouted above the noise of the marketplace. We use cordless lapel microphones. He wore a toga. Aren't you glad we don't? Same message; different culture. Different times call for different methods.

The business world has learned to be responsive to the needs of the consumer. Huge companies like Sears are dropping proven branches of business such as mail order so they can compete in the twenty-first century. Dot-com companies are flooding the Internet to capture their market share of cyberspace consumption. Corporations such as Wal-Mart are now using computers that allow them to analyze day-to-day marketing across the country for ordering new products, pushing certain items, and keeping costs ultra competitive. These pursuits allow retailers and wholesalers to stay current with cultural shopping tastes. If businesses can be so responsive in order to make a profit, why shouldn't those of us in the church learn to be as sensitive and responsive to the culture around us? Souls are hanging in the balance!

Reevaluating how to communicate and connect with people does not mean we water down the gospel. It does mean we value God's command to reach people so highly that we do whatever it takes to creatively reach the lost.

THE URGENCY OF THE MOMENT

If current trends continue, with young people showing disinterest in the church and the message of Christianity, thirty years from now church attendance among those born today will hardly be measurable. Therefore, at this pivotal moment, we have an opportunity to partner with God and alter the course of history. If we are open to being catalysts for change and to being changed by the power of the Holy Spirit, we can reenergize, refocus, and renew our churches. We can reach this soon-to-be-lost generation. Wouldn't it be something if your church—with its rich past, committed people, and strategic resources—could be reignited for a new era of ministry at the start of this new millennium? That is the vision we are committed to, and we can help you on this journey.

In a speech given at the Nazarene Conference on Evangelism held in Kansas City in January 1999, Haddon Robinson reminded us of a biblical account that highlights the problematic mindset of many in churches who are overly attached to ways of the past. According to Numbers 21, during Moses' ministry God sent a plague of snakes that bit scores of people. When the people cried out to God, he told Moses to cast a bronze snake and raise it on a pole. Anyone who looked at it was healed from snakebite.

Seven hundred years later, Israel had forgotten the purpose behind the bronze snake, had strayed from God, and had elected to worship this God-given symbol. Fortunately, a godly king named Hezekiah arose who saw the danger of this practice: "[Hezekiah] did what was right in the eyes of the LORD, just as his father David had done. He removed the high places, smashed the sacred stones and cut down the Asherah poles. He broke into pieces the bronze snake Moses had made, for up to that time the Israelites had been burning incense to it" (2 Kings 18:3–4).

Throughout history, people have taken the new thing God was doing and elevated it to an unhealthy level, so much so that their affections became attached to the method instead of to God. The bottom line is, change is good—change is essential. But it is often met with resistance. When Jesus suggested that healing on the Sabbath was okay, the response of religious leaders was, "We've never done that before." Thanks to Martin Luther and the Guttenberg press, the masses could have their own Bibles, an uncomfortable first for the church leaders. When Charles Wesley put words of worship to the barroom tunes of his day, it seemed sacrilegious. We now call them hymns. When John Wesley suggested we confront old ways and adopt a new style of evangelism and discipleship, he was disallowed to speak in church buildings and forced into the fields of England. Thus began the Methodist revival. When Robert Rake, the initiator of Sunday school, suggested we begin teaching boys and girls how to read and write by using the Bible on Sunday mornings in church, he was considered a radical.

Throughout the ages, the diffusion of innovation cycles from rejection to gradual acceptance to popular acceptance to enshrinement and refusal to let go. As Haddon lovingly reminded us, when good snakes become bad snakes, they need to be destroyed.

THEOLOGY OF NEW, NOT NEW THEOLOGY

The Bible is full of creative, innovative approaches that God employs, some of which are logical, while others seem quite far-fetched. A multitude of biblical scenarios show God implementing or commanding a unique approach and the people responding, "We've never done it that way before." Countless Mosaic events, from the plagues to crossing the Red Sea, to getting food and water in the desert, indeed had never been done that way before. Abram and Sara's geriatric-spawned child, Jericho's fall, Sodom and Gomorrah's destruction, David's giant slaying, Gideon's army of three hundred, Jonah's sea salvation, Jesus' miracles, and a seemingly endless list of God-inspired actions throughout history ought to convince us that we must think outside the box. God refuses to be hemmed in by man-made ideas and even past proven methods. His newness continues long beyond creation. What haven't changed over the centuries are his desire to do new things and our human nature to resist.

A brief "theology of new" is an important consideration as we embark on improvement strategies within church life. God is frequently doing new things as well as old things in new ways. New means different, that which is not redundant or familiar. Certainly not all new and different ideas are God's. But unless they transgress biblical fundamentals, we cannot immediately prove they are not his, because he so often talks about new things in his Word.

> Sing to the LORD a new song;
>   sing to the LORD, all the earth. (Ps. 96:1)

Sing to the LORD a new song,
for he has done marvelous things;
his right hand and his holy arm
have worked salvation for him. (Ps. 98:1)

See, the former things have taken place,
and new things I declare;
before they spring into being
I announce them to you. (Isa. 42:9)

Forget the former things;
do not dwell on the past.
See, I am doing a new thing!
Now it springs up; do you not perceive it?
I am making a way in the desert
and streams in the wasteland. (Isa. 43:18–19)

Behold, I will create
new heavens and a new earth.
The former things will not be remembered,
nor will they come to mind. (Isa. 65:17)

"The time is coming," declares the LORD,
"when I will make a new covenant
with the house of Israel
and with the house of Judah." (Jer. 31:31)

Because of the LORD's great love
we are not consumed,
for his compassions never fail.
They are new every morning;
great is your faithfulness. (Lam. 3:22–23)

I will give them an undivided heart and put a new spirit in them; I
will remove from them their heart of stone and give them a heart of
flesh. (Ezek. 11:19)

Therefore, O house of Israel, . . . Rid yourselves of all the offenses you have committed, and get a new heart and a new spirit. (Ezek. 18:30–31)

Neither do men pour new wine into old wineskins. If they do, the skins will burst, the wine will run out and the wineskins will be ruined. No, they pour new wine into new wineskins, and both are preserved. (Matt. 9:17)

The people were all so amazed that they asked each other, "What is this? A new teaching—and with authority!" (Mark 1:27)

For this reason Christ is the mediator of a new covenant, that those who are called may receive the promised eternal inheritance—now that he has died as a ransom to set them free from the sins committed under the first covenant. (Heb. 9:15)

A new command I give you: Love one another. As I have loved you, so you must love one another. (John 13:34)

We were therefore buried with him through baptism into death in order that, just as Christ was raised from the dead through the glory of the Father, we too may live a new life. (Rom. 6:4)

But now, by dying to what once bound us, we have been released from the law so that we serve in the new way of the Spirit, and not in the old way of the written code. (Rom. 7:6)

Your boasting is not good. Don't you know that a little yeast works through the whole batch of dough? Get rid of the old yeast that you may be a new batch without yeast—as you really are. For Christ, our Passover lamb, has been sacrificed. (1 Cor. 5:6–7)

Therefore, if anyone is in Christ, he is a new creation; the old has gone, the new has come! (2 Cor. 5:17)

You were taught, with regard to your former way of life, to put off your old self, which is being corrupted by its deceitful desires; to be made new in the attitude of your minds; and to put on the new self, created to be like God in true righteousness and holiness. (Eph. 4:22–24)

A FONDNESS FOR THE FAMILIAR

Most of us find ourselves emotionally drawn to what is familiar—what is perceived dependable based on past experience, and comfortable. Psychologists say it is related to conditioning. We are therefore leery of the new, different, and unproven. But this natural inclination becomes a spiritual matter when we end up subtly placing our faith not in God, but in the familiar. Even sincere religious practices can become the object of our worship. The only truly safe place to be in the Christian walk is smack-dab in the middle of God's will; when his will leads us to new methods and modes of ministry, we disobey him by staying with old, timeworn forms. Christian obedience is a current affair, not yesterday's headlines, and our lack of responsiveness to accept God's new ideas results in what it has always been throughout history: sin.

Our primary goal with this book is to encourage you to hear God, the God who does new things, not the god of familiarity. Our secondary and more obvious goal is to encourage you to trust God when you hear him instructing you toward a new path and to provide processes for making that new path a reality in your faith organization. Spiritual growth is both a direct and an indirect result of putting your faith in God, regardless of where he takes you. When we allow our faith

> One doesn't discover new lands without consenting to lose sight of the shore for a very long time.
>
> —ANDRE GIDE

to become rooted in the routine, we run the high risk of missing out on great fruit.

QUESTIONS AND ANSWERS

Q: We're not growing, but we feel we are pretty healthy. What defines church health?

A: Healthy systems do not exist merely to exist, but to be fruitful. The main questions to ask are:

Is our church obeying the Great Commission command to make disciples, teaching them to obey what God wants?

Is our congregation bearing good fruit? If so, what fruit and how do we measure it?

What kind of people is our church producing?

What is the cumulative personal growth among the individuals attending over time?

Are new people being led to Christ, and do they continue to mature through discipleship?

Naturally, there will be variance in the responses to these questions, but honesty and fruit inspection are stewardship issues. Denial is a strong temptation both personally and corporately.

While you can use this book for many improvement processes, our bias as the authors is that healthy churches are growth oriented and prioritize reaching the lost as a significant part of their purpose. We agree that cultural relevance is essential to creating a vibrant, health-oriented congregation. If we become too disconnected from our culture, we have little hope of building bridges between our society and God. The redemptive responsibility of the church is to be salt and light within our communities. While change principles are somewhat generic from organization to organization, our passion is to ignite the light of church leaders to see how they can become even more fruitful than they are presently.

Q: Are you advocating that every church should be a big church?

A: Size is not the issue; health is. We do not believe that every church is called to be a large congregation. We have been associated with large churches that were not healthy in terms of reaching the lost in their community and communicating with relevance. Big churches can become dinosaurs just like any other church if they do not improve themselves regularly. Also, some people will never feel comfortable in a large congregation because of the way they are individually wired.

God is not redundant. He has a unique place for each congregation in a given community. Too much emphasis is often placed on the super-growth models of local congregations that create undo pressure on others to "perform." Churches of one thousand or more in attendance make up a miniscule fraction of total congregations.

Knowing who you are to be as a local church is an important issue in terms of priorities and improvement issues. We offer the principles in this book not so much to make every congregation into a megachurch, but rather to help congregations that want to get better do so with maximum effectiveness and minimal pain and waste. Every church, no matter its size, is vital to reach the unreached in our communities.

Q: Some people suggest that traditional churches should be closed or replaced with church plants or contemporary-style congregations. What do you think?

A: While we have similar opinions as to what it means to be a relevant church in the twenty-first century, we are not advocating any specific style or program. If we put too much emphasis on one specific model, we will mislead. Models become dated and do not always fit the situation in which a church finds itself. Each leadership team must determine what relevance means in its ministry context. The decision you make will ultimately result in how effective your congregation is in reaching its community and discipling those within the church.

We are not against pipe organs, hymnals, ceremony, or tradition. We are for relevance and effectiveness. By promoting effectiveness, we do not suggest achieving gain at all costs. We do not believe there is a need to compromise on the basic tenants of the Bible or Christianity in order to bear fruit. At the same time, we know that many traditional congregations are designed to be productive in social settings reflective of the fifties through seventies—not the twenty-first century—in America. The goal of this book is to guide leadership teams through the process of determining what they need to become and then pursuing that direction as efficiently as possible.

The solution is not to plant churches *or* renovate existing congregations; rather it is to plant churches *and* renovate existing congregations. Church planting is a high-risk venture, with most church starts being led by pastors who are not entrepreneurial, leading core people who are not highly committed and/or unified, and using resources that are undercapitalized. While funding alone never results in a vibrant congregation, it is one significant factor, along with a pastor who is a visionary leader in a place that is responsive to the type of ministry he/she is striving to begin. Church planting is the best proven way to reach the unchurched, but a majority of church plants fail. Existing congregations that catch the vision for improvement are better examples of stewardship, where people and resources are already in place. The challenge is getting these congregations to understand and adopt change strategies in order to renew themselves.

Q: Our church seems to have a significant group of people who want to keep things as they are, as well as a group of folks who want to see change. How do you suggest we begin to get on the same page to work through this book?

A: Nothing beats prayer and seeking the guidance of the Holy Spirit to develop an attitude of unity and humility. Most congregations get into trouble because they do not begin from common ground. The process is just as important as the outcome. In fact, if you overlook the process, you will often not even get to the preferred outcome.

One of the most important principles for learning is to reserve judgment. Our judgments at the front end tend to close our minds to ideas that can unleash great potential.

Differences of opinion need not be feared. If you seek unanimity before moving forward, you'll hardly ever go anywhere. Do not confuse differences in opinions with disunity. The Bible teaches us that the body of Christ is filled with different parts and different functions. Recognizing that you're not all on the same page at this time is fine, but pursuing an honest, loving attitude toward learning something new is essential. We encourage leadership teams to dedicate a significant amount of time to prayer before and during discussion of change. Also make room for significant ways to communicate love and acceptance of each other in the process, so that you never give the idea that you value ideas more than individuals.

> Deep change requires more than the identification of the problem and a call for action. It requires looking beyond the scope of the problem and finding the actual source of the trouble. The real problem is frequently located where we would least expect to find it, inside ourselves. Deep change requires an evaluation of the ideologies behind the organizational culture.
>
> —ROBERT QUINN

APPLICATION TOOLBOX

Using this graph, plot the Sunday morning worship (adults/children/youth) attendance monthly over the last three years.

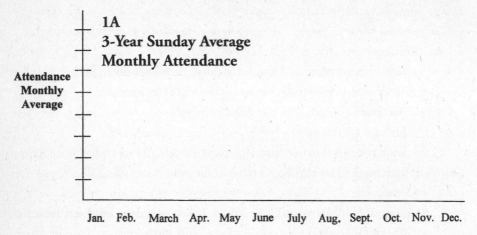

Then use this graph to plot the Sunday morning worship attendance annually over the last ten years.

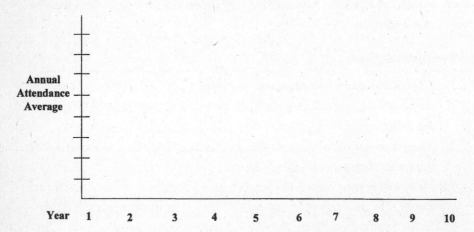

Respond to the questions on the following page by using the following scale:

1. Strongly disagree
2. Disagree
3. Neither agree nor disagree
4. Agree
5. Strongly agree

In my church:

_____ The church culture values conservative, cautious decisions.

_____ Most of the changes we see are incremental in nature.

_____ We tend to avoid deep and bold changes.

_____ There is a short-term, day-to-day operating perspective.

_____ Authority figures focus on management (maintenance) more than leadership (change).

_____ People have little hope about the future of our church.

_____ There are needed changes that no one seems to be willing to initiate.

_____ The failure to make needed changes is nondiscussable.

Having responded to the comments above, can you think of any ways or areas in which your congregation is experiencing slow death? Describe what you see happening.

Who should be on your church improvement team? How often will you meet? How do you plan to use this book as a consulting guide?

Discussion Starters

1. Ask each member of your leadership team to list the top five priorities/values of your church. Compare these lists. Is there a centrality of themes or are they diverse?
2. What percentage of newcomers are seeking Christ or are new believers after attending your congregation?
3. How well is your church meeting the needs within its immediate community? Does your current congregation match the people living nearby?
4. Learn from others. What other local congregations are growing? Why are they growing? What local congregations are dying? Why?
5. What are five things you believe your church is doing well?

6. What are five things you would like to see changed in your congregation?

7. If you're willing, list items from questions 5 and 6 among your leadership team and place a value (1-5) on each one as to the level of priority/importance (1—insignificant, 2—minor, 3—moderate, 4—major, 5—crucial). What trends emerge from these numbers?

8. What major point grabbed you from this chapter?

9. List the ten most significant personal changes you have ever made. Sort the changes listed into two categories: incremental change and significant change. Summarize your experience with significant change.

10. List the ten most significant congregational changes you have ever witnessed. Sort the changes into two categories: incremental change and significant change. Summarize your experience with significant change in churches.

> Every new truth which has ever been propounded has, for a time, caused mischief; it has produced discomfort and oftentimes unhappiness; sometimes disturbing social and religious arrangements, and sometimes merely by the disruption of old and cherished associations of thoughts. . . . And if the truth is very great as well as very new, the harm is serious.
>
> —Henry Thomas Buckle

Contemplation

Moses' father-in-law replied, "What you are doing is not good." . . . Moses listened to his father-in-law and did everything he said.

—Exod. 18:17, 24

Scripture
Read Exodus 18:1–26.

DEVOTIONAL THOUGHT

Moses had proven his God-given capabilities. Unlike any leader throughout history, Moses had led the huge group of God's people out of slavery toward free worship and the promised land. So here comes this guy, Moses' father-in-law, giving him some free advice. Jethro's opinion was well meaning—and who knows, perhaps it was even initiated by Moses' wife's complaining about how little she saw her husband. But what is interesting about this passage is how Moses responded to the criticism Jethro offered. He was being very sincere in striving to obey God and serve the people. No one could fault him for his intentions. But Jethro saw that there was a better way to accomplish his goals and meet the needs of the people. He advised that Moses divide the ministry into various groups of ten, fifty, one hundred, and one thousand. Moses would have to give up a bad habit; he would have to change.

Instead of getting defensive, rebuking Jethro for expressing a new idea, or even suggesting that his father-in-law was being antispiritual or opinionated, Moses was open-minded. He implemented Jethro's advice, and the rest is history. Moses avoided inevitable burnout, and the ministry was more efficient than ever.

Great ideas often come from people who have a fresh perspective. God often speaks through and to these people. Certainly not everyone speaks for God or utters truth, but if we are not open-minded and responsive to improvement ideas when we hear them, we will shortchange effective ministry. What might have happened if Moses had responded defensively to Jethro's advice? What might have happened if he had not changed his ministry style?

Prayer

Dear God, help me to realize that in all my best efforts and sincerity, there may be a way to improve our church and the ministry role to which I have been called. Help me to be open-minded, to consider the truth in new ideas. I pray that I will not react defensively or hastily to people who propose changes. Let me ponder my attitude in addition to my behavior. I want to be more willing to see how you can work through others and new ideas to make my participation in your kingdom more fruitful. Amen.

CHAPTER 2
Value-Driven Ministry: Examining What Motivates Us

Ultimately, deep change, whether at the personal or the organizational level, is a spiritual process. Loss of alignment occurs when, for whatever reason, we begin to pursue the wrong end. As time passes, something inside us starts to wither. We lose our vitality and begin to work from sheer discipline. Our energy is not naturally replenished, and we experience no joy in what we do. We are experiencing slow death.

—ROBERT QUINN

THE MOST DIFFICULT ASPECT of church improvement is how to change; the next is what to change. How do we consider what should stay the same, what should go, and what should begin to change? What ministry areas are we succeeding in and what areas need an overhaul? As your improvement team thinks about areas for improvement, you might find it helpful to go back to the basics in terms of what you are trying to accomplish and why. When Vince Lombardi was trying to regroup the flailing Green Bay Packers, he called the team into a locker-room huddle, picked up a football, and said, "This is a football." Starting with the essentials is key to effectiveness in any organization and church: Why are we in existence? What should we be doing? What is vital to our identity as part of Christ's body?

We prove what our priorities are by what we do. The Bible makes this clear. Several wanna-be disciples said they would follow Jesus but then decided to tend to family, new acquisitions, and other logical substitutes. Because of the God-given gift of free will, for the most part the ways you spend your time and energy will reflect your true priorities. God's Word teaches us that people value what they do, not what they claim:

> Not everyone who says to me, "Lord, Lord," will enter the kingdom of heaven, but only he who does the will of my Father who is in heaven. (Matt. 7:21)

> There was a man who had two sons. He went to the first and said, "Son, go and work today in the vineyard."
> "I will not," he answered, but later he changed his mind and went.
> Then the father went to the other son and said the same thing. He answered, "I will, sir," but he did not go.
> Which of the two did what his father wanted? (Matt. 21:28–31)

> Faith by itself, if it is not accompanied by action, is dead.
> But someone will say, "You have faith; I have deeds."
> Show me your faith without deeds, and I will show you my faith by what I do. (James 2:17–18)

Wayne Cordiero, pastor of New Hope Church in Oahu, tells the story of a Russian priest who was discouraged and disappointed about his ministry. One evening, he took a walk in the woods and wandered into a military installation.

The young, armed guard at the perimeter shouted, "Halt! Who are you and why are you here?"

The priest perked up and asked, "What did you say?"

The soldier became even more stern and said, "Who are you and why are you here?"

The priest asked, "How much do you get paid?"

The young man, caught off guard by the question, said, "Why does it matter to you?"

"Because," the priest replied, "I'll pay you that much to ask me those same two questions every day."

CENTRAL CHRISTIAN CHURCH: OUR STORY

Determining the New Direction

As I (Gene) described in the last chapter, at first glance Central Christian Church appeared successful; a closer look revealed the cracks in our foundation.

The constituency of the church in itself was telling. We had an aging congregation in a growing community. But the church was not attracting younger members.

Other problems became clear as well. I realized there had been a staff-leadership vacuum prior to my coming. The people who worked at the church had never had a staff meeting; they just did their jobs. The staff was longing to be led. They were sincere, talented people who lacked a common vision and a leader who would develop them into a team.

These issues made clear that change was essential if we wanted our church to do more than exist—to grow the kingdom of God. Fortunately, the leadership heard my concerns and supported my conclusions. I sensed that the elders were hungry for change. Hiring me was a strong sign: By selecting a twenty-five-year-old who had never pastored before, they showed that they were open-minded and ready for a fresh perspective.

Once you've established that change is necessary, though, you have to decide where to begin. I learned that the new direction is largely born in the heart of the pastor. This is because he/she has to be the main person to sell and drive it. The dream must then take root in the hearts and minds of key leaders. It has to be tested by other key leaders, but not approved by everyone.

In my early years, we tried almost anything we thought looked good. Consequently we made too many changes that could not be sustained. We were trying to create a spiritual buffet that wore us down. To avoid that mistake, start by evaluating where you are; then determine where you want to be.

DETERMINE YOUR DRIVING VALUES

Peter Drucker, father of modern management, says that the two paramount questions of any corporation are Why are we in business? and Who is our customer?[1] Although it may seem nonspiritual, the church as an organization must answer these types of questions as well: Why are we in existence? What are we striving to achieve? Another way of looking at this issue is considering what drives your church. This is an important question for three reasons. First, articulating our drive helps us understand why we do what we do. Second, articulating our drive shows us what to measure, to see if we are accomplishing our purpose. Third, articulating our drive can help us see where we need to change, what we need to stop doing, and what we need to start doing.

APPLICATION TOOLBOX

Ask your leadership team to mark on the chart below what they believe are the five primary and five secondary values that should drive your church. An organization, like people, can have many values, but which ones specifically motivate it to action? A driving value will significantly shape an organization, specifically its goals; a passive value will not. Place a P beside the five you deem primary. Place an S beside the five you consider secondary. Remember, all of the items reflect common and perhaps biblical values, but only a few are apt to be driving values within your congregation.

_____ We value reaching lost people in our community, helping them develop a personal relationship with Christ.

_____ We value reaching lost people outside our community.

_____ We value assisting people to understand the Bible better.

_____ We value tradition.

_____ We value dynamic worship of God in our services.

_____ We value spiritual growth via small-group communities.

_____ We value ministry involvement, unleashing the gifts in people to help them grow through serving others.

_____ We value discipling existing Christians.

_____ We value church life that was indicative of the fifties through the seventies, with minor exceptions.

_____ We value loving community among our membership.

_____ We value good financial stewardship.

_____ We value teaching.

_____ We value creativity.

_____ We value excellence.

_____ We value a community of love, acceptance, and forgiveness.

_____ We value good doctrine.

_____ We value the family unit.

_____ We value children and youth.

_____ We value _____.

_____ We value _____.

_____ We value _____.

_____ We value _____.

Debrief: If you are up to the challenge, discuss the values you prioritized with others in your leadership or improvement team. What similarities and differences did you note?

What does this tell you about your church?

Is there any proof or are there tangible measurements that help you verify what indeed your values are?

Is it important to have unity and primary agreement in terms of top values or is it okay to have diversity in terms of ministry values?

What are the pros and cons of each?

AND THE POINT IS . . .

The values church members and leadership embrace form their church mission. Knowing your mission allows you to create objectives and strategies for fulfilling that mission. Yet a danger exists, as William Bridges writes:

> The trouble is that people come to identify with the objectives rather than the mission. They do so because it is easier to relate their own efforts and their own self-image to the objective, which is more tangible and closer at hand, than to the mission. But that simply reminds you how constantly you must work to get people to identify with the organization's mission. That takes explanation, modeling, and reward.[2]

In other words, typically church members assume that what they are doing in their services, events, and programs reflects biblical values and missional principles. People become attached to these various actions and methods. The problem comes when the methods are no longer effective and must be changed; people may end up defending certain objectives that do not reflect or accomplish the church mission.

The next step, then, is to analyze the values you have selected as reflective of your church.

RELEVANCE: WHAT DIFFERENCE DOES IT MAKE?

Let's take one value as an example, to see how a congregation could analyze what it claims as its values. Most churches consider Jesus' Great Commission (Matt.

28:19–20) as a driving value. They wordsmith the concept into various mission and vision statements, slogans, and even logos and subtitles. "Go into all the world and preach the gospel, make disciples, teaching them to observe all things." This complies with much of the New Testament early church ministry of reaching lost people. But as we saw in the last chapter, if you do a simple analysis of how many churches are actually reaching unchurched and lost people in their communities, few could claim to be effective.

Why do so many churches claim a driving value of, say, reaching the lost but fail to do it? One reason is that stating a value is different from living it. James Collins, business and organizational expert, talks about the need to "put thorns in our laurels."[3] That way, when we go to sit on our laurels, we'll feel pain. Who is going to hold us accountable to do what we say we're about? How will we develop a system that creates pain and discomfort when we do not fulfill our mission?

Researchers abide by the principle that if it is real, you can measure it. Measuring spiritual growth is not necessarily an easy task, but there are some bench marks. The New Testament refers to them as fruit. James says that faith without works is dead and love without action is a myth. In other words, our budgets, time, staffing, programs, and statistics should reflect our driving values.

When we ask people why they don't attend church, the number-one response we get is that "it doesn't seem relevant." Because time is now the most prized commodity in our society, the primary competition of every church is any alternative use of time. If people do not perceive our services, events, and programs to be relevant, they will not attend or at least prioritize church involvement. Recently I (Alan) was looking up the word *relevant.* In copying the definition my eye fell on the fourth word down from it, *relic.* As you read these definitions, consider which word best applies to the values your church clings to and upholds.

> **Relevant:** related to the matter at hand, to the point; pertinent. Applicable to current social issues; distinctive.
>
> **Relic:** something that has survived the passage of time, an object or custom whose original cultural environment has disappeared; something cherished for its age or associations with a person, place, or event; an object of religious veneration; anything old, leftover, or remaining; the remains of a dead person; a corpse.
>
> —*Webster's Illustrated Encyclopedic Dictionary*

Relics are usually irrelevant. Relevance has to do with making something fit, understanding the role of and application of an idea, tool, or concept. People are inundated with ideas and ways to occupy their time. If they do not quickly perceive how something is relevant, they're apt to overlook it and move on.

In terms of reaching the unchurched, there is a growing problem. Most culture observers state that North America is now a non-Christian nation. Postmodern philosophy and lack of connection with authentic Christians have left a majority in our country doubters regarding biblical faith. They do not believe the basic tenants of Christianity that scores before have espoused. They do not believe in any absolute truth, but in individual, experiential truth. They do not understand how an institution that plays the pipe organ, has singers/priests in robes, and speaks in theological language could relate to their world.

What are the problems with seeming irrelevant? Let me offer an analogy. In many places along the coast, tidal pools and bays capture water and sea life when the tide is high. When the tide goes out, fish, shellfish, and creatures are trapped. As the water evaporates and seeps into the ground, many of the animals die or become easy game for predators. Churches that perpetuate a distinct style and methodology amidst a changing society must realize that their fishing pools are shrinking. Fewer and fewer people are attracted to pipe organs, gospel music and hymns, traditional sermons, and Christian-culture terminology and practices. This does not nullify the fact that these things have worked effectively in their time. But churches that choose to intentionally continue to fish within their shrinking fishing pool ultimately decide to die. The issue is not if, but when.

In the next chapter we provide some ideas on dying with dignity, on letting go of established practices while still honoring what they accomplished. Every organization has a life span. There is no shame or failure in fulfilling God's will over a designated time and place. But we must let go of the myth that one system will always work. Everything is beautiful "in its time," but the right thing in the wrong time is not so beautiful. People are attracted to beauty.

PUTTING YOUR VALUES TO WORK

We are familiar with many healthy and larger congregations that appear to be thriving in very static, Christian-saturated communities but are not reaching the unconvinced. If these congregations choose to reach only the already convinced, then they do not need significant change. A mere tune-up and oil change will suffice, instead of dropping in a new engine. But for most of us who attend churches in very dynamic and more progressive subcultures, to replicate what worked in the fifties, the seventies, or even the nineties is insufficient. Valuing evangelism and discipleship of pre-Christians forces us to improve our language, form, and methods, but not our basic essence. If you believe it is God's will for your church to thrive for many more years, then you will need to seriously consider improvement issues, which in fact you are doing with this book.

One of the most difficult issues to confront is a certain ministry or event that is performed with excellence and perceived to be effective but does not reflect the stated values of a church. For example, if you have a Christmas production that attracts hundreds or thousands of people over the course of multiple services, you might initially believe that its success warrants its expensive budget. But after analyzing how many people show up in regular worship services the next year because of the event, you may determine that it is not a wise use of money for outreach. Basically, the public just considers the production an entertainment option but does not emotionally or spiritually connect to the church. You may want to consider how you could better design the program or follow up with people in order to establish a relationship. You may also decide that you are not in the entertainment business and that the cost of money and volunteers is not effective. Therefore, you may need to drop a program that appears to be very popular.

Another example may be a preschool ministry. While the church may be providing a service to the community, families may be using it for child care alone and never enter the church family. If the stated value of the church is to provide Christian education to the community, then a church-sponsored preschool may be justifiable. If not, then perhaps the preschool should spin off on its own, apart from the church, or shut down altogether. When the pet projects of individuals become congregational responsibilities, we run the risk of straying from our core values. Perpetuating programs and events that do little for our ministry effectiveness, regardless of their success, convince us that we are doing more than we really are for kingdom building.

JESUS' PURPOSE STATEMENT

For I have come down from heaven not to do my will but to do the will of him who sent me. And this is the will of him who sent me, that I shall lose none of all that he has given me, but raise them up at the last day. For my

Father's will is that everyone who looks to the Son and believes in him shall have eternal life, and I will raise him up at the last day. (John 6:38–40)

WHAT A VALUE-DRIVEN CHURCH LOOKS LIKE

A church that is value driven must separate values from practices; essence from form; content from culture; message from methods; staple from style; principle from tradition.

When a baseball pitcher throws an incredible game, he is likely to look for minute differences surrounding his stellar performance to explain and to be able to repeat the success in the next game. If, for example, he discovers that one of his socks is inside out, he may attribute some of his success to his attire on that day. Psychologists refer to this as superstitious behavior—associating a certain consequence with an unrelated occurrence that happens at the same time.

Less whimsical than superstitious is the idea of conditioning. Pavlov popularized this idea when he "trained" his dogs to salivate when he rang a bell. The bell had nothing to do with salivating, other than being run initially when food was present. A conditioned response can occur when a factor occurs at the same time as an experience, whether or not the factor actually caused the experience. We mentally draw the conclusion that there is a causal relationship based on its proximity to the experience.

In a similar fashion, when we come to know Christ under a certain leader, worship style, music type, or church, we are apt to believe that this is a more preferred way to know God than other ways. This does not diminish the fact that we have come to know Christ personally, but we tend to confuse what is form with what is essence. Thus, when someone suggests a different form, we sincerely believe we are defending the essence and regard any variances as compromise.

Just for fun, on the list below mark each item with an F if it represents a stylistic form or method, with an E if it represents essence—a biblical staple or principle that reflects a church value.

____ Altar calls at the end of worship services
____ Sunday evening worship services
____ Bible teaching
____ Sunday school
____ Discipleship

___ Reaching the lost in one's neighborhood

___ Baptism

___ Official local church membership

___ One- to two-hour worship services

___ Hymnals

___ Wearing suits, ties, and dresses to church

___ Putting song lyrics on a screen

___ Drama

___ Reaching the lost in other cultures

___ Midweek prayer services

___ Small groups

___ Pastors with seminary degrees

___ Priesthood of all believers; every Christian having a ministry role

___ Pipe organs

___ Choir robes

___ Praise teams with a contemporary praise band

___ Financial giving to the local church

___ Denominational structure

___ Accountability

___ Worshiping in buildings with pews and stained-glass windows

___ Using movie clips in church

___ Promoting loving relationships full of forgiveness and unity

___ Caregiving among believers

___ Teaching from the King James Version of the Bible

___ (Add your own items)

___ _____

___ _____

Discuss your responses with others as to whether these are cultural characteristics or enduring, fundamental principles that mirror church values. There is nothing wrong with specific or general cultural forms, as long as we do not confuse them with genuinely biblical principles when it comes to change and improving our impact.

BLIND SPOTS: WHAT ARE WE MISSING?

Whenever you consider your own personality, a variety of perspectives exists. For example, there is what you know about yourself that others know as well (public). There is that which only you know about yourself (private). Then there is what others know about you that you are not aware of yourself (blind spot).

The same is true of organizations and churches. We do not always see ourselves as others see us. If we are going to do a valid assessment of how we are doing in order to develop an improvement plan, we need to consider what we may be overlooking.

Blind spots are what others know about us that we are not aware of ourselves. Many churches have large blind spots, and this is dangerous. When we fail to consider how we appear to our community, we often overlook significant knowledge as to how we might reach them effectively. Within a church, blind spots are unknown attitudes and sacred cows that may derail an improvement process. They represent information we must seek out if we want our improvements to be effective.

We emphasize blind spots here as a reality check. Most of us overestimate how well we know ourselves and our churches. The exercises in this book are designed to reduce the size of the unknown areas in your self-perception. When we have critical issues in our blind spots, we will probably not see effective change implemented. Discovering the unknown can be scary. We all like to think of ourselves in a better light than reality sheds.

Familiarity often creates significant blind spots. For example, let's say that you walk into your bathroom one day and notice a large crack in the corner of the mirror. To you, it seems like a huge imperfection. Now how did that happen? I've got to get that fixed. You get busy with work and family and put off the repair for later. You see it again and think, Hmm, I really do need to repair that mirror. After several weeks of your daily routine, you are all but oblivious to the Grand Canyon crack in the corner of your mirror. The reticular activator in your brain has filtered out that information as unimportant. And others may be reticent to mention the problem. One day, you may have a friend over who uses your restroom and thinks, Wow, what a huge crack in that mirror. I wonder if John knows it's there. I wonder why he hasn't fixed it. I'm sure he is aware of it. I'll just keep quiet.

The fact is, the longer we attend a church, the less aware we become of chipped paint, mediocre music, boring messages, dim lighting, unfriendly ushers, weedy lawns, and alienating small groups and Sunday school classes. Gleaning information solely from within your family is a sure way to create huge blind spots.

After you have done what you believe to be a thorough job of congregational analysis, ask the following questions:

- What are we missing?
- Who might help us consider blind spots—areas that we have missed?
- Why do we think these people can give us different perspectives? (It is tempting to find people who will tell us what we want to hear: the emperor without clothes syndrome.)
- Once you have gained fresh perspectives from outside sources, ask: What do these people think about our programs and services in terms of the values we claim to prioritize?

In the analysis of your church, every time you describe your church a certain way, ask the question, How do we know this? How confident are we that we are correct? When you suggest that your church is not a certain way, ask again, How do we know this?

NEGOTIABLES VERSUS NONNEGOTIABLES

Based on the value list you created earlier, what are nonnegotiables? What are you not willing to give up regardless of the relevance factor? List these. Have each person on the improvement team provide his or her opinions of ministry nonnegotiables. The list should probably be ten items or less. (God refined his nonnegotiable list to ten and Jesus later refined the list to two.)

Once you write your list, ask yourself this question for each item: What makes this a nonnegotiable? Are there biblical grounds for this rating? Is it based on personal opinion and your unwillingness to compromise or negotiate? Personal preferences are not unimportant in considering what you keep and what you are willing to change. They are a part of our culture, personal self-image, and life experiences. But life is too full for us to wage war over many things. Establishing a short list of nonnegotiables will help you avoid trivial pursuit and ultimately determine what you are willing to change and how much you might be willing to change it.

Once you have come to some sort of consensus on what is and is not nego-tiable, you are ready to consider reconfiguring all negotiables. You do not need to create stress and conflict over items that you have predetermined not to alter. Understand that what you agree upon as nonnegotiables will ultimately deter-mine the core of your existence, reflecting why you do what you do.

No one can do the hard work for you, to determine what it is that does and should drive you. Your church is unique. The bias of us as authors is that we raise the value of outreach and evangelism in addition to discipleship improvement, because so few congregations are doing that effectively today. We as churches do not need to be singular in our value(s), but if we become too broad, we cannot hope to fulfill our goals, which are reflections of what we value. Remember, pri-orities are not what we say we do but what we actually do. Asking and answering blunt questions about measurements, criteria, bench marks, and fruit bearing helps us be honest with ourselves.

In short, coming to terms with what you believe should be the driving force behind your congregation is key to seeing the discrepancies between what is and is not happening. These discrepancies serve as the focal points for potential change and improvement. Without the apparent discrepancies, change processes will likely be weak and minimal in effect.

> Beware of worshiping the teapot instead of drinking the tea.
>
> —Wei Wu Wei

Improvement Story: Soul Grow Inc., Scottsdale Family Church

At Scottsdale Family Church, we recently celebrated our three-year anniversary. The church has grown to between five and six hundred in attendance at each Sunday worship service, with just under one thousand active members; 60 to 70 percent of those were unchurched prior to coming to SFC.

Those statistics delight me, but they were not easily won. For about nine months, we were stuck around the five-hundred mark. We began asking ques-tions about our purpose and values. We did some in-house consulting, which included the leadership analyzing what was and was not taking place. This set the ground for bringing in an outside consultant to see where we might have blind spots.

After a prayer retreat, I (Alan) sensed that God had some new things to teach us as a congregation. Our church had somewhat prided itself as being contemporary, relevant, and a real nineties organization. But our analysis showed us that actually, we had more or less exchanged a traditional box for a contemporary one. The point is that it was still a box, revising much of what we had inherited from centuries of church culture. Most of the things we did were not directly related to biblical principles.

For example, there is no specific job description for a pastor in the Bible. Nothing in Scripture tells us to meet for worship on Sunday mornings for one to two hours, sing a few songs, have a thirty- to forty-five-minute message, take an offering, and make a few announcements. Altar calls, musical style, Sunday school, and the like are generally concepts that have come to us through tradition. My suggestion was not that we get rid of the contemporary church box, but that we break down the walls. In other words, I suggested we ask, What would it be like to not have a pastor or a church, because these are loaded with stereotypes and preconceptions? What if we were to begin an organization designed solely to help people grow their souls and experience radical change based on biblical principles of connecting with God?

As a result, we began the year 2000 with a new series called Radical Living and a kickoff message on becoming a Radical Church. I outlined eight great traits of a saint, biblical principles that reflect characteristics of mature followers of Christ. These traits include evangelism, discipleship, care via groups, ministry/servanthood, compassion, stewardship, corporate worship, and private worship. While these are not the final list of character traits of the mature believer, we believe that they are the 20 percent that results in 80 percent of fruitfulness. These then became the bench marks around which we designed our events and programs. We call this new viewpoint and goal Soul Grow Inc. We are now working on measuring tools that will help us better quantify spiritual growth and improve what we do. While we are just getting established in this process, Soul Grow Inc. is significantly changing how we go about ministry development, assessing needs, measuring growth, and whom we look to for ideas and modeling. Even contemporary churches, to a certain degree, have become somewhat predictable and redundant. Perhaps there is a better way to do what we do, a more effective means to seeing people grow and become radically different because of their God experiences.

By merely tweaking centuries of traditions, we often fail to see the sort of early church dynamics that so many of us long to realize in our local ministries.

Thinking outside the traditional and contemporary church boxes is what SFC is about these days. The jury is still out, but the process has taken us along some pretty significant lines of change and renewal.

Improvement Lessons:

- Even new, growing churches can get stuck and need to perpetually improve. Take a hard look at what your church is doing that may be becoming outdated.
- Study your church's health in terms of the traits it inspires in people rather than its numerical attendance growth.
- Approach any restructuring with intentional, concentrated effort. Don't make knee-jerk decisions.

> The leadership of change does not depend on circumstances; it depends on the attitudes, values, and actions of leaders. Leaders must begin by setting aside that culturally conditioned "natural" instinct to lead by push. Leaders must instead adopt the unnatural behavior of always leading by the pull of inspiring values.
>
> —James O'Toole[4]

QUESTIONS AND ANSWERS

Q: You mentioned putting thorns in our laurels, ways to hold our church accountable for what we say we value. Do you have some practical ideas for how to do this?

A: Someone said, "Money talks." One way to reward growth is with increased budgets, withholding money from programs that are not tangibly reflecting the values of a church. For example, if you are funding an annual community outreach event, whether it is a revival series or a family carnival, analyze how many visitors attend your church in the next three to six months as a result of this event. When we finance outreach programs that produce little or no fruit, we should consider cutting the funding, regardless of the tradition or affection for it. Another example is recruiting a youth pastor to develop leaders in order to staff a vibrant youth ministry. If you consistently find that the youth pastor is running the program himself and investing little effort into leader development, you can decrease future youth ministry funds and make salary raises contingent on proven leader development. You may also need to release staff members who are unable or unwilling to develop ministry along the lines of stated values of the church.

While finances are some of the most powerful ways to provide pain with ineffectiveness, here are four other ideas for establishing thorns.

1. Develop an ad hoc team that analyzes ministry effectiveness according to the values of the church. This team may need to be appointed by the pastor and include various ministry representatives, meeting quarterly to report results from the services and ministry programs. Feedback from this team can be used to direct ministry leaders toward more effectiveness in line with stated values.

2. Reward ministry effectiveness when you see a person or ministry fulfilling church priorities. Elevating models and publicly esteeming people and ministry teams are intangible and inexpensive ways of encouraging what you want to see happen. The lack of recognition will become a thorn for many people.

3. Hold the ministry directors and leadership teams accountable for measuring results and planning programs and services around the stated values. Provide a list of the stated values and ministry objectives of your church. Compare this list with the events and services planned over the next two to three months for each ministry. Let each ministry director defend how the calendar events and meetings reflect items in the value list. When a person is unable to adequately establish a connection between an event and a value, the discomfort of accountability is often sufficient to motivate changes.

4. Hire an outside consultant to ask church growth and health questions of pastors, staff members, and ministry leaders. Sometimes internal relationships entangle objective analysis. When a loved and/or influential person defends the effectiveness of a ministry, others will oblige and compromise. By using a neutral person from the outside to help staff analyze and confront their own ministry dysfunctions, you can often avoid family conflict as well as get to the bottom of ministry ineffectiveness.

Q. Our church seems to do a lot of things that have little purpose. For

example, after a big event, some of us think, Why did we go to all that effort? What good did our work and money do?

A. Good thinking. These are stewardship concerns, and God consistently teaches about the importance of time, money, and resource management. Once you decide on the values of your church, planning the calendar and events is a much easier process. Everything you do should somehow reflect your values. By putting these values in writing, you can better hold program staff accountable for their planning.

As a leader or ministry team member, constantly raise the question, How does this event reflect one or more of our core values? People will try to justify their pet projects and programs, but when challenged a bit to provide proof, they will reveal whether there is substance there or just hot air. By simply talking about connecting programs with values, we begin to mold ministries around our values.

In addition to planning programs and events around values, we must look at how effective the program or event is. Measuring results requires creativity, pre-planning, and follow-through. Most churches are very inefficient because they fail to determine proposed outcomes and fruit measuring—they don't set tangible goals.

It's a touchy situation: How do you talk about event/program ineffectiveness when so many people have volunteered time and energy to make it happen? How do you communicate honestly with leadership without hurting feelings? To tell the emperor that he is not wearing any clothes is a gutsy and often controversial action. Sometimes the only person who can do this is a well-respected and loving supporter, whose commitment to the leadership and church is not questioned. Another person can make the same comments regarding ministry efficacy and be considered a troublemaker and boat rocker.

If leadership will okay challenging stewardship effectiveness, everyone comes under the same criteria for ministry development. When a church formally or informally disallows accountability, then it becomes dysfunctional and usually harbors all sorts of pet projects and ineffective programs and events.

Q: So how do you measure ministry effectiveness? How do you know if your programs are reflecting your values without getting into a debate that no one can win or prove?

A: Whew! Measuring spiritual growth and intangible effects can be challenging. In business, the bottom line quite often is profit. Because churches are faith communities, we tend to place an inordinate amount of weight on the two tangible measures, attendance and offerings. Yet a growing number of corporations are service oriented (like the church) and their values include intangibles such as excellence and customer satisfaction.

Churches are beginning to experiment with various ways of measuring program and staff effectiveness, as funding and available time appear to be shrinking. Gathering various ministry leaders to brainstorm ways of measuring effectiveness is a good first step. Creating surveys and event feedback reports, hiring third parties to interview newcomers and regulars, and providing forums where leaders can gather grass-root information are some measurable ways to analyze ministry effectiveness. (See Appendix A for resources on this topic.)

Q: We have some dinosaur ministries and events in our church that do not reflect our values, but axing them will cause a lot of hassle. Is there some way to avoid this?

A. Knowing when and how to pull the plug on a ministry that has run its course is very difficult. As a rule, once a ministry has been determined not to either reflect the values of a church or produce desired results, let it continue to exist as long as it does not drain funding, calendar space, or significant staff energy. Sometimes people need pet projects and find fulfillment in low-key participation. There is no need to rock the boat over ministries that have run their course but are not significantly distracting the church from its main purpose. For example, maybe a women's missionary group has been wrapping bandages for years. They gather monthly for a luncheon where they talk and work. If you determine that this ministry is not effectively reflecting the values of the church, there is no need to create a negative stir by canceling this ministry as long as it is not siphoning off money or staff energy. Don't give it inappropriate public attention, but just let it run on its own.

Too many church leaders hamstring themselves by creating conflict over matters that do not significantly impact a church. A church, like people, can only handle so much stress and change. If you overload a congregation with stress that does not enhance effectiveness, you will reduce the amount of improvement that will create positive momentum.

APPLICATION TOOLBOX

Take a ministry inventory. First, list all the events, programs, and meetings that fill the church calendar. In smaller churches one person can do an entire church inventory. Larger congregations will need to ask ministry directors to do an inventory for their specific ministries. The congregational leadership team can look at the larger church events, programs, services, and meetings. This alone is a helpful process—each ministry considering how it spends its time in meetings, event planning, and actual ministry service—and it is crucial to analyzing how the church is doing in terms of reflecting its stated values.

Second, assuming you have a written list of your church values, take the inventory list and write beside each item the value it fulfills.

Third, using the system below, rate each item's effectiveness in fulfilling the value. Naturally, if you have done little or no measuring, your rating will be subjective, but work at placing some initial rating beside each line item:

* Not vital; we should consider lopping off this item

** Seriously consider why or how we do this item; is it needed?

*** How can we do this better, to make it more effective?

**** Good, but can we improve anything to make this item even more effective?

***** What other things like this can we do to expand on this effectiveness?

> One of the greatest pains to human nature is the pain of a new idea. It . . . makes you think that after all, your favorite notions may be wrong, your firmest beliefs ill-founded. . . . Naturally, therefore, common men hate a new idea, and are disposed more or less to ill-treat the original man who brings it.
>
> —WALTER BAGEHOT

Discussion Starters

1. Why is it important to be a value-driven church? What is the danger in not considering the value behind what you do?

2. What are the top five values of your church? Do these reflect biblical principles as opposed to church or personal traditions?

3. How can you bring your leadership team to a point of agreeing on at least the top five values in your church?

4. If you are having a difficult time articulating and agreeing upon a value list, what might this tell you about yourselves? Why is it difficult, if not impossible, to work together toward too many directions?

5. What "sacred cows" might be roaming your church: practices, events, or styles that you consider sacred but that, in and of themselves, are not really essential? What things do you not even consider talking about for fear of creating conflict and hurting feelings?

6. List any examples of ministries, programs, or events that you have effectively discontinued because they did not appear to be relevant or reflect your mission/values.

7. What ways do you have of ascertaining the effectiveness of your current ministry calendar?

Contemplation

[Jesus] said to Simon, "Put out into deep water, and let down the nets for a catch."

Simon answered, "Master, we've worked hard all night and haven't caught anything. But because you say so, I will let down the nets."

When they had done so, they caught such a large number of fish that their nets began to break.

—Luke 5:4–6

Scripture

Read Luke 5:1–11.

DEVOTIONAL THOUGHT

Simon had every reason in the world not to let down his nets. He was tired, for he'd fished all night. As far as he knew, Jesus was not a fishing expert: carpentry, yes; fishing, no. Plus, they had just been in those waters and experience told them that more fishing would be a futile waste of resources. But out of faith and perhaps a budding friendship, Simon agreed to Jesus' suggestion. Lo and behold, the catch was not just a few fish. The nets were about to break.

When we begin thinking about doing old things in new ways, we are tempted to rely on past and even present experiences to avoid the suggestion. After all, our experience tells us that it will not work, that it will be a waste of precious energy. But limited experiences tend to box in the possibilities of improved ministry. God is not confined by our thoughts or experiences. Sometimes he has the nerve to get in our boats and recommend we try the same old thing in a brand new way.

What would have happened if Simon had argued with Jesus or graciously declined to obey his suggestion? No one could deny Simon's logic, but logic is limited, usually to our mental framework. Jesus is constantly pushing the limits of our experiences and our thinking. He transcends old, proven ways of doing things. Our nets are designed to catch fish, not adorn the side of our boats. Let's be open to using them perhaps in new ways.

Take time now to ask yourself: What are some things I am doing now that are not catching many fish? What might I do differently that would reap far better results?

Prayer

God, you called us to be fishers of people. Empty nets are not your will or your design. Help us to consider new ideas, new methods to promote old but proven truths. Even though my experiences may suggest that an improvement idea will not work, help me to consider the possibilities. Expand my faith. Allow me to break out of my boxed-in thinking that is based on recent experiences and even weariness. I trust you in the deep waters of life and ministry. Amen.

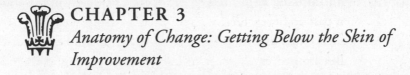

CHAPTER 3
Anatomy of Change: Getting Below the Skin of Improvement

> *There is nothing more difficult to plan, more doubtful of success, nor more dangerous to manage than the creation of a new order of things. . . . . Whenever his enemies have the ability to attack the innovator, they do so with the passion of partisans, while the others defend him sluggishly, so that the innovator and his party alike are vulnerable.*
>
> —NICCOLO MACHIAVELLI

A N OLD STORY depicts the situation of many churches. A young girl was watching her mother prepare a holiday ham for the oven. Mom cut off the ends of the ham before placing it in the pan.

"Mom, why did you cut off the ends?" her daughter asked.

"Well, I'm not sure," she answered. "That's just the way my mom used to do it." Her curiosity motivated her to phone her mother. "Momma, why did you always cut off the ends of the ham before baking it?" she asked.

Grandma thought a minute and then replied, "I'm not sure. I guess I saw my mother do it. Let me call her and ask why." Grandma called Great-grandma. "Mother, why did you always trim the ends of the ham before you put it into the oven?"

Great-grandma replied, "Because my pan was too small."

Knowing why we do things will help us determine whether they are really worth doing. Tradition and habit motivate a good number of our practices when effectiveness and practicality should be key. If we can understand how these habits become established, we are more apt to help initiate new ones.

Establishing new habits is harder for churches than for other organizations. When you compare churches with for-profit corporations, you will begin to think that churches are genetically inclined to be slower. There are a few reasons why this is so.

WHY CHURCHES CHANGE MORE SLOWLY THAN OTHER ORGANIZATIONS

First, churches see themselves as tradition keepers, preservers of the past. A felt responsibility of the church is to perpetuate values of the historical church such as Scripture teaching and time-tested doctrines. The problem is, we tend to confuse ageless truths with cultural traditions. The latter change while the former should remain in their purest form.

Second, culture plays a huge role in the way churches operate. Because culture tends to be a habitual and emotional environment, we process change in the church more slowly. In order to pay bills, perform services, and organize people, we must be structured somewhat professionally. But we tend to feel and respond more emotionally in congregational settings. When our emotions become a significant part of change processes, those processes become much messier. In order to avoid hurting feelings and damaging relationships, we tend to avoid issues that can create conflict, such as ideas for improvement.

Third, the church is not as in touch with its bottom line. For-profit corporations measure their effectiveness in profit margins, sales, and more tangible outcomes. When an organization is clearly missing its mark, people can understand when change is recommended. Churches are not for-profit service organizations. Their effectiveness is more difficult to measure. Because churches are muddy about measuring growth and effectiveness, there is rarely a clear-cut perception that significant improvement is needed. Exceptions of course are crises, where the threat of extinction or existence of great pain creates a readiness for change.

Fourth, change-weary people view churches as bastions of relief. Many pastors hear comments such as, "In this world of change, it's nice to know there is one place that stays the same: the church." Because the people who attend church are undergoing significant changes and turmoil at work, they approach weekends and evenings feeling stressed. The last thing many of them want to talk about or experience is change in their faith community. Change creates tension, and people's desire for church to be an island of tranquility amidst a whirling society creates a negative response to significant church-improvement strategies.

People can handle only so many changes in their lives at one time. Because work tends to be seen as mandatory and church voluntary, the voluntary change effort is usually low in priority.

Fifth, churches tend not to be leader led. Old-paradigm pastors are usually gifted at teaching and nurturing, not leading. Church managers abound, but leaders are needed when change is required. Because only 5 percent of pastors identify leadership in their gift mix[1], they are apt to either avoid change efforts, feel intimidated by lay leaders who promote change initiatives, or bungle improvement projects because they do not understand the leadership process. When pastors who are not wired to think and behave as leaders supervise congregations, they foster status-quo ministry or incremental changes, which rarely are sufficient for transformation.

> Most of us seek quantum leaps in our performance levels by pursuing a strategy of incremental investment. This strategy simply does not work. The land of excellence is safely guarded from unworthy intruders. At the gates stand two fearsome sentries—risk and learning. The keys to entry are faith and courage.
>
> —ROBERT QUINN[2]

CENTRAL CHRISTIAN CHURCH: OUR STORY

Making Change a Gradual Process

When I (Gene) arrived, the church was just concluding a capital campaign that had not gone well. They needed a new building, but the finances were not happening. They had set a building-fund goal of one million dollars and commitments of only ninety thousand dollars had come in. I recognized a ripe opportunity to chart a new course where one wasn't working well.

The first thing I did was get on the phone and call my mentors. They helped me realize that the goal was too high—we needed a more reasonable ambition. The elders agreed, and we decided to revamp the whole program. We introduced "Charting a New Course" at a special banquet and set a goal of four hundred thousand dollars. Along the way we supported the program with teaching on evangelism, the priorities of Jesus, outreach, and the results of maturity.

As we kept the issue present before the congregation and reiterated reasons for the proposed change, the church's momentum grew. When we finally tallied the contributions after a second pledge challenge, people had made commitments of just more than four hundred thousand dollars.

This win got us looking forward, established my leadership ability with the congregation and the leadership team, and provided the financial capacity to address our facility needs.

That gave me personal momentum. The first year and a half I preached through the Book of Acts to help the congregation see what the power of prayer and the Holy Spirit can do. We began to look at more radical change. I started to develop a vision of a church with a seeker-targeted ministry. I had grown up in Illinois and had known of Willow Creek Community Church, the congregation that excelled in this type of ministry, since 1980. I had also led a seeker-style youth ministry in Illinois before coming to Las Vegas. With so many lost people in our city, I knew such a ministry could be a powerful tool for the kingdom. I began to study models of the seeker-sensitive church, and the seeds of deep, lasting change began to take root at Central Christian Church.

WHY CHURCHES CAN CHANGE MORE EFFICIENTLY THAN OTHER ORGANIZATIONS

When we know that churches are slow to embrace change, our first temptation is to feel doomed. But we need to look at the bright side if we are to mobilize our congregations toward improvement. If implemented, there are some factors that allow churches to be more responsive to change than other organizations.

First, churches possess the Holy Spirit. While possessing God's Spirit and being led by that Spirit are different issues, most faith communities at least recognize the possibility of supernatural activity in their midst. That includes divine guidance, faith obedience, and spiritual empowerment. The pursuit of and reliance upon the Holy Spirit allow us as individuals and groups to move beyond our comfort zones and rational means of decision making. If we let God be God, we are apt to follow him into areas where we would never go naturally. If we gave the Spirit more room to lead in our congregations, undoubtedly we would see many things changed in churches across America. While most corporations run by human logic, we potentially march to the drumbeat of a different drummer.

Second, churches tend to have lower overhead. The primary asset of most congregations is its people. We are by nature a service-oriented organization. We provide a service of faith community whereby people connect with each other to evangelize and disciple. Other than buildings and some tangible resources, most churches have pretty low upkeep costs, making them leaner and more flexible for implementing change. In corporate counterparts, where huge factories and significant overhead make changes more costly, change issues can threaten organizational existence. While every ministry dollar may seem bigger than the same dollar in the marketplace, money tends to flow toward new ideas and good stewardship, which makes improvement issues potentially more fundable.

Third, family sticks together. Because churches emphasize relationships and tend to function somewhat like a family, they also tend to be more resilient to internal and external stress. While employees in for-profit corporations are becoming more consumerlike in their attitudes, making them less committed to stick with stressful work conditions, church attendees are often more dedicated. If friendships are established beforehand, people will often endure the pain and discomfort improvement processes can create. If we approach change from a unified position and ask people to hang in with us during the temporary construction, they will often go further with the church than they would with other organizations.

Fourth, our history and higher calling prepare us for change. Faith communities have frequently undergone revival, persecution, and expansion. Our history is full of stories where God moved his people into promised lands and created fresh ministry opportunities for them. If we do just a little investigation, we will find that most status-quo situations are detrimental to our faith in God. We grow best when on the move, not, as I mentioned in the last chapter, sitting on our laurels. If our experience is true to that of our biblical counterparts, we will expect God to lead us into new territory. We need not fear; most local churches can think back a few years to when they crossed rivers and accomplished significant breakthroughs. Because congregations must live by faith more than many other organizations, they can be more responsive to change.

Fifth, churches have a higher call. Although our bottom line is often less defined, faith communities are motivated toward deeper causes than dollars and cents. The intangibles of helping people develop a relationship with God, pursue heaven versus hell, and rise above a life of sin and self-centeredness are second to none. The power of our call and our passion to fulfill it make us more open to change in order to see God's purposes completed. Our responsibility is huge. According to the Bible, God's plan of salvation takes place through his church.

We are vendors of hope. The local church is the neighborhood franchise for God and his ministry of grace to our world. By promoting the higher cause, many churches can capitalize on improvement efforts, challenging people to make sacrifices that other organizations would not dare make.

Sixth, churches tend to be more personality responsive. Highly relational communities are affected more by the influence of individuals. When individuals within a church use their leadership gifts to bring about improvement issues, people respond. More bureaucratic and policy-laden organizations find their people slow to respond because people are motivated not by intangibles like increased company revenues, but by an inspiring leader. Also, individuals in companies often feel impotent to catalyze change due to so many checks and balances. Too much structure thwarts flexibility. Because churches are more personality sensitive, they tend to be more responsive when a leader effectively casts the call for improvement.

LIFE CYCLES

There is a time for everything,
and a season for every activity under heaven:
a time to be born and a time to die,
a time to plant and a time to uproot,
a time to kill and a time to heal,
a time to tear down and a time to build,
a time to weep and a time to laugh,
a time to mourn and a time to dance,
a time to scatter stones and a time to gather them,
a time to embrace and a time to refrain,
a time to search and a time to give up,
a time to keep and a time to throw away,
a time to tear and a time to mend,
a time to be silent and a time to speak,
a time to love and a time to hate,
a time for war and a time for peace.

. . . He has made everything beautiful in its time. (Eccl. 3:1–8, 11)

LIFE CYCLE OF A CHURCH

Life consists of a series of cycles: conception, birth, childhood, adolescence, adulthood, old age, death; spring, summer, fall, winter. Organizations such as churches go through cycles as well. The most common life cycle of an organization is the S-curve.

3A
Organizational Life Curve

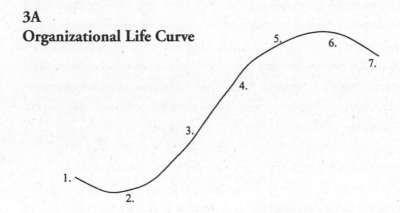

At point 1 in the curve, the organization begins with a vision, a crisis, or a new discovery or innovation. The initial excitement of responding to the potential creates the burst of energy that is necessary to get a new venture off the ground.

At point 2, reality hits the dream. The scary, life-threatening aspects of beginning a new venture are enough to destroy many fragile visions. When a venture is understaffed, inadequately capitalized, and weakly led, it will often die at this point.

If the dream survives, at point 3 the organization (church) takes off. Early growth replaces the tough, frightening phase as the team strives to perpetuate the increase and organize the chaos. These are exciting days for any organization, even though it is still young and vulnerable.

At point 4 in the organizational cycle, structure begins to catch up with growth. Church leadership begins to implement procedures and policies that help stabilize the organization. If the leadership is able to maintain a balance between stability and growth, the organization will continue to be healthy for some time.

At point 5, overmanagement becomes a danger. Emphases on budgets, buildings, incremental improvements, and general maintenance issues tend to overcompensate for the growth and result in a focus on self-maintenance. As a majority of energy and resources move toward perpetuating stability and status quo, the conditions are becoming established for plateau and decline. Like most businesses, churches tend to be overmanaged and underled.

At point 6, decline has begun. Quite often it shows up in statistical analysis (declining attendance, newcomers, offerings), but the process actually started much earlier. By the time most organizations recognize their failing health, a lot of damage has already occurred, making turnaround a difficult process.

At point 7, death is unavoidable and imminent (outside of a miracle). Many churches are basically on life-support systems. Flatlined congregations can go through the perfunctory behaviors of faith communities such as holding services, scheduling meetings, and carrying out religious activities, but for all practical purposes, vitality is gone.

Spiritual museums, where people reminisce about the "good ol' days" but take no action to discover a new promised land, abound across America. This is where the church adage fits: "It's easier to give birth than to raise the dead." Church planting is certainly an alternative to the problem of dying churches and avoids much of the pain that can come from pursuing church-change issues, but starting new churches is a high-risk process. Entrepreneurial pastors, leaders who are wired to start new works, are even harder to find. Far too much potential remains in the scores of churches that have reached the zeniths of their current organizational cycles for us to overlook their renaissance.

You can chart this S-curve in lives and organizations. Churches, parachurch ministries, denominations, spiritual movements, and educational institutions all experience the S-curve effects. The duration of each phase differs per organization. Some have steeper, shorter curves. Others reflect flatter, longer curves. Obviously, some organizations never experience the full curve because they either die before they mature or recreate themselves prior to death. The latter is the focus of this book. The most critical place for renewal is between points 4 and 5, not 5 and 6. By the time an organization reaches the latter, it is often in a negative momentum phase where turnaround emphases are too little, too late. Unfortunately, sometimes the painful motivation to change doesn't occur until points 5 and 6.

3B
Timing of Renewal

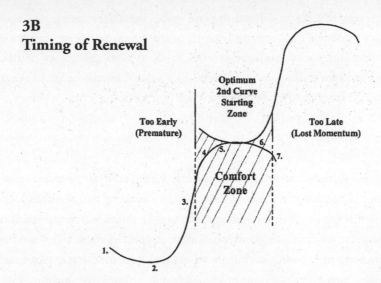

The exception to the inevitable S-curve demise occurs when organizations create another S-curve before losing critical momentum and resources. Self-renewing churches and corporations usually do this intentionally. Occasionally, an organization will happen upon a new product or leader or, in the case of a faith community, experience a God-given revival. But the chance approach to renewal is very rare. A much higher percentage for succeeding comes when leaders proactively plan how they can avoid decline and pursue growth and renewal. The best time to do this is when things appear to be stable and well.

Unfortunately, we often occupy ourselves with doing business and management as usual so that we take little time or effort to think ahead of the curve. The deception of perceived health and vitality creates a comfort zone. In this zone, we label change agents as boat-rockers, troublemakers, and naysayers and either ignore them or run them out of town. Like a person suffering from hypothermia or carbon-monoxide asphyxiation, churches find the desire to fall gently asleep very tempting. But to do so is to guarantee our eventual demise.

Churches that are best positioned for renewal are those that understand the life cycle of all ministries and organizations and work ahead of the curve. A self-renewing organization will go through several of these S-curves, not just one or two. During times of change, leadership must initiate multiple change processes if the church is to stay vibrant and relevant.

The half-life of a ministry is much shorter than it used to be. Bill Hybels recently said that at any given time, one-third of the subministries at Willow

Creek Community Church are undergoing significant change and restructuring. The feeling of constant chaos is more of a norm than an exception in organizations that are adequately responding to the needs of a changing society around them. This in no way suggests we change our values, but in order to preserve them, we must be retooling our methods and practices.

Improvement Story: Grove City Church of the Nazarene, Grove City, Ohio

When I (Bob Huffaker) came to the church in the fall of 1989, the services averaged around six hundred attendees in Sunday morning worship. Although they were very traditional in style of worship, the people were visionary in their attitude and had searched for a growth-oriented pastor. So right away, we began using contemporary music, adding it to the choir/hymn/organ custom. We began implementing choruses and mild media such as screen projection of lyrics. I invested the first part of my ministry there to educating the congregation on the concept of praise.

As we began to implement other changes, I spent time almost daily with a teacher of the older adults. We went on walks and prayed together for the church. He did a lot to communicate to that group what we were doing, and we all agreed to give them exactly what they wanted in their own Tuesday evening Bible study. That kept them happy and in favor of other changes.

Over time we changed the focus of our church from programs and events to ministry. We were not numbers motivated. We emphasized children and youth programs. As a result, there was some fallout among our more rigid attendees. We gave people permission to leave so that no one would feel guilty. We lost a pianist of seventeen years, but not more than six or seven families. Some who remained with us complained at first, but we did not have a significant loss because the leadership was on board with the staff.

We held our services in a multi-use facility, but when asked to do a traditional service in the old sanctuary, I agreed. The leadership encouraged me not to do that: "That's not our niche, Pastor. There are thirty other Nazarene churches in the Columbus area if people want a more traditional ministry." At that moment, I felt as though our leadership had formed a unified team. We were in sync with each other and the vision. We knew that we were called to be different and that those who did not feel the same were free to pursue church homes where they could freely worship.

Keeping to our vision of a more forward-looking church, we grew. Fortunately the church was not ingrown, so when new people came they were welcomed. Our growth has remained consistent over the years. In the fall of 1999, we moved into our new 3,200-seat sanctuary and sixty-five-acre campus. Our average morning attendance is now more than 2,700. Approximately 50 percent of those attending are unchurched; in October 1999 we baptized more than one hundred people and celebrated more than two hundred verified decisions for Christ.

Improvement Lessons:

- People have to know the reasons behind changes. Continually educate and make an effort to love people. Purposefully drop in and ask for prayer. Talk about the new families and fruit of the changes being made.
- Don't become fainthearted. Don't back off if a few people oppose the vision. You must be both strong and loving.

> The art of progress is to preserve order amid change and to preserve change amid order.
>
> —ALFRED NORTH WHITEHEAD

CHANGE SEQUENCE

Understanding the stages of change will make us wiser, stronger, and more patient change agents. When we are unaware of change anatomy, we are apt to rebuke people, ideas, and barriers and view them as enemies instead of processes that can make us healthy and stronger. We often see leaders who are incredibly frustrated with how change is going and feel paralyzed about what to do. Oblivious to the anatomy of change, they blindly grope their way through the process with marginal effectiveness and sometimes very negative results. This failure creates a fear of change and gets passed along the grapevine; others lacking confidence then decide not to pursue change because they are afraid that they will be just another church statistic and holy war story.

In *Diffusion of Innovations,* Everett M. Rogers gives us a model of stages in the organizational-change process.[3] The first two stages make up the initiation phase. At the end of the initiation phase, you decide whether or not to pursue the change. If you decide not to make the change, then for all practical purposes, the idea has died. If you make the decision to pursue the change, then you enter the second phase—implementation. Be warned: You will never get to stages three, four, and five until you effectively progress through the initiation phase. Church leaders who try to ignore this process often find themselves in hot water. Even though they may be right in suggesting what needs to be changed, their lack of awareness of change anatomy will usually result in an idea miscarriage.

Stage 1: Setting the Agenda

This is where a person or group of people brainstorm or suggest change that would benefit a ministry. You might think that ideas are generated by people who perceive a problem, but studies show that most ideas sprout from a model of success. Seeing or hearing of others who are doing well in ministry often motivates an effort to replicate that success. Innovations can develop from someone's attending a conference, reading a book, or visiting another church. Most organizations are more aware of ideas than they are of specific problems within themselves and how to effectively address them.

Ideas gained from outside sources are more difficult to implement than ones gained from within the church or ministry. Why? Because some will view the idea as foreign and therefore questionable if not threatening. You can combat this prejudice through research, analysis, and fact finding. At any rate, don't dismiss spontaneous suggestions or ideas from "outside" before examining their plausibility and potential effectiveness.

Stage 2: Matching the Solution to the Problem

People sometimes are not aware of a problem in their church until they hear of another church that is doing well. That is why taking a group of people to an effective church conference to hear another church leader speak or suggesting that they read a book as a group can do wonders for educating people in reaching their potential.

Andrew invited his brother to "come see" Jesus. Seeing often precedes believing. A fundamental of the gospel is that we must realize our sin before we recognize our need for God and his solution, grace. In organizational terms, identifying a problem is a prerequisite for the willingness to consider a new idea.

The natural sequence is to see something we want, look at what is blocking us from having it, and then pursue the change needed to obtain it.

One of the most common errors leadership teams make in catalyzing effective change is failure to sell the problem. Our initial excitement tempts us to rush into selling a solution, for which many people are not ready. If they haven't seen the need, they're not prepared to meet it. William Bridges writes in *Managing Transitions,* "People let go of outlived arrangements and bygone values more readily if they are convinced that there is a serious problem that demands an ending."[4]

You may be tempted to just inform the congregation that you plan to make changes. Bridges warns that although the authoritarian, autocratic approach to leading appears to be a much faster way to implement change, in the end it is longer and harder. You have to do a lot more explaining, mopping up of messy emotions and relationships, slugging it out through conflict, and motivating to adopt a change that people do not feel they needed because they were unaware of a problem.[5]

Incidentally, recognizing a performance gap is often the beginning of identifying a problem. When we establish few or no ministerial goals other than to merely survive, we are not apt to develop any recognizable gaps between what we are doing and what we want to achieve. That is why the values identification and ministry evaluations we suggested in previous chapters are important.

Stage 3: Redefining and Restructuring

At this point, the church decides how the idea will need to be shaped to adapt it to its specific setting, as well as how the church structure will need to change to implement the idea. The problem with many ideas brought from other ministry situations is that they are adopted without being adapted. Rarely can you lift an idea from another context and use it as it was discovered. Even when the idea comes from within the church, you nearly always need to modify the initial concept to make it functional.

Does the change involve an existing ministry or will you need to create a new structure? For example, when you want to add a room to your home, you have to figure out where it will go, what walls will be modified or removed, and how far you'll extend the roofline. Building a totally separate guesthouse may be an alternative to adding square feet and disrupting the existing house. Understand that when you add the new idea, it will change the structure of the total house. You'll use more water, electricity, energy, and money. Sometimes we cannot realistically determine how much the new idea will affect us until after we have implemented it. Some uncertainty is a given. The good news is that we also sometimes underestimate the benefits that can occur by implementing the new idea.

In terms of contemporary church music, for example, is there a need for an entirely different musical style in the existing worship, or should we blend styles, using a couple of hymns with two or three contemporary praise songs? Do we need to devote an entirely unique worship service to this new style or is there enough latitude within the congregation for both styles? Will we be making everyone happier with this blending or will we be frustrating everyone in the process?

Part of the redefining and restructuring process is the development of a leading change agent or champion. At this point, every significant change will need a champion who will see the change process through to the end. The law of physics says that a body at rest tends to remain at rest. Organizations are structured to perpetuate what they have previously done. Their very strength, preserving what has been, becomes a liability when the need for change arises.

> Every organizational system has its own natural immune system. If the organization didn't have such an immune system, every germ of change would take root, and the organization would not have enough stability to get anything done or enough continuity to give people the identity they need. But the cost of an immune system is that even good germs get filtered out or killed off. The old immune system choked off creativity in its own manner.[6]

The champion of an idea must have stamina. When you are camping, driving the tent pegs deeply into the ground, tying the ropes securely to nearby trees, and placing weights strategically in the corners can make a tent very secure from the elements. But if there is a crisis—a bear or a storm approaches—taking down the tent quickly can be difficult. To use another metaphor, initiating a change is like pushing a wagon uphill. If no one is pushing, gravity will take the wagon back downhill. Acknowledging who the champion is will make a significant difference in the effectiveness of implementing the change. An innovation without a champion is almost doomed to die. The champion must be a person of influence but does not need to be the official leader. History is spotted with examples of passionate underdogs who catalyzed change from roles of little authority (for example, Ghandi, Martin Luther King Jr., John Wesley, and Martin Luther).

The leadership's attitude is pivotal. Even though change can take place with a champion who is not in a formal role, a vast majority of church improvement languishes due to the official leadership's lack of support of or resistance to a new idea. If the senior pastor and leading laypeople do not embrace a new idea, it is highly unlikely that significant change will occur.

Understanding what changes are needed to revive health and vitality and a willingness to risk failure and rejection are key characteristics of champions. Obviously, just because a person advocates a certain change or idea does not mean he or she is right. The idea can be a stupid, ineffective one. But the larger of the two problems is that of fear of rejection. Idea champions are often labeled troublemakers and instigators. The Bible tells the plights of many who faced rejection because they promoted unpopular ideas (Moses, Joshua and Caleb, Jesus, and Paul). Risk taking and championing a cause or innovation are part of this stage of change.

Stage 4: Clarifying

When the new idea is introduced into the church, a significant need exists for people to understand how it relates to the purpose of their church and ministry as well as what impact it will have on them as individuals. When leaders strive to implement changes too quickly, they often fail at this stage because people have questions that demand answers: "How does the idea work?" "What purpose does it serve?" "Who will be affected by the change?" "Will it affect me?" Rushing past these questions will nearly always harm a change process and tends to snag a lot of well-intentioned, productive ideas.

New ideas are often muddy. Therefore, effectively communicating, understanding various social circle concerns, and allowing people time to individually and socially process are nearly always essential. The more widespread a proposed change is, the more time people will need to process it.

Stage 5: Routinizing

After a change has been implemented in a church or ministry, people begin to own it. The change itself loses its identity as a separate "thing" as members become familiar with it and new people enter the church assuming that it has always done things this way. The more people who begin attending after the changes are implemented, the greater the stability of the change because the new thing becomes an expected tradition for them. Many of us can think of small or large ideas that we now consider church traditions, but we also remember when the ideas were new and perhaps even the topic of argument. Former opponents of the then-new idea are now avid fans and will fight to change the once-controversial improvement. Routinizing is the last stage of an innovation and marks the end of the change process.

Everything we accept as "old" in our congregations was at one time new. Altar calls, pipe organs, hymnals, stained glass, Sunday school, praise bands, projected lyrics, Sunday night Sunday school, small groups—nearly every short- or long-term tradition was at one time an infant. We should not be surprised, then, that new ideas are so often seen as strangers, intruders. Just as existing children often see a new baby as competition, the natural response in an organization is to perceive the new idea as something that will compete for valuable attention and resources, and that could potentially replace something dear.

The improvement process tends to be the same, whether small or large, regardless of what the change involves. Progress leaders often want to jump from new idea to routinizing without adequately transversing stages two, three, and four. But to disregard this process either out of ignorance or blatant disregard is to significantly decrease the chances of an effective improvement process and thus lose the potential benefits of the new idea.

Here in graph form is Everett Rogers's change sequence.

3C
Rogers's Change Sequence

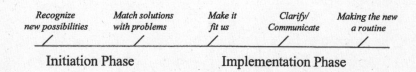

| Recognize new possibilities | Match solutions with problems | Make it fit us | Clarify/ Communicate | Making the new a routine |

Initiation Phase   Implementation Phase

THE PRIMARY REASONS CHANGE INITIATIVES FAIL

Author John Kotter lists eight primary reasons why change initiatives fail in corporations:

1. Allowing too much complacency. You've gotta wanna change.
2. Failing to create a sufficiently powerful guiding coalition. The improvement team must have strong leaders and those in power must either provide personal vision or grant permission to change agents.
3. Underestimating the power of vision. People need to have a clear, compelling picture of a preferred future.
4. Undercommunicating the vision by a factor of 10 (or 100 or even 1,000). Make it redundant, mediated, visual, emotional, logical, and repetitious.
5. Permitting obstacles to block the new vision. . . . Realize that pushing improvement initiatives means swimming against the current. Constantly strive to remove barriers and problems.
6. Failing to create short-term wins. Providing hope and momentum are key elements to new beginnings. Nothing motivates like success, big or small.
7. Declaring victory too soon. New ideas take awhile to not only implement, but to become a part of a culture. Initial success must be followed up with continued achievement and recognition for some time in order to become habitual and part of our new self-image.
8. Failing to anchor changes firmly into the corporate culture. Improvements take awhile to become family, so never assume that people have become familiar with new ideas until you have made significant effort at establishing them and measuring feedback.[7]

THE PRIMARY REASONS CHURCH IMPROVEMENT MEASURES FAIL

While Kotter's eight reasons reflect typical corporate-change failures, additional considerations exist when the change is being proposed in a church. Here are ten common problems in church-change implementation:

1. Inadequate leadership. Leadership is about changing organizations, while management is about maintaining them. Since most pastors are not gifted as leaders and most churches rely heavily upon pastoral supervision for

guidance, many churches never see change for lack of leading. Leadership, whether it be pastoral, lay, or other, must be in place for significant change to take place. The number-one reason by far for most improvement failures is inadequate leadership. (See chapter 5.)

2. Lack of compelling, defining vision. You can't expect people to travel where they cannot see. Vision casting is a natural expression of leaders, but with so few churches led by leaders, getting at a compelling, well-defined vision is the first major hurdle for most would-be change agents. (See chapter 6.)

3. Failure to address biblical essentials. Church improvement is not just change for change's sake. If our improvement is not based on biblical values and ministry essentials for impacting our culture for Christ, then our primary motivation for change is lost. The Bible is a vital tool for pursuing improvement in a faith community, where hopefully we value such teachings. Even the most ardent person against change should be willing to consider improvements that have a solid, biblical foundation.

4. Unwillingness to confront ailing issues. Fear of conflict and rejection are basic human nature responses. They are the primary reasons we are unwilling to spotlight practices in our churches that are ineffective. We all want to feel successful and productive, whether or not we really are. This desire often keeps us from seriously analyzing our time and energy expenditures. By avoiding sacred cows, not recognizing what elements of our church are ailing, and running from potential areas of conflict, we hamstring significant change initiatives.

5. Poor grasp of timing (too fast or too slow). When an improvement initiative moves too fast or too slowly, it is apt to get stuck. As we read in Ecclesiastes, everything is beautiful in its time. There is a ripeness about change; if we push too hard or wait too long, we miss the window of opportunity. Managers tend to wait too long, waiting for consensus before moving forward. The problem herein is that your more motivated people, who serve as catalysts and supporters, will sometimes not wait for significant improvement to take place. Letting fruit rot on the vine is the typical failure of most fearful leaders. Strong, entrepreneurial leaders, on the other hand, often try to push change through before it has had a chance to ripen. Fruit that is picked too green often rots faster. People and processes need to be in place before change can have lasting effect. The rubber-band effect can occur where the old ways snap back with even

more resistance to future change ideas. Effective change agents understand the importance of timing.

6. Lack of team development. Effective improvement requires a team of people working together. As an individual, you cannot make lasting change happen. Vision casting, participant ownership, and adequate team development make enduring improvement possible. Getting people to own a proposal means more than getting their vote or okay to begin implementation. Many leaders think that as long as people give them permission to drive the bus, the people are actually on the bus. Many improvement objectives are driven over the cliff with no one besides the bus driver on board. Understanding who needs to be on the team and adequately training and working as a team are vital to seeing your change implemented and last.

7. Overly divided people groups. We all like to listen to people who say what we want to hear. We naturally gravitate toward those who think the way we do. The weakness of many leaders is that they are not in tune with various groups, especially those with differing views. Every organization has various circles of influence within it. Bringing about effective church improvement means identifying these social circles, knowing who is in them, and addressing the various concerns of these people groups. Each group will have its own priorities and concerns. When a leader is unable to adequately gain permission and/or address the needs of the groups, he or she will be ineffective in the change effort.

8. Poor handling of conflict. Conflict is a part of any healthy relationship. Where no conflict exists, people are either walked on or controlled. Conflict is about working through different opinions and ideas. Keeping peace at all costs is an excuse many nurturing, managerial leaders use for avoiding improvement initiatives. At the same time, when a leader has poor people skills or runs from a conflict, the potential of messing up an improvement issue increases. When relationships become secondary to changes, we run the risk of distorting the biblical principle of love. Practicing love requires working through conflict, even if it results in agreeing to disagree. To let conflict go without addressing it often means sabotaging the change effort. (See chapter 9.)

9. Carnality: a spirit of pride or self-centeredness. While some pastors might jump quickly to this conclusion, we cannot deny the reality that selfish,

flesh-controlled individuals derail many church improvement initiatives. An unwillingness to give up control to God and the Holy Spirit has created problems throughout history in the church. We cannot ignore the existence or influence of people who call themselves Christians but who are not in step with God's Spirit. Unity is not so much agreeing with each other as it is agreeing not to let disagreement mar the local church or God's kingdom. When a self-righteous person becomes a block in a church, even the best of leaders is often impotent to initiate lasting improvement.

10. Poor understanding of the change process. An old joke seems fitting here. A Baptist and a Methodist pastor invited an Assembly of God pastor (you can add your preferred flavor) to go fishing one day. They rowed out to the middle of the lake. After a few hours of no bites, the Baptist pastor said, "I'm going to shore for something to eat." The Methodist minister said, "I think I'll join you." Each pastor proceeded to climb out of the boat and walk across the water to the shore. The Assembly of God pastor was amazed. How in the world did they do that? he thought. Not to be outdone, he got out of the boat and immediately sank to the bottom of the lake. The Baptist pastor turned to the Methodist and said, "Do you think we should have told him where the rocks were?"

When we look at effective change agents, we sometimes get the feeling they can walk on water, when in reality they just know where the stepping stones are located. Understanding the anatomy of change—the difference between a transition strategy and change strategy—and being able to identify the various factors in an improvement process are vital for effectiveness. Natural, strongly gifted leaders can often catalyze change in spite of themselves, with little conscious understanding of what they are doing. But the rest of us look like the proverbial deer staring at the headlights.

THE IMPORTANCE OF TRANSITIONING WELL

One of the most significant anatomical characteristics of change is that the transition process of change is unique to the change itself. Next to leadership, most change processes get hamstrung on this single point!

Every relay-race runner understands the importance of the hand-off, transitioning the baton from the current runner to the next. If the runner does not pass the baton smoothly, the race can be lost. If the pass does not take place within a certain distance or if it drops to the ground, the team may not win. Track coaches drive the point home to relay team members: Races are won or lost in the transition.

The same is often true within improvement processes. Regardless of how much effort we put into determining what it is we need to change in order to become more effective, relevant, and fruitful, we are apt to lose the relay if we do not work on the transition.

> Unless transition occurs, change will not work. That's what happens when a great idea falls flat. The starting point for transition is not the outcome, but the ending that you will have to make to leave the old situation behind. Situational change hinges on the new thing, but psychological transition depends on letting go of the old reality and the old identity you had before the change took place. Nothing so undermines organizational change as the failure to think through who will have to let go of what when change occurs. Transition starts with an ending.[8]

Transition starts with an ending—and ends with a beginning. In the middle is a very precarious area between old reality and new reality called the Neutral Zone.

3D
Transition Phases

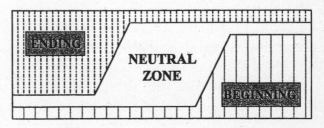

(William Bridges, *Managing Transitions,* © 1991, Persens Books, p. 70)

> It's not so much that we're afraid of change or so in love with the old ways, but it's that place in between that we fear. . . . It's like being between trapezes. It's Linus when his blanket is in the dryer. There's nothing to hold on to.
>
> —MARILYN FERGUSON, *American Futurist*

SAYING GOOD-BYE

Someone said, "It's not the changes that kill us; it's the transitions." The most dreaded stage or phase in the change process is the time of transition. The people of Israel complained the most between Egypt and Canaan. This no-man's land, Bermuda Triangle, twilight zone, is equivalent to the space between the roof of a burning building and the safe roof of an adjacent building. For a time during the transition, chaos, confusion, insecurity, and apprehension reign. We know what we must do, but the fear of the jump can create a lot of havoc.

Any analysis of the change process must take an honest look at the most difficult in-between zone. Managing the transition is different from managing the overall change. Transition management emphasizes personal impact and role definition; it is more relationship oriented.

You can't erase the transition phase, but you can make it easier. An overused illustration is worth a mention here. It's about the guy who is hiking along a cliff when all of a sudden, he slips. He's about to plummet to his death when he grabs a straggly tree that is growing out of the side of the rocky face. Looking far below at his certain end, he yells, "Help! Is anyone there?"

Suddenly, a giant hand emerges from the sky and a booming voice from heaven says, "Let go!"

The climber looks down again and then back up. He screams, "Is anyone else there?"

The joke describes the plight of many churches and congregational members who cannot grasp the new thing God is wanting to do, because they are unwilling to let go of the past. We discussed in chapter 1 the way God calls us constantly to newness and the way Jesus modeled this characteristic. Still, many people embrace the familiar even more tightly when faced with the unknown quantity of a change.

We will discuss just one aspect of the transition phase here. Your role as a change agent requires that you honor those who love the "old" ways. Before any significant change can take place within a ministry or a church, you must initiate a period of letting go, of burying the dead, of mourning their loss, of celebrating memories—but then move forward. Too many leaders and progressive types err when they do not allow for suitable mourning and when they do not arrange for a respectful memorial of the things they are about to change.

Some leaders fail to honor the past because they weren't around when a certain ministry or style of worship was successful and effective. Out of insensitivity to others, they forge ahead, lopping off ministry elements with no apparent awareness of the memories and meaning to others.

Most of the time, before a new change occurs that will become fruitful, we must allow the death of something else. Hanging on to outdated ministries and religious traditions because of the meaning they used to provide can be a morbid practice. Until Israel let go of Egypt, it could not grasp the promised land. We cannot take hold of God's kingdom until we release our own. The same is true of change. Before we see the benefits that a new program, style, strategy, or ministry will bring, we must let go of some of the things of the past. (See chapter 8 for ways to do this.)

> All changes, even the most longed for, have their melancholy; for what we leave behind is part of ourselves; we must die to one life before we can enter into another.
>
> —ANATOLE FRANCE

QUESTIONS AND ANSWERS

Q: Why are there so many crash-and-burn stories of churches that have tried to implement change but have split, or lost staff, or gone through significant conflict?

A: Lots of issues can so plague a church that significant losses occur. Perhaps the biggest one stems from the fact that leaders, managers, and pastors tend to grossly underestimate the unique characteristics of the change process. They do not realize that the DNA of the transition is different from the DNA of the old and new organizations. Change is akin to a hall, or a stairwell, elevator, or escalator. These transitional spaces have different dynamics from the rooms or areas they connect. Because few people invest much time and effort into studying the change process, they quite often work in ignorance.

The key is to understand how change works, from beginning to end, and especially how to ease the transition, so that the change agents, leadership, and members can work in tandem toward a common goal successfully.

Q: The idea of organizational change seems so corporate and sterile for some of us who think of church as a spiritual family. Aren't we missing something if we take too much of a business look at change and improvement?

A: As a rule, church people overestimate how much faith communities are uniquely different from other social structures. Because we talk about God and less-tangible issues, we sometimes deceive ourselves into thinking that systems, good management, leadership principles, and other organizational characteristics do not apply to us.

At the same time, businesspeople sometimes overestimate the similarities between corporate structure and faith communities. There are idiosyncracies in churches that separate them from their for-profit counterparts. The interaction with the Holy Spirit, theology as a determiner of values, volunteer-driven efforts, and spiritual growth as a means and objective all require that people work together differently in a church than they would in a secular business.

Still, many in leadership have learned much from leading thinkers in the corporate realm. With a little bit of translating, we can often apply cutting-edge ideas from more aggressive corporate situations. The fact is, solid structural and organizational principles work wherever they are applied, and the church is wise to take advantage of these guidelines.

Q: As a pastor looking at the daunting challenge of catalyzing change within my church, I have to think about the potential career risks if things do not turn out so well. How do I do this honestly?

A: It is good that you take the challenge seriously. A person who takes improvement issues lightly is foolish and foolhardy. Still, life is a series of risks. In most professions, job security used to be a matter of putting in your time. Now, it is rarely an option in any. Family conditions, age, finances, stability of the church, and any number of other factors must weigh into a leader's decision whether to move forward, at what speed, and with what gusto. The best advice is to know as much about the change process as possible beforehand, consult God on a serious level, and if needed, seek the advice of wise and discerning leaders.

Q: Why isn't there a simpler, single-method model for implementing improvement?

A: If you find one, use it. If someone tries to sell you one, run. Some of the church-change books we have reviewed are built around a single best approach. But one size does not fit all. That is why we have focused more on concepts, principles, and making sure that you and your improvement team are not blindsided by careless mistakes or overlooked issues. Most churches get into trouble because they underprepare for significant improvement. While you will not need to implement all of the recommendations we discuss in this book, we want you to be aware of them in case they do apply to you. Sometimes you do not know whether they do or not until you get in the middle of the process.

APPLICATION TOOLBOX

First, on a piece of paper draw a large S-curve. Mark the points. Then answer these questions:

- How do these correlate with various times and eras in your church (ministry)?
- At what point would you say your church/ministry is on the S-curve presently?
- Can you think of times in your ministry when a second (subsequent) curve was begun that allowed your ministry to experience renewal before seeing a decline or plateau?

Discussion Starters

1. Can you think of a change implementation that went bad? In what stage did the change begin to go haywire?
2. Think of a potential change issue for your church. Discuss the various components that will influence the effectiveness of the change: amount of time needed, amount of change proposed, leadership capabilities, and readiness of the congregation.
3. If you had to start your church from scratch, which ministry components would you keep?
4. One of the best ways to peel back outdated, ineffective practices is by asking the five Whys. Look at something specific you're doing and ask, "Why is that?" Then do it again, and again, and again, and again. You might irritate

some people, but at least you will get to a deeper level of answering the question Why do we do what we do?

5. Imagine the change process as two rooms connected by a hallway. Think of a change situation and determine where you are in the process:
    A) in the old room with a locked door (closed to change);
    B) in the old room with the door open (open to change);
    C) in the hallway (transitioning);
    D) in the new room with the door open (transition complete but still settling);
    E) in the new room with the door locked (transition complete and at home).

If you answered E, how is this different from A?

6. Why does it help to consider the transition as a unique experience of the change process? Do you agree or disagree that it is the transition more than the change that creates the most problems?

7. Why is the letting-go part of the change process so crucial to the success of the transition? Why do we have such a difficult time leaving familiar places (events, traditions), even when logically we know they have ceased to be highly effective?

8. What sort of strategic plan or process exists for changes you are pursuing in your ministry or congregation?

> Great is the art of beginning, but greater the art of ending.
>
> —Henry Wadsworth Longfellow

Contemplation

> Some men came carrying a paralytic on a mat and tried to take him into the house to lay him before Jesus. When they could not find a way to do this because of the crowd, they went up on the roof and lowered him on his mat through the tiles into the middle of the crowd, right in front of Jesus.

—LUKE 5:18–19

Scripture

Read Luke 5:18–26.

DEVOTIONAL THOUGHT

What are friends for? These guys saw a window of opportunity closing when they could not get their invalid friend into the presence of Jesus. Imagine how devastated the paralytic must have felt: Even the word *invalid* says "not valid," or "You don't count." But these buddies didn't take "no" for an answer. They chopped a hole in the thatched roof and lowered their lame friend right under the Messiah's nose. He had to take notice then.

Sure enough, he did. Jesus, impressed with the faith and perseverance of the men, healed the lame man so that he could carry his own bed out of the impacted house.

What would have happened if the friends of this man had looked at circumstances and not pushed the envelope, so to speak, to get Jesus' attention? They could have justified the failure to their lame friend: "It's far too crowded. We're too late. He's too busy. A hole in the roof is too much work, too much trouble, too much risk. What if it doesn't work? Oh well, it was a nice idea." Unfortunately, the paralytic would have gone to his grave as a lame man, a wanna-be, a could-have-been-healed person. But the man's friends persevered and took the risk to think outside of the norm in order to be effective.

Circumstances should not be our guides as Christians. Faith requires us to seek out new strategies, new ways of accomplishing our goals. If one way is not working, find another one that will. There is little or nothing sacred in means and methods themselves. Getting people to Jesus is what matters most. Cutting holes in roofs is not the norm, but then, these are not normal times. Taking risks means potentially failing, but not taking risks often guarantees failing.

Prayer

Dear God, help me to have such a passion for the spiritual invalids around me that I will do nearly anything to get them to you. Forgive me for taking "no" for an answer so easily. Help me let go of my fear of appearing foolish and being rejected by others. Drastic times call for drastic means. We must bring people to you, regardless of the circumstances. Let me be a better friend to the lost. Help us do what it takes to bring people to you, regardless of the mess and unconventionality. It will be well worth the effort. Amen.

CHAPTER 4
Why People Respond as They Do: Understanding the Emotional Side of Change

A friend of our was a disciple of William Edwards Deming, who did more to bring the era of people-as-cogs to a close than anyone. One evening, at a dinner for Dr. Deming, our friend asked him if he could sum up his entire theory of work, production, statistics, variation, systems, knowledge, and control in a single sentence. Deming did it in two words: "People matter."

—HARVEY ROBBINS AND MICHAEL FINLEY

Why are there so many books on leadership and change, and yet no one has a corner on the market for bringing it about? Why is there no cookie-cutter recipe for doing what needs to be done, with limited loss of time, love, and energy? The primary difficulty with change is that it is 90 percent social/emotional and 10 percent logical/physical. No matter how much we try to justify our proposed change with logic, spirituality, resources, and common sense, change is tough because it is primarily cultural in nature. Cultures are mainly emotional, not logical. Those of us who value logic like to explain our preferences from a sensible framework, but when it all boils down, emotion runs deep.

Let us add: By *emotion,* we do not just mean feelings, such as anger, sadness, happiness, or joy. A part of personal identity, our self-image, is based on what we have experienced, and that too colors our emotions. Our perspectives are biased, twisted to our individualized views, and not necessarily grounded in truth or reality.

Here is an example. The leaders at a large company tried to figure out how they could save some money and shave costs from everyday operating expenses. They determined that by faxing paper horizontally instead of vertically, they could save as much as 15 percent because the transmissions would be faster. They never pushed the change, however, because they knew that to get people to adjust their habits would be too much work.[1]

This is a common example of how we fail to behave logically and sensibly because of habits and emotional bonding with traditions. That is why change is such a controversial topic. When you suggest a change of habits, environment, relationships, or even spiritual direction, you are questioning each individual's personal preferences and the beliefs that back them. Even as Christ followers, we try to spiritualize our preferences, believing that God is on our side and certainly supportive of our opinions—otherwise we wouldn't have them. It is important to remember that those of us who receive change well tend to be a minority; the majority of people resist change because of the way they are emotionally wired, not because they are negative, bad, or faithless.

CENTRAL CHRISTIAN CHURCH: OUR STORY

Negotiating Emotional Change

When we initiated our changes, we didn't really know how people would respond. If you are a new pastor, like I (Gene) was, knowing is doubly hard. Every church says that it is open to and ready for change, but it is still really difficult to assess. It's only when you start navigating actual change that people's readiness—or lack thereof—becomes apparent.

One tool that helped smooth the way for us was incremental introductions to big change. These gave us an opportunity to test-pilot how prepared our people really were. We started by adding a second Sunday morning service and Sunday school program. The congregation adjusted well and the improvements seemed to work, and the church grew. Slowly, over time, we introduced more contemporary choruses to our worship music and experimented instrumentally; when we added drums, they did not sit well, so we backed up.

If you want to implement sweeping change, start small: Push the envelope and respond when people are ruffled. Another example is that women had never helped with offerings or Communion. Some of the ladies began asking to do this. The board recognized that no biblical teaching forbade women to do these things, but the board also recognized that the church was not ready for this change. After letting the issue rest for a year or so, I did some teaching on the subject. After that, we sensed the congregation was prepared and we began using women to take the offering and serve Communion. No significant opposition arose.

I learned from that experience that I needed to use wisdom regarding what change to push right away and what to implement gradually. It was clear that beginning incrementally and respecting the readiness of the congregation were two keys that unlocked the door to major and lasting change.

SEVEN UNCHANGEABLE RULES OF CHANGE

Mark them well. In forty thousand years, they have not changed one iota:

1. People do what they perceive is in their best interest, thinking as rationally as circumstances allow them to think.
2. People are not inherently antichange. Most will, in fact, embrace initiatives provided the change has positive meaning for them.
3. People thrive under creative challenge but wilt under negative stress.
4. People are different. No single "elegant solution" will address the entire breadth of these differences.
5. People believe what they see. Actions do speak louder than words, and a history of previous deception octuples present suspicion.
6. The way to make effective long-term change is to first visualize what you want to accomplish and then inhabit this vision until it comes true.
7. Change is an act of the imagination. Until the imagination is engaged, no important change can occur.[2]

CHANGE AND SOCIAL WIRING

Every organization is made up of people who differ in the way they view new ideas and innovation. Birds of a feather flock together. While we tend to prefer people who are most like us, it's important to understand that diversity need not disrupt unity. Ephesians 4 and 1 Corinthians 12 help us see how God has given his church a variety of gifts and abilities, manifested by a single Spirit for the cause of Christ. Everyone changes throughout life and ultimately has to respond to different situations and relationships. But people tend to respond to new ideas at different speeds. These are natural inclinations and do not make some people better or worse than others.

Understanding the different wirings helps us see the big picture of how change does and does not take place effectively. Social scientists and leadership scholars tell us that most groups of people have certain leanings, all of which can enhance and diminish any organization's health.

APPLICATION TOOLBOX

Answer the following questions to see how you tend to view changes. There are no right or wrong answers. Following each question, place an A beside those to which you answer "rarely, only occasionally." Write a B after the questions to which you respond "usually, quite often." Do this as a team as well as with people of influence within your church.

1. I prefer to improve existing things rather than to initiate something new. _____

2. When someone throws out a new idea, I get energized. _____

3. When someone advocates a new idea, I'd prefer not to get involved. _____

4. I don't go looking for change, but I am willing to figure out how new ideas might work. _____

5. I feel most comfortable when I'm around familiar friends and settings. _____

6. I feel irritated when people seem to have little reverence for tradition and heritage. _____

7. I like to take someone's idea and see how it might work. _____

8. *Inventor, innovator,* or *entrepreneur* are words that describe me well. _____

9. I think we should stick to what is proven and tested. _____

10. Unless you can prove to me an idea is trustworthy and proven, I'm apt to stick with what I have already. _____

11. I'm pretty good at seeing the potential in a concept or idea. _____

12. Traditions and routines make me feel comfortable and secure. _____

13. I don't have a lot of tolerance for those who are negative about new ideas/change. _____

14. I get bored with routine and tradition. _____

15. I grow weary of all this change talk in society. _____

16. I think we'd be better off if we stayed with what has worked in the past. _____

17 I am not afraid to try new things in life. _____

18. I have effectively started various career ventures and projects. _____

19. The idea of change and innovation is at times scary. _____
20. I'm more comfortable with what is proven and widely accepted than I am with pioneer work. _____
21. I tend to buy into an idea after a majority has accepted it. _____
22. If someone I respect accepts a new idea, I'm open to hearing his/her view. _____
23. I get excited about brainstorming sessions. _____
24. I'm not opposed to innovations, but I like to see how they can pay off before I adopt them. _____
25. I like a variety of the arts. _____

Tabulating Responses: For every question that you answered with B, "usually, quite often," place a check in the corresponding blank. Count the number of checks in each vertical column and place the total at the bottom.

	Creator	Progressive	Builder	Foundational	Anchor
	2_____	7_____	1_____	3_____	5_____
	8_____	11_____	4_____	10_____	6_____
	13_____	17_____	20_____	15_____	9_____
	14_____	18_____	22_____	16_____	12_____
	23_____	25_____	24_____	21_____	19_____
Totals	_____	_____	_____	_____	_____

Primary category (column with the highest score)

_____

Secondary category (column with the second highest score)

_____

Although this is a very brief self-analysis, it gives you an idea of how you respond to innovation. If in doubt, ask others who know and work with you to answer the questions on your behalf.

The following are descriptions of these five categories.

FIVE TYPES OF CHURCH MEMBERS

Each church body will contain a combination of these personality types.[3]

Creators are relatively few (2 to 5 percent of the general population), but we need not have many of them to make an exciting and stimulating world. They are the out-of-the-box thinkers, artists, inventors, and prophets. Creators have very little loyalty to history. They think new thoughts, look at life differently from the way others do, and peer into the promised land before anyone else does. Creators tend to thrive on new ideas and bore easily with the commonplace. The sheer element of newness attracts them to ideas, sometimes regardless of the ideas' value or necessity. While a majority of people consider Creators to be mavericks and loose cannons, most of us would live extremely dull and ineffective lives without their cutting-edge thoughts.

Progressives are not so much originators of new ideas as they are the ones who see an idea they like and strive to act on it. Progressives serve as editors and refiners of Creators' ideas and tend to see how they can make the ideas practical in order to keep up with and even stay ahead of changing times. Progressives tend to be better appreciated than passion-driven Creators because they are a bit more logical and safe. New ideas for improvement do not threaten them. In fact, they embrace them, as long as the ideas seem reasonable and have the chance of significantly adding to the church or organization. People with this wiring make up about 10 to 20 percent of society.

Builders are good-hearted people who strive to keep an organization from tipping over from new ideas and the risk that comes from giving up proven ways. Builders are not so much resistant to new ideas as they are dependent on the Progressives to show them how an improvement will work and benefit an organization. When they initiate improvement, it is nearly always incremental. Think of the chaos we'd be in if it were not for these people, who help us fully implement new changes and improve them as we go. Those who are level-headed, not prone to knee-jerk reactions, help stabilize a group. Creators are explorers, Progressives are pioneers, and Builders are settlers. While Creators are dreaming new dreams and Progressives are busy figuring out what is and is not a viable idea, Builders are active carrying out the ideas and making them realistic parts of the present so we do not regret the past. This large group consists of 25 to 40 percent of a typical organization.

Foundationals make up those who prefer to keep things as they are. They move into the frontier town once the infrastructure is in place and homes and commerce established. Foundationals help us avoid losing our past values and meaningful history. Like Builders, Foundationals provide stability and overall strength by keeping the Progressive minority from taking the organization down any cow trail they desire. Unlike their Builder siblings, they are more cautious and conservative about changes. While Creators and Progressives often see Foundationals as old-fashioned, closed-minded, and resistant to change, Foundationals believe they are strengthening the future by preserving the past. Foundational people are very dependable. Once you get a Foundational going a certain direction, loyalty and consistency follow. This large group consists of 25 to 40 percent of society.

Anchors benefit us by making us think through our change issues. They are in love with our heritage and have a great appreciation for historical effectiveness and values. They highly esteem routine and rituals. Other types often see Anchors as sticks-in-the-mud and downright deadwood, when in reality they push Progressives and Builders to synthesize and plan innovations so as not to wreck an organization. Just as a pendulum requires an equal weight to bring it back to center, Anchors keep us from flying off into wrong directions and also from prematurely implementing a change before thinking through the processes and outcomes. With regard to the explorer-pioneer metaphor, Anchors represent those who stay in the old country, turning out the lights when the rest have gone. They make up about 10 to 20 percent of the general population.

Of all these types, who is right? No one is—neither is anyone wrong. Every group of people is wired differently from the other, but working as a unified team is essential.

> The body is a unit, though it is made up of many parts; and though all its parts are many, they form one body. So it is with Christ. For we were all baptized by one Spirit into one body—whether Jews or Greeks, slave or free—and we were all given the one Spirit to drink.
>
> Now the body is not made up of one part but of many. If the foot should say, "Because I am not a hand, I do not belong to the body," it would not for that reason cease to be part of the body. And if the ear should say, "Because I am not an eye, I do not belong to the body," it would not for that reason cease to be part of the body. If the whole body were an eye, where would the sense of hearing be? If the whole body were an ear, where would the sense of smell be? But in fact God has arranged the parts in the body, every one of them, just as he wanted them to be. If they were all one part, where would the body be? As it is, there are many parts, but one body.
>
> The eye cannot say to the hand, "I don't need you!" And the head cannot say to the feet, "I don't need you!" On the contrary, those parts of the body that seem to be weaker are indispensable. (1 Cor. 12:12–22)

Authors Harvey Robbins and Michael Finley write, "In developing strong teams, understanding and valuing differences is essential. But in adapting to change, understanding and valuing commonalities is the key. We grow by focusing on how we are unique; we progress by focusing on how we are similar."[4]

4A
Responsiveness to Change

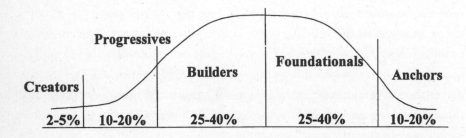

You may have noticed the range of percentages within each category. These exist because churches and organizations have varying ratios of these kinds of people. Entrepreneurial, upstart churches and businesses tend to have higher percentages of Creative and Progressive types. More static and long-term churches and organizations tend to have more Foundationals and Anchors. It might help to think of a church's change orientation like the weight distribution of a boat. When a boat has a lot of weight in the front, it will sink lower in the water at the bow. When the weight is unevenly distributed in the rear, the front will be out of the water and the stern submerged. The center of gravity will affect how the boat sails.

Similarly, the percentages of these types of people will affect a church. That is why certain churches are quicker to adopt new strategies and forms: They have larger numbers of Creator/Progressives who establish a critical mass toward change. When a disproportionate number of opinion leaders are Foundationals and Anchors, slim is the chance of inaugurating an aggressive improvement program. The center of gravity is too far back in the boat.

For any significant new idea to become adopted, it must first be accepted by a critical mass of the opinion leaders. A biblical example of this is in Numbers 13, where the twelve spies were sent into Canaan to explore the new territory. Only two, Joshua and Caleb, came back with positive reports. Ten were not in favor of the transition. No matter how motivated Joshua and Caleb were, they were not influential enough to dispel the fear incited by the ten. Perhaps the people of Israel had spent too much time in slavery. The Progressive leaders had either been eradicated or beaten into submission. They had been conditioned to think, Don't rock the boat.

As a result, the children of Israel wandered for forty years in the wilderness. What would have happened had half or three-quarters of the spies returned with hopeful reports? When a critical mass of the opinion leaders does not affirm a good report, a church will not likely adopt the new idea.

In some smaller churches, the critical mass may be just one or two people. One pastor told us the story of how frustrating his Sunday evening services had become. They seemed to be mediocre reproductions of Sunday morning. At the same time, Sunday mornings were going so well that they were packed. He wondered how the congregation would respond to going to double morning services to allow for more growth. He shared his burden with a key opinion leader who simply said, "Pastor, let me take care of it."

The next Sunday, this key layman stood in front of the congregation and said, "Folks, you know that when we hired our pastor, we hired him to do two services, Sunday morning and Sunday evening. It's not fair for us to change what we asked. But as you can see, we're out of room. We have to make more space for people to come to our church. Starting next Sunday we will not be having Sunday evening services, but we will have 9:30 and 11:00 A.M. services."

The man sat down and the next week, the changes were made without a hitch. Certainly that may be a unique story, but the concept of getting the opinion leaders to adopt the new idea is clearly seen in this church.

The bottom line of any church improvement issue is coming to an appreciation of differing gifts and abilities to respond to new ideas and improvements. We all need each other if we are to grow as Christ desired. Elevating love above any other agenda is paramount.

One church was striving to implement new forms of worship and discipleship. The congregation failed to recognize the benefit of differing ways of thinking and looking at improvement and ultimately lost a large group of discontented people. The anger, gossip, and bad-mouthing of those left in the church must have saddened our God of love. When our Father's children cannot get along, he is disappointed. Ultimately, the church failed to grow, and the pastor left a few years later. The congregation has not recovered from this division.

If I speak in the tongues of men and of angels, but have not love, I am only a resounding gong or a clanging cymbal. If I have the gift of prophecy and can fathom all mysteries and all knowledge, and if I have a faith that can move mountains, but have not love, I am nothing. If I give all I possess to the poor and surrender my body to the flames, but have not love, I gain nothing. [If I pursue or thwart change issues in my church, but am not loving, I am nothing.]

Love is patient, love is kind. It does not envy, it does not boast, it is not proud. It is not rude, it is not self-seeking, it is not easily angered, it keeps no record of wrongs. Love does not delight in evil but rejoices with the truth. It always protects, always trusts, always hopes, always perseveres. Love never fails. (1 Cor. 13:1–8)

THE STRENGTHS AND WEAKNESSES OF THE FIVE TYPES

Many of us understand the idea that our strengths can also become our weaknesses. You can't be strong in all areas. The human tendency is to compare our strengths with others' weaknesses and become frustrated. Similarly, we tend to overlook our own shortcomings.

Creators' strengths involve getting the rest of us to see into the future, to shake loose from the past that can keep us from being effective and even surviving in the future. God is a Creator in his work and keeps doing new things. Creators are often the ones who introduce to us the new wine that requires new wineskins (Matt. 9:17).

Creators' weaknesses can include their lack of tolerance for those who do not readily see things their way. They often alienate others by pushing risky, unproven ideas. Then they label the less-creative people closed-minded, stubborn, and the demise of the organization. They are also sometimes too quick to bail out on practices that have productivity left in them, merely because they are not new.

Progressives' strengths include their ability to be open to new ideas and to help weigh the risks and viability. They tend to demonstrate their faith by trusting God for things that are yet unproven. Most organizations would not move forward without the influence of Progressives.

Progressives' weaknesses include those of their Creator cousins: They can have low tolerance for those who are not able to see what is invisible, who are unwilling to move into the promised land in spite of the giants and risks. This intolerance can often reduce communication, alienate people with different opinions, and work against the change the Progressives promote.

Builders' strengths include being stable and loyal. They avoid being swayed by fads. Builders focus on settling the land after the pioneers have spied it out and secured the borders. The settling effect does a lot within a church or organization for making the improvement a lifestyle and a fully functioning, productive idea.

Builders' weaknesses include tending to gain their security and sometimes even their identity from the present setting. Thus they can be resistant to change in untried ways that God is leading, because they do not have their own experience to give them confidence. Sometimes they can lose the importance of the new idea in trying to figure out how to apply it.

Foundationals' strengths include the desire to honor valuable heritage. These are people who are very loyal, who will be just as loyal to new ways once the new ways are explained, established, and experienced. Foundationals with good attitudes lovingly raise caution flags to help Progressives maintain essential values as well as practices that still may be productive in the right setting.

Foundationals' weaknesses include the fact that more than any group, they can thwart the progress that the Holy Spirit wants to make. Foundationals sometimes get pickled in antiquated forms and practices. They are apt to lose the perspective that change need not be bad and that effectiveness today means moving out of yesterday. To leave the past does not require giving up on eternal values but recasts them for contemporary application.

Anchors' strength is loyalty, even beyond that of the Foundationals. Their love for the past allows us to continue to celebrate our heritage. They cause us to think through our processes, motives, and ideas. Loving Anchors create an environment that causes others to think about long-term values and to remember the lasting good things of the past.

Anchors' weaknesses include their fear of the future and change, which can make them a thorn in the sides of those who believe that occupying the promised land is crucial. Anchors with bad attitudes can be divisive. They can earnestly believe that they are right when in reality they have created idols out of their traditions and religious practices.

Any number and combination of these people can exude an attitude of self-righteousness when they feel they are the most spiritual and pleasing to God. At the same time, any number and combination of these people can be truly right with God in their own minds and can be earnestly seeking to obey God as individuals. The goal is to recognize that these natural differences exist and that all of us types must work together in unity, emphasizing love but moving as God leads. Because we are human, we are not all the same. But because we have God's Spirit in us, we make room for others' differences and appreciate what each brings to the table. Those less comfortable with change must recognize that God often introduces new things via more progressive brothers and sisters. At the same time, the more progressive people need to understand that the others can love God just as much as they do and that less-change-oriented people help qualify the improvement process for it to be effective.

NEW-IDEA KILL ZONES

Growing up on an Iowan farm, I (Alan) remember harvesttime, when Dad would put the sideboards on the wagon, which extended the capacity to hold more grain. Sometimes he'd put on double sideboards, but that was as far as he would go.

In the same way, certain people can't manage as much newness as others can. These people would add one sideboard to their wagon to hold the overflow, but not two. The fact is, none of us can handle endless changes. You can put only so many sideboards on your life to handle the overflow of family, career, social, financial, physical, spiritual, and ministerial demands. When people are near capacity stresswise, they will avoid all new-change demands, regardless of how good, logical, and potentially beneficial they may be.

> The more stress your situation piles upon you, the smaller your change space becomes. It is a paradox: instead of getting better at change, the more of it you are asked to do, the worse you get at it. Piled-on change, with no time allotted for re-energizing, causes most people's change potential to diminish: burnout. As we prioritize some things in, we prioritize others out: unknown people, unfamiliar situations, difficult ideas. We call it the kill zone, the overlap space that shrinks or expands as the circles move in our lives. In the kill zone, resistance is our religion. Moving things from the kill zone to the comfort zone means reversing a decision already made. We do not do this lightly.[5]

A kill zone is equivalent to a foul zone in a baseball game. No matter how good the hit is, if it goes into the foul zone, it does not count. Regardless of how good an improvement idea seems, a person will reject it if it falls within his or her new-idea kill zone.

PERSONALITIES OF CHANGE

Authors Harvey Robbins and Michael Finley combine elements of the Myers-Briggs and DiSC tests, which help us understand personality differences and how they facilitate or obstruct the process of change. They differentiate between who responds to what kind of motivation. Approximately 20 percent of people are reactive against change. These are the people who would rather fry than jump off of a burning platform. Another 60 percent tend to respond best to being pushed—informed about the pending bad news if change is not pursued—and then motivated by pull—seeing the potential rewards. The final 20 percent tend to be motivated best purely by seeing the potential rewards and encouraged to dream and imagine.[6]

Like many personality observers, Robbins and Finley categorize people who vary in their response to change according to four categories. They compare the elements of reactive/proactive with task oriented/people oriented.[7] In the next section we will look at these four personality categories (Driver, Analytical, Expressive, Amiable), which have varying sizes of new-idea kill zones.

Please don't be confused by our introducing another lens through which to understand why people respond as they do to change. The purpose of mentioning the temperament concept in addition to the previous discussion of the five change-responder categories is twofold. First of all, it is beneficial as a tool to understand various nuances of change, helping us predict how people will respond to change. Each instrument and framework gives us new insights for understanding people. The categories of change-responder types we just used look at people specifically from the angle of how they react to change. This other approach looks at how different personalities respond to change in terms of how they respond to life in general. The second benefit of this material is that many of us are more familiar with the four primary temperaments through popular books and seminars. Our basic personalities affect so many ways we see and perceive that it only makes sense to consider how our emotional wiring affects our perception of change and improvement.

As you identify these different types among your congregation, you can better select who should be on the improvement team and how they should serve. The larger the kill zone, the more likely a new idea will die. The smaller the kill zone, the more likely a new idea will survive.

4B
Personalities of Change

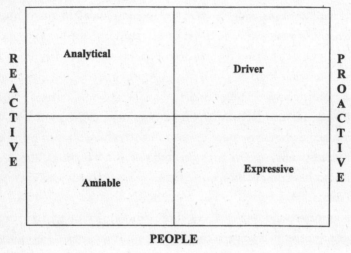

PEOPLE

Drivers are proactive and task oriented. They are individuals who have very small new-idea kill zones and who often pursue change because they are easily bored with the status quo. While Drivers can be tyrannical if pushed, they tend to enjoy striving after improvements and creating more effective ministry. These are the people who will initiate and maintain the momentum behind an improvement process. Make sure they are discipled and loyal, then let them loose.

Expressives are proactive and people oriented. They are often so enamored with change that they need constant change to function. These people bore easily. They tend to be very creative and fresh and do not dive deeply into life or projects, floating from one to another. Expressives can attack if pushed. Expressives can add a lot of energy and help sell an improvement emphasis, but they are not the ones you want doing the detailed implementation.

Amiables are reactive and people oriented. They are easy to love and enjoy life as it comes. They shy away from any change and enjoy the status quo. The uninterrupted life tends to be the preference for most Amiables, but if pushed, they tend to become passive-aggressive. They demonstrate their anger quietly by resisting change and digging in their heels. When you find Amiables who like an improvement idea, include them as team members, but don't expect them to initiate the change.

Analyticals are reactive and task oriented. They are very detailed, organized, and reflective, but they can also be antichange, resisting it because they do not understand how the benefits can outweigh all the reorganization work it requires. When pushed, they tend to run or hide. When you have an Analytical who supports an improvement idea, let him or her help you design the plans and details. This will help diminish the fears of those who need to know you are not flying by the seat of your pants before they buy into the improvement.

GENDER DIFFERENCES

The brains of males and females are noticeably different in terms of how the right and left hemispheres of the brain interrelate. The female mind is better at crisscrossing the space between the two brain halves. The result is that the two genders change in different ways. Women's skill at crisscrossing proves that women are natural multitaskers—able to think about more than one objective at a time. "This multitasking ability helps explain why women have historically been ghettoized into pink-collar professions—hospitality, health-care, teaching, telephone work, homemaking. The conclusion is inescapable: our most change-capable people are not being allowed to play their logical role in leading organizational change."[8] If our congregations included women more frequently in improvement processes, we would tend to find more resources for adopting and adapting to the transitions required.

A shortcoming in many congregations is that the decision makers are often males, who unconsciously fail to consider how the women might respond to the improvements and to the way they are communicated. Because women are great social catalysts, they can often make or break the improvement processes with their involvement. One significant reason to include women on the Dream Team is to include the female way of thinking and processing. This is more important in today's culture because now more than ever, we know women are qualified and savvy assets to the change process. To alienate them intentionally or unintentionally is to bring on unnecessary miscommunication and potential conflicts.

Crash-and-Burn Story

I had become the associate pastor of a fifty-year-old church with three hundred in worship attendance. We were the typical, traditional church, which meant Sunday school and event driven.

When I joined the leadership, the senior pastor felt dissatisfied with the church's sensitivity to the lost. He, I, and some lay leaders studied the problem of churches seeming irrelevant to the culture around them. As a result, we determined that we needed to employ some new ways of doing ministry. We formed a Dream Team that read books on contemporary ministry and discussed the principles. We decided that the following year, we would begin a new style of worship service for an entire month. It would be called Seeker Month, and it would occur once per quarter. We thought this would introduce the concept to the people and that they would allow it if they saw it as a short-term outreach emphasis.

The transition was tough. We created opportunities such as forums and pastor breakfasts where people could talk to the pastor about why we were doing what we were doing. People under forty seemed to like the idea and were uncomfortable with the element of change and creativity. But the people over forty were not. They said, "We don't want the change. You're taking our worship from us."

My job as associate pastor was to help support the senior pastor and handle some of the negative feedback. As a result, we decided to hold the traditional service at 8:30, Sunday school at 9:45, and contemporary worship at 11:00 A.M. Between services, the pastor changed clothes from a suit and tie to a polo shirt and Dockers. Initially, the change went very well. Attendance grew to nearly 450.

But then everything seemed to go bad. Old church members began complaining about the changes. People began verbally attacking the pastor and his wife in the hallways at church. Some saw him as Satan personified. They began wearing out his family. After a few weeks, the pastor abruptly resigned. Within weeks, the church called me to serve as senior pastor. During the pastoral transition, the church had gone from 450 to 280 in attendance because of the dissension and lack of leadership.

After three or four months, we were back up to four hundred in attendance and were improving the quality of both services, still with different styles. Things looked good externally, but internally we were still experiencing squabbling over service and musical styles. We were trying to replicate what church-growth successes such as Willow Creek and Saddleback did, but we had failed to realize our uniqueness. I began to feel trapped between the opposing groups and could offer no solutions, so after a year, I left.

The next pastor returned the church to a traditional service format. More than one hundred people left because they did not feel I was treated with grace and acceptance during my stay there. The church now has less than two hundred in attendance on Sundays.

Crash-and-Burn Lessons:

- Our biggest mistake was that we did not establish a foundation of values for why we were doing what we were doing. This takes time. Take enough time to make sure your people understand and support what you're doing. We should have spent more time in teaching, preaching, reading, and talking with people.
- Every church is unique. I tried too much to emulate what I had seen and heard from teaching/model churches, which was not healthy. My gifts, church, and community provided a unique chemistry: principles transfer; practices may not.
- Before pursuing change, be sure the people have prayed and sought God's will in small groups. Have key leaders of all ages lead these groups and make sure they are spiritually broken and focused together to seek God's will. It is his church and not ours. We were too busy doing and growing, and we died from the inside out.

EMOTIONAL PASSAGES

As we mentioned earlier, what makes grieving and the emotional aspect of change so difficult in a local congregation is the fact that a church is a blend of corporate/organizational elements as well as family-like relationships. In most congregations, where relationships are esteemed and promoted, the stockholder influence is significantly higher than in nonfamily-oriented organizations. Thus, the very thing that we need and enjoy the most, relationships, often makes improvement and vitality more difficult. While strong webs of friendships and family relations can enhance change processes if the people are motivated to improve, human nature being what it is, these same relationships often thwart change.

When endings take place, people get angry, sad, frightened, depressed, confused. These emotional states can be mistaken for bad morale, but they
aren't. They are the signs of grieving, the natural sequence of emotions people
go through when they lose something that matters to them. You find them
among families that have lost a member and in an organization where an
ending has taken place.[9]

In his book *Managing Transitions,* William Bridges lists common negative emotions that occur during the transition process.[10]

The first is anger. This emotion can range from mild muttering and occa-
sional grumbling to friends, to outright rage and physical response. (If you don't
think church people are capable of this, you haven't played in a church softball
league.) The problem with anger is that like water, it can flow both constructively and destructively. When anger is directed at a specific source, it can be
resolved more effectively than when it is misdirected toward people or things not
related to the change, or when it is undirected, settling within a person. When
people feel powerless in transition processes, they will often drag their feet, make
"mistakes," and even sabotage the success of a new venture. That is why gathering feedback, communicating well, and developing a team approach to change is
always better than a single edict to change.

The second is bargaining. When an improvement idea looks like it is building steam and will be difficult to avoid, people are often tempted to resort to
unrealistic attempts to get out of the situation or to make it go away. Side meetings at coffee shops, in homes, and in church parking lots are often the pools for
deal striking. In order to diminish the impact of a suggested change, or to totally
eradicate the threat of change, people may strive to negotiate a compromise. At
times, these meetings can appear to be problem-solving efforts, but improvement-team members need to keep a realistic outline and not be swayed by
desperate arguments and impossible promises from those who are not keen on
the change.

The third is anxiety. Anxiety is a form of a low-grade fear, a gnawing nervous-
ness. It can vary from mild and silent concern to dramatic and expressed
phobiclike responses. We are naturally a bit fearful of the unknown, especially if we
perceive that there are difficulties in the near future. This anxiety can also help us
create unrealistic fantasies of catastrophe and destruction. The Bible is full of
acknowledgements of our fears, using the words "fear not" 365 times (one for

every day of the year). Because anxiety is natural, improvement-team members need to make sure they do not make people feel stupid or unspiritual for having or expressing it. Keep communication strong and compassionate and express empathy, not disgust or reprimand. "You shouldn't feel that way" statements increase the negative emotions of guilt and alienation and rarely alleviate the worry.

The fourth is sadness. Good grief is a natural, healthy part of living. When people deny their sadness or get stuck in a grieving mode, they become unhealthy. Stilted grief often rears its head later in depression or anger that eats away at attitudes, relationships, and self-esteem. Sadness can range from silence to tears to an outright broken heart. Encourage people to say what they are feeling, and share your feelings too. When a loved one passes away, you don't counsel a griever by saying, "Come on, it's no big deal. Get with the show. Grow up." Convey hope, but avoid reassuring people with unrealistic suggestions of hope.

The fifth is disorientation. Organizational transitions feel a bit like getting on and off a moving escalator, merry-go-round, or other amusement ride. Transitions into new environments raise the stress level, taking attention away from normal activities. When you get off the plane in a new airport, you automatically try to become oriented, looking for the baggage claim, restroom, ground transportation, or the connecting flight's gate. Confusion and forgetfulness, insecurity and feelings of being lost are common during times of transition even among organized people. Give people extra support—opportunities to get things off their chests and reassurances that disorientation is natural and that other people feel it too. Don't get frustrated over details that seem to be overlooked. Be a grace giver. Give people extra attention and provide directions for next steps.

The sixth is depression. A common result of these other emotions is a feeling of hopelessness and being tired all the time. Like sadness and anger, depression is difficult to be around. But you often can't just say a prayer or have a single talk with a person and make it go away. People have to go through it, not around it. Make it clear that you understand and even share the feeling yourself but that work still needs to be done. Do whatever you can to restore people's sense of having some control over their situation. One way to do this is to clarify a role in the change, whether it is in the planning and development phases or in the implementation. Providing ownership and small arenas of control are therapeutic ways of blowing away the clouds of depression.

GROWTH OPPORTUNITIES IN THE NEUTRAL ZONE

Seize the opportunities that lie within the neutral (transition) zone, between what is old and new. The in-between area is certainly stressful, but it is also filled with unique potential for growth and development, which will be lost once the transition is over. Keep the big picture in mind. The temptation is to focus on the trivial irritations. The goal for us in a faith community is not just to go through times of personal and community change, but to grow through them. Transitions provide vibrant, fertile opportunities for fruit bearing.

The pruning that God does to make us more productive for his kingdom often happens within our churches as we confront issues of power, control, self-ishness, letting go of the past, releasing personal ministry preferences, and mourning the loss of comfort zones. Far too many churches get so consumed with getting through the transitions that they fail to capitalize on the inherent personal growth within them.

> The neutral zone isn't just meaningless waiting and confusion—it is a time
> when a necessary reorientation and redefinition is taking place, and people
> need to understand that. It is the winter during which the spring's new
> growth is taking shape under the earth. The neutral zone is like the wilder-
> ness through which Moses led his people. That took 40 years, not because
> they were lost but because the generation that had known Egypt had to die
> off before they entered the Promised Land.[11]

Look at it this way: The personality differences make improvement processes more dynamic. Someone said, "Ministry would be wonderful if it weren't for the people." You may agree that this is true, yet it is the people who make the change both possible and needed. In spite of all the personality dynamics that go into church improvement, remember to keep the main thing the main thing.

In my book *Broken in the Right Place,* I (Alan) write about the need to let the challenges and negative circumstances in life break you, so that your capacity for God can increase. There are many places where we can be broken in life: in our finances, emotions, physical body, mental capacity, relationships, career, and even church and ministry life. But all of these are ultimately designed to break in one right place, our soul. If we allow church life and ministry transitions to make us broken in the wrong places, we'll wind up like so many old, bitter, cynical people who line our churches or worse, give up their faith—the walking wounded. Is it possible for everyone to grow from these times of faith testing? Perhaps not. But if we all take the attitude of Christ (Phil. 2) and seek to humble ourselves and wash the feet of others, we will ultimately be elevated by God.

> If you have any encouragement from being united with Christ, if any comfort from his love, if any fellowship with the Spirit, if any tenderness and compassion, then make my joy complete by being like-minded, having the same love, being one in spirit and purpose. Do nothing out of selfish ambition or vain conceit, but in humility consider others better than yourselves. Each of you should look not only to your own interests, but also to the interests of others.
>
> Your attitude should be the same as that of Christ Jesus:
> Who, being in very nature God,
>   did not consider equality with God
>   something to be grasped,
> but made himself nothing,
>   taking the very nature of a servant,
>   being made in human likeness.
> And being found in appearance as a man,
>   he humbled himself
>   and became obedient to death—
>   even death on a cross! (Phil. 2:1–8)

People who are broken in the right place wind up being more fruitful, joyful, peaceful, and mature than those who are not. Their productivity increases sharply. There is no comparison. Work hard at not letting the outcome of change take priority over the process of change. Our goal is not just to get from here to there, but to accomplish it via deepening our love for each other as well as personally growing in our relationship with God. When the agenda supersedes this, we can still accomplish the change plan and yet diminish the kingdom. Let go. Let God lead. Give up the power, the manipulation, and the self-centered focus on what you want. Let tough love prevail as you remain unified amidst your differences.

> Know that the LORD has set apart
>   the godly for himself;
>   the LORD will hear when I call to him.

In your anger do not sin;
>   when you are on your beds,
>   search your hearts and be silent.
> Offer right sacrifices
>   and trust in the LORD.
> Many are asking, "Who can show us any good?"
>   Let the light of your face shine upon us, O LORD.
> You have filled my heart with greater joy
>   than when their grain and new wine abound.
> I will lie down and sleep in peace,
>   for you alone, O LORD, make me dwell in safety." (Ps. 4:3–8)

"In your anger do not sin": Do not let the sun go down while you are still angry, and do not give the devil a foothold. (Eph. 4:26–27)

Discussion Starters

1. Fill out and tabulate your scores on the change-response tool in the Application Toolbox. What were your category totals?
2. If you're game to do this as a team, go around the group and share what you believe your strengths and weaknesses are in terms of how you are wired regarding innovation and new ideas.
3. What did you learn about the leadership and influencers in your congregation from their scores on the questionnaire?
4. Think of and discuss a personal time in your past when you and/or your family faced a new situation. How did you respond to it?
5. Think of and discuss a time in your history as a church when the congregation faced a new challenge (pastor change, new building, new ministry). How did the church respond to this?
6. How can you as a church emphasize unity within diversity? How have you accomplished this in the past? What have you learned from doing it poorly in the past?
7. Talk about the concept of brokenness and discuss how you can maximize maturity and spiritual growth during the transition.

A single rower can easily alter or impede the group's progress simply by rest-ing on the oars. It's the same in organizations. A few people, with no particular malice in their hearts, can prevent good changes from taking place. It is called resistance, or foot-dragging, and it is the veto privilege even the humblest worker can use.

—HARVEY ROBBINS AND MICHAEL FINLEY[12]

Contemplation

These are the things God might want to say to members of each of the five change-response types:

Dear Creator,

We have a lot in common; both of us enjoy the creation of something new. I applaud your desire to break out of the mold, to be different, and to pioneer new areas. Throughout history, I have used people like you to cast the vision for change and announce to the masses what I have in store for them. You are not intimidated by change, or the transitions that new ideas create. You are very comfortable with the new wine I talk about in my Scriptures; you are the new wineskin. I do not fault you for your willingness to hear new ideas and think new thoughts.

Many Creators have gone the way of the martyred prophet, at times because people were stubborn and scared but at other times because the Creator did not have enough sense to communicate with caution. Be bold, but also be wise. Understand that until certain people catch the vision you possess, you will not progress very far. By championing a cause with too much zeal, you can actually harm it by creating unnecessary resistance. Remember the law of physics, which says that for every action, there is an equal and opposite reaction. Change rarely happens quickly.

Those who do not grab onto a new idea immediately are not necessarily stubborn or mean-spirited. They are just different. Just as some soils are porous and allow water to flow freely through them, others retain moisture and hold it to water plants. There are many soils within my garden. Yours is not the only one, nor the best. Each serves a different and yet important purpose in my grand plan.

So be patient with those who are slower to understand and pursue a new idea. Your responsiveness is a plus, but your openness can also be a weakness when you pursue ideas that are untried and potentially harmful to my work. Temper your shallow roots in the past and present with the wisdom embedded in the cautions and concerns of Foundationals and Anchors. Hear their thoughts with grace and acceptance.

Your insight into the future is beneficial only if it finds a home in the minds and hearts of those without such vision. Learn the ways of others. Do not let your strengths become a weakness by hindering your love for those who do not see what you see. It is no sin to have different eyesight. Less-creative people are no less children of mine. Work to bring unity, even while you push the envelope for innovation and progress.

I know your intents are good. You seek the health and welfare of my work. You have been blessed with an inner wiring that makes faith a matter of life and ministry in addition to your soul. Do not let go of your dreams, your spirit to plow new furrows for tomorrow. The new things I have for my church are most apt to come through creative types like you, but do not make that a matter for pride or an excuse for bullying others. For just as I am a God of new things, I'm also a God of longsuffering and love.

Your burden for change is heavy, I know. Count the costs. Consider the outcomes. Don't overlook those who have something to lose, but also don't give up on those who stand to gain from the change that I bring. Keep the faith.

Love, God

Dear Progressive,

What a key role you fill in my kingdom work. While not always possessing the prophetic voice of your Creator brother, you bear the burden of hearing the new thing and bringing it to fruition through the respect that others have for you. You are not swayed by schemes and crazy ideas, but you are motivated by the hope in the potential of ideas. You sort out the best innovations and begin to think of how they can benefit others. You are a vital link between new ideas and those who would build the structures that will allow my people to cross the river into the promised lands of the future.

Understand your critical position in the big picture of change. You are designed to take an idea from a Creator and see how you can implement it.

You have the ability to see into tomorrow, to count the apples in a single seed, and your faith stretches beyond mere belief in my ways. You strive to make a way in the wilderness, a stream in the desert, and a bridge into the future. You legitimize the potential in an idea that threatens those who do not have the innate capacity to see its benefits.

While I want you to be encouraged, I also exhort you to keep your eye on the Mission Giver, not the mission. Progressives like you can get so caught up on the new idea that you lose your focus on me. Just as I had to test Abram to see if he loved me or his son more, I want you to keep your hand in mine so that you do not go about my mission in your way. Don't go too fast or too slow. The process is often as important as the outcome. Keep pace with my Spirit.

Although you relate best to your Creator brothers and sisters, keep patience with those who do not see what you see. Do your best to communicate the directions with care and detail. Bring along Builders and Foundationals who are your allies to make the dream a reality. Do not alienate yourself from these needed team members. Know that their resistance is usually not rebelliousness but caution and at times, fear. Learn from their suggestions, but don't be intimidated by their perceived resistance. They want to make sure you have thought through the process. They are tempering the idea, refining it with their challenges and questions. Do not resist the purging of what is unimportant, but also do not compromise on what you know and believe in your heart.

You have to be about progress, ushering the people into promised lands and avoiding wilderness wandering. Caleb and Joshua are your models, but do not let pride in your position in line keep you from humbly seeking me for wisdom and accepting others who are not quick to adopt your suggestions.

Stay close to me. Keep your heart pure of pride, self-sufficiency, and conflict. You can turn a cause for or against me by the way you handle new ideas. Do not lose ground by pushing too far, too fast. Trust me to lead the way. As I led my people through the desert with a pillar of cloud by day and fire by night, I will give you what you need to find the land of promise.

Do not become weary in well-doing. Stretch your wings and let me be the wind beneath you. You are the trusted steward of my dreams and aspirations for your spheres of influence.

Love, God

Dear Builder,

The new things I declare for you and your people cannot come about without your work of faith. You manufacture the systems and structures that will make the new things realities for my people. You help the Creators and Progressives strategically plan their schemes. You are responsible for developing the hows, the applications, bringing dreams to reality. While you must prayerfully trust Progressives to lead the way, you must be next in line to create the process. Do not overlook your importance.

While you are usually not the originator or messenger of innovation, you should not allow this to create a closed-mindedness. I am a God of new things. I have never stopped creating, since the beginning of life itself and the birth of planet Earth. I have made humans in my image, which includes the aspect of creativity, making something from nothing or virtually nothing. No one people-type is wired to pull off the operation alone. You are all members of a larger team—my team. Fill your role with confidence and boldness, but do not thwart progress. Do not let your search for solutions keep you from confronting the problem. Do not let your respect for the present and past cause you to disrespect the future.

If we do not pursue new ways, we will soon become extinct in our faith. Our churches will become little more than holy museums for yesteryear's ministry practices. I do not need any more of my houses to become restaurants or antique stores. I need vibrant, relevant, gardens of fruitfulness. I am the one who makes a practice, building, or person sacred. My presence sanctifies the style. I am not confined to any given culture or practice.

Be conservative in your beliefs, but liberal in your methods. Work hard to confront your fears of the future. Your security is in me, not the traditions of faith. The best way to preserve the faith of your fathers is to help today's society to connect with me.

Embrace your Creator and Progressive siblings. They have a purpose in my plan just as you do. If each fulfills his and her niche, we will progress together. Do not fear what is ahead just because you cannot see how it will impact your life. Trust me. Take my hand.

Love your brothers and sisters. I am your God, and I have created you with the flexibility to respond to what I call you toward. Go the distance. Do not give up. Take one step at a time.

You must somehow connect the more progressives with the less progressives, so stay in tune with me. Do not rely on your own energies, rely on mine. I will give you the wisdom you lack. Seek me. Be encouraged as you build ways into the wilderness.

Love, God

Dear Foundational,

I want to thank you. I so appreciate your unwillingness to leave my ways just because of some new fad or bandwagon driving nearby. You are a person of faith and convictions. You stand for what is right, even if it seems that you are bucking the tide of society. You are essential for my church to avoid becoming a wishy-washy group without a rudder. I have placed you on the team to constructively challenge the Creators and Progressives in their new ideas. Your job is to make sure we do not compromise on the future because of harebrained schemes and knee-jerk reactions.

But as your responsibility is to stabilize my kingdom, please know that you are also not intended to be a barrier against progress. Please don't claim to be my spokesperson in thwarting a new idea. Old isn't better, just older. The tried and proven of the past is quite often the burden that creates the failure of the future. Times have changed, and I have kept pace . . . so keep in step. Don't lag. Don't fall behind and self-righteously suggest that you are leading the way. My role for you is not as leader, but as strong follower. I need you in that role to create balance, not dead weight.

I am a God of new things, responding to the needs of my people and the lost in our world. Do not hold me back. Work hard not to mistake your celebration of the past for my leading in the present. Do not keep my people from fulfilling their call.

I need you to lovingly encourage and support the Spirit-filled Progressives and Builders in your midst. Provide input. Hold them accountable, but act in unity with them. You are the peacekeeper in my camp. Your peers and Anchor siblings rely heavily on your opinion. They can catapult you into the promised land, or lunge you into wilderness wandering. Believe it or not, you hold the key. Unlock the door to the future. Shut the door on the past, not to forget what I've done in years gone by, but as a memory to spur you forward into tomorrow.

I am not yet through with you or with my church. I am not about to lose more ground to the enemy. Keep your faith from dying. I am with you, even when you walk through the valley of the shadow of change. My rod and my staff will strengthen you.

And know that I am with you always. Turn your fears over to me. Celebrate our victories and practices of the olden days, but rest assured that the good ol' days are yet to come. Fan the flames of hope.

Trust my Progressive leaders to hear my voice and risk what is necessary to keep joy and faith alive for coming generations. Fill your role on the team with boldness and love. I believe in you.

Love, God

Dear Anchor,

I love you. Thank you for your diligence in watching out for those who would rob my people from their heritage, their moorings. There are many thieves today who are bent on destroying the present and future by maligning the past. I have worked in days gone by, and none should negate that fact.

I have empowered you to a special position of historian, teacher, and holder of the fort. Do not be intimidated by those who seem to care less about bygone times. Lovingly help them to see my hand yesterday, so that they do not miss it today and tomorrow. Many fail to recognize my voice in the future because they never recognized it in the past. But you do, and I so appreciate your energy.

At the same time, know that just as I was alive in old ways, I am alive in new ones as well. Do not assume that yesterday's success will produce the same fruitfulness tomorrow. You can legitimately preserve the past by progressing in the future. Know the difference between messages and methods, essence and form, ageless truths and cultural preferences. When you mix these categories, you run the risk of worshiping traditions and habits instead of me. I do not make my dwelling in cemeteries. I am the author of births, rebirths, and resurrections. Dreams, like people, all have life spans. A strategy that has worked before may be ready for retirement or burial. Let it die naturally, in peace.

I know your fears regarding the future and the unknown. You fear the loss of good times, of position and comfortable ways. I do not fault you for your resistance. We all desire the security of the known. Peter and John wished to stay on top of the mountain when I appeared to Jesus. They wanted to camp out and savor the moment for days to come, but I did not let them. They had work to do, a mission to fulfill. So pull up the stakes and pursue the new mission. Endure your Creator siblings and put up with weaknesses.

Hold the Progressives and Builders accountable. Do not let them stray from my ways. Teach them about their heritage, but do not try to repeat yesterday. I am a God of new things.

Trust me. Place your faith in me, not the familiarity of past traditions. You'll see the new fruit I'll bring. Let me prune. You'll heal.

Do not divide my family. Hold your fears. Keep the peace. And I will be most proud of your faith. Take my hand as we cross the river into the land of promise. I am with you.

Love, God

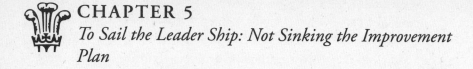

CHAPTER 5
To Sail the Leader Ship: Not Sinking the Improvement Plan

The present is a time of great entrepreneurial ferment, where old and staid institutions suddenly have to become very limber. The only things that evolve by themselves in an organization are disorder, friction, and malperformance.

—PETER DRUCKER

The primary reason improvement issues fail or succeed is leadership. The primary reason improvement issues fail or succeed is leadership. No, the editor did not miss an error. In spite of all the complexities of church improvement, leaders and the way they catalyze change are key. Mechanics tell you that when your car won't start, you should begin tracing the problem at the battery. Leadership is the place to start when something is or is not happening in your church. While leadership is not everything, it is by far the most important single factor in effective improvement processes.

The reason a majority of churches never make it to the harbor of healthy ministry is because their "leader ship" sank on the way. Many churches relate more to the *Titanic* than the "Love Boat" when it comes to effective change strategies. "Making space in others for change goes to the heart of leadership. It reminds us that in order to lead we must first know. Leaders accustomed to distancing themselves from followers and striking meaningful poses will find they have no luck enlarging their organization's change space because they have no knack for knowing people and their change potential."[1]

The Bible recognizes leadership as a spiritual gift.

> We have different gifts, according to the grace given us. If a person's gift is . . . leadership, let him govern diligently. . . .

> Love must be sincere. Hate what is evil; cling to what is good. Be devoted to one another in brotherly love. Honor one another above yourselves. Never be lacking in zeal, but keep your spiritual fervor, serving the Lord. Be joyful in hope, patient in affliction, faithful in prayer. (Rom. 12:6, 8–12)

By *leadership,* we refer to the process by which change issues are initiated by people of influence within and among groups. In nearly every social setting, members have varying amounts of influence. Not all influence is leadership, but leadership is the special kind of influence that significantly affects decision making, direction setting, and speed. Not all organizations need leaders in the specific sense. Leaders are people who help create, manage, and develop change within groups. When change is not needed, managers will do. Managers are people who help maintain a system, improve processes incrementally, and try to keep things on an even keel. While you always need good managers, leaders are necessary only to create and perpetuate change.

CENTRAL CHRISTIAN CHURCH: OUR STORY

Leading the Charge

The call to lead a church through change, to do the hard work to bring a congregation to a fuller and richer place of ministry, is awesome and occasionally overwhelming. The best way to describe it is to liken it to the work involved in a favorite family trip. For example, every summer my (Gene's) family vacations on a lake in northern Minnesota. It's a great time of year to be away from the 112-degree heat of Las Vegas. (I know you've heard it's a dry heat, but so is a blowtorch!) Our favorite fishing spot is on an isolated lake about twenty miles from our cabin.

To fish on this lake you have to be determined to get there. We trailer our boat. Since there's no place to launch on this lake, we have to go to a connecting lake. We cross the first lake, lined with cabins and boats, where people are fishing and water skiing. Then we come to a winding channel about the length of two football fields. The pathway is approximately six feet wide. Lily pads rub against both sides of the boat in this channel that is closely walled in by tall, white birch trees. Going through this natural hallway makes you feel like you're on a Ponce de Leon expedition.

The water gets so shallow in this channel that we have to raise the motor and paddle. In the last fifty feet, the bottom of the boat starts dragging on the channel bed. When we get to that point, my wife and kids get out of the boat and pull me through (in my dreams).

Getting this far is quite an ordeal, but the end of the narrow, shallow channel opens up to the most peaceful lake that you can imagine. I've seen some of the most beautiful sunsets, eagles soaring overhead, deer drinking at the water's edge. And the fishing—well, it's incredible! In spite of the breathtaking beauty, there are only a couple of cabins and seldom more than three or four boats on this entire lake.

If this paradise is so beautiful and the fishing is so great, why aren't there more boats, cabins, and people lining the shores? Why doesn't everybody fish on this lake? The reason is that it takes so much effort and hard work to get there! You've got to launch in one lake, cross it, maneuver through a channel, raise your motor, paddle, and then get out and portage your boat. And you have to take other people to help you. But the best fishing is on the other side of the hassle. Only those who are willing to endure the tremendous effort of going through the channel enjoy the better fishing.

In the same way, leadership is about doing what it takes to gather a team of inspired people, enlist their support, and get to the fishing lake.

THE ROLE AND LEVELS OF LEADERSHIP

While the most common reason that churches do not effectively improve is a lack of leadership, the most significant misperception regarding leadership is that those in positions of authority are leaders. Basically, there are three kinds of leaders. We'll refer to them as L1, L2, and L3. L1 leaders are individuals who are not gifted at leading but are perceived as good leaders because of the positions they fill. Church members often look to pastors, paid staff, elder-board members, and ministry directors as leaders, primarily because of their organizational roles.

The trouble is, L1 leaders do not intuitively understand leading. Most pastors, for example, tend to be teachers, managers, nurturers, and spiritual technicians. They do much of the ministry themselves, which is the main reason the average church in America right now sees just ninety people in Sunday morning worship.[2] (Remember that in Exodus 18, Moses was an L1 leader who wore himself out providing inadequate service because he was trying to do it all himself.)

L2 leaders are leaders by gifting, whether or not they fill official positions. Change is commonly thwarted when L1s occupy decision-making positions and/or when L2s are not in favor of certain ministry improvements. An L2 leader is good at team building, which involves identifying ability, recruiting, motivating, and unleashing. L2 leaders intuitively seek out leadership roles early in life and often gravitate toward situations where they can make a difference with their gifts. Sometimes L2 leaders diminish their abilities because they do not make room for other leaders who have the ability to rise in a church or organization. Talented L2 leaders tend to build organizations around their own gifts, which actually weakens an organization over the long haul. When the leader retires or moves on, the company or church is hard-pressed to replace the person, and the infrastructure suffers as a result. But L2 leaders are important because they are born with abilities others can only wish they had. They too can help a change initiative, but only in tandem with other types of leaders.

The third level of leadership is rare but ultimately the most productive over time. L3 leaders are people who intuitively and/or consciously understand leadership and develop other leaders. You do not lead leaders the same way you lead followers. Leaders and followers are different kinds of birds. Sparrows flock; eagles do not. The fact is that just as the best coaches are not always the best players, some of the best leader developers may be only above-average leaders themselves. For example, in Exodus 18, God told Moses via Jethro the principle of ministering through others: "Select capable men from all the people—men who fear God, trustworthy men who hate dishonest gain—and appoint them as officials over thousands, hundreds, fifties and tens" (Exod. 18:21). Jethro convinced Moses to move from L1 and L2 leading to become an L3 leader. This was a whole new ball game for Moses. L3 required far less time on the front line of ministry and much more time behind the scenes, so that everyone would be served better and he would avoid burnout.

All of these leaders, despite their flaws, can be an effective part of a change process. While gifting is a matter of degree and development, L1 leaders who lack intuitive skills to align people, create vision, and catalyze change can gain an understanding of the change process. By understanding this process, they can help catalyze the improvement changes by unleashing L2 leaders and creating ministry teams that are empowered to set in motion the structure, zeal, and handles for making improvement a reality. While not naturally gifted, L1 leaders need to be involved in leadership by working through L2 leaders, whether or not they ever become true L3 leaders. All levels of leaders need to identify, develop, and deploy opinion leaders in a congregation to achieve significant ministry improvement.

The best change agents over the long haul seem to be L3 leaders—pastors and lay leaders who are secure and savvy enough to identify influencers, disciple them, and engage them in local church leadership. Most pastors invest far too little time in leadership development because the urgent demands of ministry seem overwhelming. A pastor who wants to become an L3 leader must usually first invest in L2 leading, getting a team of people together to carry the load of weekly ministry, so that he can proactively invest more time in training, recruiting, and mentoring those with leadership potential. While L1 leaders add to ministry, L2 leaders multiply, and L3 leaders bring an exponential increase.

Pastors and lay leaders who desire to lead at the L3 level need an array of leadership training resources. Helping Christian men and women think like spiritual leaders is a specific goal with specific demands. While user-friendly leadership-development resources from a Christian perspective are limited, a good L3 will seek to blend the best of discipleship materials with cutting-edge leadership books, tapes, and resources. But be careful: not everything with the word *leadership* in the title is about leadership. The topic is so popular that marketing strategists drop the name into the titles of any number of nonleadership resources. Leading should not be confused with counseling, preaching, pastoring, discipling, or ministering in general. It is a very special ministry with unique characteristics. (See Appendix A for help obtaining leadership-training resources.)

Although the majority of this book is about church and organizational change, to see ministry come alive and attract the lost, leaders must change the way they lead as well. If you want different results, you have to employ different actions. Because leading is such a key factor in any change and improvement strategy, what makes us as leaders think that we can avoid being at the core of change ourselves? James Belasco and Ralph Stayer talk about leading differently in their book, *Flight of the Buffalo*. They use the buffalo as a metaphor depicting the typical American organization. In the early days of the Wild West, Native Americans killed numbers of wild buffalo by shooting the lead buffalo. Because the animals were such good followers, when the leader was killed the entire herd stopped in its tracks. Then the pursuers moved in easily for the slaughter. Belasco and Stayer's advice to organizations that want to last is to become more like geese, who rotate leaders and who work as a team.[3]

In another useful book, *Built to Last,* James Collins and Jerry Porras emphasize the importance of the organization not building itself around the gifts and personality of a charismatic leader. When the leader goes, the organization weakens and loses its focus.[4]

Church leaders need to follow these examples. Lead differently and strive to get out of the way for other leaders to emerge as a team. Deep and significant change never happens via one individual but through a team approach.

PUMMEL/PAMPER/PUSH/PULL

What is the most effective leadership approach to implementing an improvement idea? In their book *Why Change Doesn't Work,* Robbins and Finley define four popular means for motivating change, called Pummel, Pamper, Push, and Pull.[5] Pummel refers to a terroristic attitude: "Do what I say or you will die." This manipulative approach works only for short periods of time and is effective in emergency situations but few others. This sort of physical and emotional coercion can be used by both change agents and those who resist change.

The Pamper approach, "Do what you feel like doing," is nonthreatening and can often be misunderstood as loving behavior, but in reality it lacks spine and tends toward the dysfunctional idea of codependency. Pampering may bring about some change, but the improvement rarely lasts because significant change creates stress and requires perseverance that pampering does not promote.

The Push attitude tends to be more fear and pain oriented but not as pushy as pummeling: "Do what you must do or the ministry will die." Push focuses on the negative, promoting improvement to avoid the reality of loss or pain. Because pain avoidance is a very strong motivator, Push often creates a moderate amount of long-term change. At the same time, we need to beware of the doctor who cures the disease but loses the patient. Too much scaring can work against you in the long run. When the pain subsides, the tendency is to lose motivation and return to the status quo, which is why Push alone often does not create long-term change.

Pull makes the statement, "Do what you must do to achieve the future of which you dream." When a leader implements imagination and inspiration, people are motivated by what they can yet experience in a positive sense. The Pull approach to encouraging change tends to create the longest lasting effect, because people feel the least manipulated and the most compelled to enjoy a better life, whether it be church, career, or family. Pursing a dream is a powerful motivator. "The best hope organizations have for making successful change lies in utilizing a balanced combination of the more temperate two—Push and Pull. Push to get people's attention and start them thinking. Pull to leverage people's knowledge and creativity to put the change over."[6]

When you think about it, you can easily see these motivational styles in many facets of persuasion and sales. Take evangelism, for example. Some people like to pummel people with the gospel, wrestling them into submission to God. This Bible-thumping approach is useful for some, but the results are often temporary, with the new convert often leaving the faith for lack of lasting resolve. The Pamper approach is so laid-back and nonforceful that the recipient often fails to understand how to accept Christ personally, or perceives the lack of passion to mean there is little benefit to accepting Christ. Push evangelism warns the person of impending eternal doom, which is biblical, but by itself it can be negative. Quite often, it takes a Push in life such as brokenness to help us confront our need for Christ. But Jesus wants people to follow him primarily out of love, not fear. The rewards of eternal life, heaven, spiritual fruit, and the gift of Jesus as a companion are the best long-term motivations for a healthy relationship with God (Pull).

SITUATIONAL LEADERSHIP IN THE CONTEXT OF CHANGE

The Pummel/Pamper/Push/Pull idea shows us that there are various styles within leadership. Learning to be appropriate as a leader is a big challenge. Quite often, when you hear war stories of improvement efforts that self-destructed, you can trace the cause to an inappropriate leadership style. Most leaders by nature are comfortable with one or two styles. There are General Patton, take-charge, bull-in-the-china-closet-type leaders; animated directors; player-coaches; and relaxed facilitators. The best leaders are those who are able to read situations and respond appropriately.

Organizational guru Ken Blanchard designed a situational leadership model that helps leaders know when they need to be individually aggressive and take charge, when they need to be laid-back, and when they need to be in between.[7] When you know how to vary your style according to the need at hand, you can be effective in a variety of situations.

The fact is that during the life of an organization, different styles are needed at certain times. During a time of crisis, a congregation needs and wants strong, aggressive, individual leadership. During times of passivity or high member commitment, the congregation would reject that same style. Leaders who are not aware of appropriateness will often find their leading ignored; they rarely understand what went wrong. Their tendency is to blame any number of factors, usually people, when the main cause was an inappropriate style. Following is a simple grid I adapted from Blanchard and Hershey's concept to help leaders and improvement teams discern what might be a more appropriate leadership style per change-readiness level.

5A
Appropriate Leadership Response

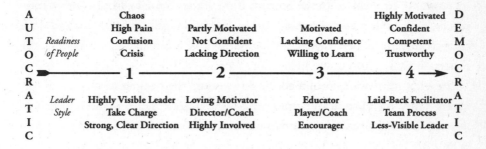

Level 1: Motivated, Unprepared: The congregational atmosphere is negative in terms of pain, desperation, and discouragement. The fear of a split, closure, or emotional confusion makes a church ready for a leader who is lovingly aggressive and at times authoritative in style. This is the best situation for immediate change, but congregations in crisis mode often wait too long to find such a leader. If a leader here is too laid-back and participatory, the church will often flounder and fail. This is a congregation in emergency status. Time is of the essence. The leader must help the patient stop bleeding and apply first aid promptly. He must be assertive and can be autocratic, giving orders and taking bold charge.

The challenge here is that many leaders who are good at this style cannot move into other styles after the patient has made it out of ICU. Thus you see congregations that either split or plateau after being saved, or let the pastor/leader go so they can seek a kinder, gentler person. Since pain is the strongest motivation for change, leaders can move their congregations great distances while the crisis mode exists and should implement as many positive changes as possible, since future changes will be slower and more difficult to adopt.

Level 2: Partly Motivated, Partly Prepared: Here, the overall congregational response toward change is positive, but there is a strong sense of not knowing how to change or what to improve. If the members voiced their need, it might be: "We give you the freedom to roll with it; show us what to do!" In this context, a leader needs to respond like a Director/Coach, providing assertive direction and team instruction. He is in the trenches with the people, showing them what to do as well as directing. An entrepreneurial mindset is welcome here. The people are somewhat dependent on a strong leader who will include them in the process but provide very adequate direction and how-tos.

If this leader is overly aggressive, the people will tend to shrink back because they want to be involved in the process. If the leader is too laid-back and participatory, the people will lose respect for him/her and results will diminish for lack of overt direction. Here the leader is high hands-on but includes people in the process as well.

Level 3: Motivated, Equipped: In this setting, the congregation is predominately ready for change and the people have a good sense of what needs to happen. The role of the leader here is one of a sideline Player/Coach. Because the people are basically motivated and competent, the leader is a permission giver, consultant, and cheerleader. If the leader does not include team members in the process, people will turn him off and reject his leading. Authoritative leadership here will alienate people and reduce the ownership of members. If a leader is too laid-back and does not provide direction and regular encouragement, the people will languish and become discouraged. The leader is low hands-on and primarily works through others.

Level 4: Highly Motivated, Highly Equipped: For most leaders, this is a dream situation. The people are educated on the improvements to be made and are excited to see them implemented. At this level, the leader should be primarily a facilitator, encourager, and team captain. In meetings, it may seem difficult to pick out the leader right away, because there is a much more democratic process at work. Members are collaborators, equals working as a team. If a leader comes on too strong in this setting, he will alienate himself from the team members and synergy will not happen. Some members will become frustrated with the process and check out. Others will endure the leader's attempt at control but will lose respect and hold back on their energy.

A TIME FOR EVERY LEADERSHIP STYLE

Do not confuse laid-back leading with weakness or managerialism. In all of these settings, strong, loving leadership is needed. Leadership is not stronger when it is more autocratic. Nor is it more loving when it is more participatory. Rather, strong, loving leaders have the ability to be appropriate. There are times to be firm and resolute and times to be soft and loving. The best leaders have a wide range of stylistic behaviors along with an innate wisdom to discern appropriateness. Within the course of a single day or week, a leader might find himself going from meeting to meeting, employing a different level of leading in each. The bottom line is, when leaders fail to choose a style appropriately, followers withdraw.

These style descriptions are obviously brief, but they provide a template from which to work. You can see this effect, for example, in church planting. A common trend is for a new congregation to hire a post-founding pastor who does not have entrepreneurial gifts. When a church planter has been in a congregational start for less than ten years, the congregation usually needs to hire a similar, high-energy, visionary, assertive leader for it to survive the transition. The changes that take place within the first ten years of a new, growing congregation are significant. There is little room for maintenance or laid-back leading at this point.

New and established congregations often find themselves weary from aggressive leadership styles and go too far the other direction: They hire a laid-back leader, or more common, a pastor who is not a leader but a manager, nurturer, or teacher. They eventually long for greater progress and seek stronger leadership, so that the next hire is more of a visionary person. This back-and-forth cycle is very common, but it is unnecessary if the leader is able to read the situation and respond with a range of appropriate styles. A leader cannot lead the same way as the organization progresses through various stages and circumstances.

> In Italy, for thirty years under the Borgias, they had warfare, terror, murder, bloodshed. They produced Michelangelo, Leonardo da Vinci, and the Renaissance. In Switzerland they had brotherly love, five hundred years of democracy and peace, and what did that produce? The cuckoo clock.
>
> —ORSON WELLES

HOW TO DISCERN AND USE OPINION LEADERS

God has given both spiritual gifts and natural talents to certain individuals who in turn exude influence over small and large, formal and informal groups. We refer to these people as *opinion leaders*. In nearly any group, regardless of the culture, certain individuals will emerge with more influence than the rest. Opinion leaders may or may not fill formal positions. Yet church members listen to and seek out their views more than others'.

Opinion leaders are vital to the improvement process because of their influence. A variety of sources create this influence, such as personal charisma, expertise in a certain subject, access to information, natural authority, a network of relationships, and a proven track record.

Church leaders need to understand the importance of opinion leaders in a congregation. Some leaders rely on surveys and popular vote to determine how far and fast changes should be made. But surveys and votes provide little significant input, because what the total congregation believes is actually immaterial. What does matter is what the opinion leaders believe. If you have 90 percent of the total congregation with you but few of the opinion leaders, the idea is doomed to fail. Conversely, if you have a large percentage of people who initially vote against an idea, yet the opinion leaders are in favor of it, the improvement is apt to happen. (Obviously, such a situation rarely occurs because the influence of opinion leaders keeps certain groups from straying far from their ideas.)

Here are five questions to help you detect your group's opinion leaders.

1. Who holds official positions of authority? Although position does not make a leader, organizational structure often determines that whoever holds the position of power wins. Staff members who want to bring about transformational change in a congregation with little or no senior-pastor support are impotent, not because of their gifts or ideas, but because of their lack of organizational authority. When the staff members who favor such change try to take over, the result is division. You cannot ignore those who fill elected or selected positions of influence. If you want to succeed, sometimes you have to consider the influence of position and include these people in the process. The opinions of these people matter because they can promote or thwart improvement processes by the power invested in their position.

2. To whom do people turn in conversations? Watch how people listen and speak in social settings and meetings. Not everyone gets the same attention, the same response. Sometimes people confuse opinion leaders with

those who express their opinions. Outspoken individuals can draw attention to themselves and their ideas without changing opinions. We probably all know people who by their very outspokenness move people away from their views. Talkers are often not opinion leaders, but when a person of influence is silent, someone will ask, "What do you think about this?" Group members look up and at an opinion leader when he/she speaks. They also tend to quote this person in subsequent conversations: "Well, Bill said that he thinks. . . ."

3. Whom do people miss at discussions of change? Although everyone is needed and loved in the body of Christ, not everyone is recognized as an opinion leader. Sad to say, there are many people who, when they are absent from a meeting or event, are not significantly missed. When an opinion leader is not in a group, his or her absence is usually noticed: "Where was So-and-So this week?" Be careful not to confuse activists, people who are extremely loyal and involved, with opinion leaders. Being present and seen are not the same as being influential. A person who is constantly involved in a ministry or project may have little or no influence with others in that group.

4. Who has demonstrated leadership in past situations? Even if you do not know a person well, you can learn about potential influence gifts by interviewing the person regarding his or her history. Leadership tends to emerge early in life. Influencers may have been playground leaders, determining what the kids do at recess. They often filled roles as captains on the basketball team, student-body presidents, and club chairpersons. Past and present work experiences are reflections of leadership abilities. Look for people who have led change and improvement successfully in the past, not merely held positions of authority.

5. Who has the proven ability presently to cast a vision, create structure, catalyze people toward a cause, and make progress? Opinion leaders sometimes quietly go about making an impact in your church with little fanfare. Sometimes it is by their choice. They may be weary of their secular work and social influence, so they step back in church. Look for people who have run with a ministry project and succeeded. Get to know them and recognize opinion-leader gifts so you can unleash their abilities. They may be new and undiscovered while they are proving themselves in a sideline ministry. Perhaps they demonstrated influence by running a single event.

Opinion leaders are not always leaders per se, but they do influence. As we said before, not all influence is leadership. Leaders influence by organizing followers around a cause. An opinion leader may not be a people organizer, but people value his or her views and seek him or her out for advice. One small group of people who are often misperceived as leaders but may be opinion influencers are those with selling abilities. Salespeople have great people skills and can cast vision, but they do not do well in organizing people and often loathe others' selection of them as leaders. Salespeople are good to have on an improvement team, but understand their role as communicators and bridge builders versus key leaders. Another overlooked group is some (not all) family members of leaders. Certain leaders rely heavily on the opinions of their spouses, even when the spouse is not overtly recognized as an opinion leader. When considering how to influence and communicate with opinion leaders, do not skip over the gatekeepers (children, secretaries, peers).

Discerning the opinion leaders is crucial because good or bad, right or wrong, they are the individuals who will persuade others to go either for or against proposed improvement suggestions. Their influence varies in degree and area. By *degree,* we mean intensity. By *area* we mean the size of the social circle, or network. In one church a man who had a very strong influence shaped the views and behaviors of nearly all of his extended family members who were active in the church. This man's degree of influence was high in this circle. The area of his influence was not broad, however, because the size of the church had outgrown this extended family and the man's influence had not grown with the church. Certainly the man could thwart an improvement idea, but he would not likely terminate it if others outside his social network approved it.

That brings us to the point of identifying where various people groups and opinion leaders are in their attitude toward improvement ideas.

DEVELOPING A SOCIAL GRID: AN INFLUENCE CONSTELLATION

Topics such as leadership, opinion leaders, and attitudes toward change can seem subjective and difficult to transfer from concept to reality. One of the best ways to visualize the change process in terms of social influence is to plot opinion leaders and their natural inclinations on a graph called a social grid or influence constellation. To do this requires a certain level of maturity and understanding so that you don't hurt feelings. Your goal is to understand the complexity of your church and its readiness to respond to improvement ideas. You may feel awkward, trying to determine who is and is not an opinion leader and to what degree. A pastor or small team may want to do this confidentially.

The reason for preparing a constellation is to see whom you should consider as part of a team for an improvement issue. When a change issue fails in a church, chances are very high that leaders were oblivious to certain opinion leaders, their degree of influence, and their attitude toward an improvement idea. In order to avoid being blindsided and to adequately prepare a church for change, leaders need to understand the configuration of influence in the church. (For convenience, we will abbreviate opinion leader as OL.)

Step 1: Influencer List

Begin by making a list of the perceived OLs in your congregation, based on the five criteria we listed. In congregations of seventy to one hundred fifty, strive to list four to ten. In congregations of two hundred to four hundred, try to list ten to twenty. In congregations of five hundred to one thousand, list twenty to forty. For every one thousand active attendees, you can expect twenty to forty OLs—this would be equivalent to Jethro's recommendation for Moses to find people who can oversee groups of fifty and one hundred. Congregations vary along socioeconomic lines. Higher-income and educated communities will have a higher percentage of OLs than will moderate- and lower-income areas.

Step 2: Influence Source

After each name, try to describe the social circle of the OL. If you want to code the type of circles of influence, you can use the following abbreviations or make up your own: *F* for family, *O* for office or formal role, and *P* for personal influence via relationships, giftedness, or resources such as money. While being optional, this exercise might help you know how to address each opinion leader.

Step 3: Influence Direction

Decide where you think each OL is in terms of his/her view of a certain change issue. A triangle represents a person in favor of change, a circle is neutral, and a square is negative to change. You might think up a specific new idea or change in general to determine this.

Step 4: Influence Size

Look at the size of the social circle and/or the degree of influence an OL has in the group to determine the size of the symbol representing the OL (small, medium, large). The purpose of this is to develop a feel for the cumulative influence and the OL's attitude regarding change, since not all OLs have the same impact. Longer-established and more static congregations will typically have OLs with stronger influence than newer and growing ones.

Step 5: Influence Pattern

Next, create an influence constellation by placing each member onto a chart of three concentric circles. The purpose of this is to see where people fit in their basic comfort level regarding change. The inner circle is for Creators and Progressives. The next is for Builders. The outer circle represents Foundationals. Anchors are located outside the circles.

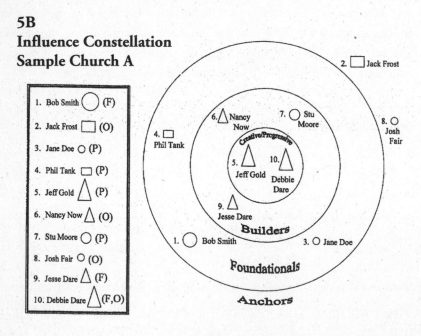

5B
Influence Constellation
Sample Church A

1. Bob Smith ◯ (F)
2. Jack Frost ☐ (O)
3. Jane Doe ◯ (P)
4. Phil Tank ☐ (P)
5. Jeff Gold △ (P)
6. Nancy Now △ (O)
7. Stu Moore ◯ (P)
8. Josh Fair ◯ (O)
9. Jesse Dare △ (F)
10. Debbie Dare ◁ (F,O)

Key to Influence Constellation

Influence Direction

Triangle represents an OL in favor of the change.
Circle represents an OL neutral to the change.
Square represents an OL negative to a change.

Influence Size

Small shape represents an OL of a small social group or low influence.
Medium shape represents an OL in a medium-sized social group or moderate influence.
Large shape represents an OL in a large social group or large significant influence.

Influence Source

F: Family network
O: Office/position held
P: Personal influence (charisma, talents, money)

Personality Regarding Change

Inner circle: Creatives & Progressives
Middle circle: Builders
Outer circle: Foundationals
Outside area: Anchors

According to this influence constellation, what sort of change orientation exists in this congregation? What kind of communication needs to take place before you move too far down the road of improvement? How much time might this group need before it sees tangible results of improvement?

Overall, the influence constellation reflects a pretty positive environment for change, so long as you do the necessary work to communicate with the fringe opinion leaders.

A good Dream Team captain would be Jeff Gold, who has a significant opinion group, is positive about the idea, and is a position-holding Progressive. Debbie, Nancy, Jesse, and Stu would be good team members as well.

A potential problem is Jack Frost, who appears to have a medium influence group and is an Anchor opposed to the idea at this time. The goal is not to convince Jack to be in favor of the change, but merely to persuade him to become neutral. The goal is *not* to make everyone favor the improvement. Rather, the goal is to *reduce the influence* of those who might block it. Dissolving opposition is different from raising support. As long as people are neutral, they will not prevent an improvement from happening. The people in favor of the idea can carry it forward.

Nancy Now and Jesse Dare might persuade Stu Moore to move toward adopting the idea.

Heavily include Bob and Jane in communication so that they can pass on the information to their spheres of influence among the Foundationals. The same goes with Phil.

Now, let's use the same names of opinion leaders and create a different influence constellation for another church and see how this influence constellation is posed for change.

5C
Influence Constellation
Sample Church B

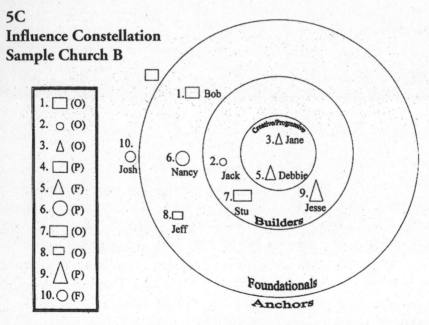

What sort of change orientation exists in this congregation according to this influence constellation? What kind of communication needs to take place before you move too far down the road of improvement? How much time might this group need before it sees tangible results of improvement?

Overall, the influence constellation reflects a church that has some work cut out for it before it publicly announces any sort of significant improvement plans. Depending on how the church government is structured, a potential blockade exists with Bob, Jack, Josh, and especially Stu being officeholders who are either against or neutral regarding the change.

Your Dream Team captain would be Jesse, along with Jane, Jeff, and Jack.

A potentially significant opinion conflict exists between Stu and Jesse, as well as Stu and the other Dream Team members. Therefore a change agent would want to invest significant time with Stu, to understand his concerns and to help him catch the vision of what they want to see happen at the church. If Stu becomes neutral or even in favor of the change, the constellation will change significantly.

A change agent would also want to spend plenty of time teaching about biblical values underlying the change, in order to help Phil, Bob, Nancy, and Josh get on board.

If Jesse and Debbie Dare are related, Jesse can positively influence Debbie, who in turn can communicate with other concerned Anchors, such as Phil.

Obviously, the first congregation is poised for pursuing new ideas faster and more significantly than the second one. If a pastor or leadership team ignores the differences in these groups, it would result in either offending and alienating people or not creating enough sense of direction and improvement to satisfy the opinion leaders.

While this is far from being a cookbook recipe, it is a tool for understanding the social setting in your congregation, which is key to approaching the improvement strategy with the right speed, size, and direction. We'll later talk about communicating the vision. Effective communication begins by knowing the audience, which is what an influence constellation provides for us.

APPLICATION TOOLBOX

Make copies of this blank Influence Constellation and complete it to reflect your own congregation. To do this well requires some thought, but the process alone will take you a long way toward considering who the opinion leaders are in your church and where they stand at this time. The constellation will change as the readiness for improvement ripens. Leaders may want to do this alone at first and then add people who they feel can handle the subjectivity maturely.

5D
Influence Constellation

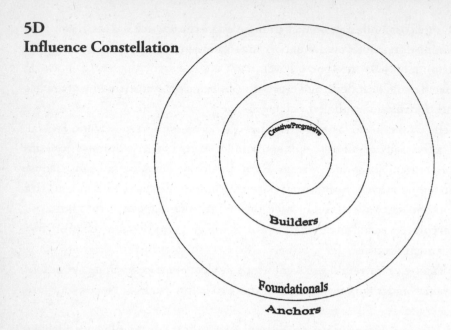

Improvement Story: Sugar Creek Church, Sugar Creek, Ohio

I (Dwight Mason) came in 1985 to a very traditional church of seventy, which had a fifty-minute, suit-and-tie Sunday worship service consisting of organ music, hymns, a mediocre choir, a sermon, announcements, and an offering. Sugar Creek is a rural church, approximately six miles from the closest towns of Dover and New Philadelphia. I quickly realized that if I wanted to bring about improvement, I had to be willing to pay the price. For example, when I arrived, the sound system consisted of car speakers placed in wood cabinets. I started small. I took out a personal loan for a new sound system and installed it for the first Sunday I was in charge of the service. I did that to demonstrate that some change could be quick and positive and that I was committed to healthy innovation.

We began to change the first year, but we chose it very carefully. On Sunday evenings, I began speaking on reaching our community. The format changed to more of a seminar/workshop style, where we equipped Christians to witness and minister. Wednesday evenings became a time of prayer, which elevated our sensitivity to God. We started using praise choruses and periodically brought in outside singing guests who also introduced more contemporary music to our people, whetting their appetite for more. Eventually we began employing background tracks to expand our musical selection and style. We gradually added one musical instrument at a time, so that we eventually had a full band. As a result, we had to move our Easter and Christmas celebrations to a community gymnasium to accommodate the crowd. In these we incorporated bands and celebrative music. The people enjoyed these so much that they began suggesting we do this more in our regular weekly services.

We have made other changes as well, such as incorporating other worship elements, focusing on outreach, and prioritizing home groups. Over the course of about four years, we have experimented with small groups, workshops, and taking off various Sunday nights so that people could have family time and small-group Bible studies. The result was that our congregation unanimously agreed to do away with our Sunday evening service, which had become ineffective. One of the ways we made changes like these was to introduce our leaders, not just the pastoral staff, to various books and conferences. These new ideas began to grow in our people so that together we harvested the desire for improvement.

Although we were running around seventy people when I came, Sugar Creek is now breaking the one-thousand mark in Sunday morning attendance, with about 40 percent of the people being unchurched, even in a highly religious area. We are pursuing the purchase of seventy-five acres of land next to a freeway and sale of our current campus. I believe that country churches still have potential to be thriving congregations, if pastors are willing to make long-term commitments and intentionally introduce a vision that exudes excellence and excitement.

Improvement Lessons:

- An effective change agent needs to seek change over the long haul. If you seek just quick fixes, people will think you are committed more to ministerial success and personal agenda than to them and their well-being. You can do less than you think you can in one year, and more than you think you can in five years.
- Don't let education alienate you from your people. You may have been exposed to ideas for ministry that your congregation hasn't. Bring your people along with you as you examine improvement concepts. One way to educate is to expose them to other models for vision casting and idea sharing.

SOCIAL BANKING

How embarrassing! I (Alan), the pastor, had given our tithe check to our church and it had come back with three nasty letters on it: NSF (Nonsufficient Funds).

I could have reduced the amount and gotten by, but I could not have increased the total or the results would have been the same: NSF. There was not enough money at the bank in my name to cover my request.

Leadership is basically social banking, whereby certain individuals with influence resources are entrusted by others to lead them well. Trust, granted influence, and power are the results of an array of sources, such as personal charisma, professional competence, experience, relationships, and who is within your network. Whenever a leader affirms followers, accomplishes tasks, and demonstrates competent leading and decision making, his recipients make emotional deposits into the leader's social account. When the leader asks people to make sacrifices, take risks, and push harder, he withdraws from that account. If he is effective in using that withdrawal, he can turn it into a profit and wind up with still more in his social bank account.

Good leaders are investors, taking small deposits and turning them into large assets. In Matthew 25, Jesus told the story about the foolish steward who buried his treasure in the ground. When the owner came back, he reprimanded the one who hid his asset: "You should have at least put it in a bank where you could have collected interest."

People in leadership roles who basically bury the trust and influence they have been given by others are foolish. To enjoy being liked and respected without ever making demands that build God's kingdom is akin to hoarding what is not yours. Such leaders could take that investment and bring great returns, if only they would use it wisely. When they do not want to take the risk or challenge people to follow a vision, they lose what they could have gained. And like the foolish steward in the biblical account, they will be held accountable.

The best leaders are those who are not satisfied with the low interest rates of insured accounts, the guaranteed wins. They are the venture capitalists who go after high-risk opportunities. When these opportunities succeed, the payoff is huge. Obviously, when leaders squander the investment or if circumstances sour the opportunity and potential success "goes south," even well-intentioned leaders can be touted as incompetent and never trusted again. Conversely, a mediocre leader can be heralded as a genius if he is the right guy in the right place and circumstances blossom with very little effort on his part as a leader.

Technology allows us to go on-line to check our bank balance at any given time. In the same way, a leader needs to be able to check the balance in his social bank account. Conflict, poor service, and personality issues subtract from the total. Change requires withdrawals as well. When the changes pay off, the original deposits return and interest and net profit accrue. When they do not, a leader must start over. When a leader makes too many withdrawals, the group he governs will basically put a freeze on his leadership. The leader will be forced to leave or rendered bankrupt (impotent). Large changes require large withdrawals. Small changes or improvements that are widely adopted cost less.

When our kids are saving money to buy something, we help them as parents to make the right decisions. If our ten-year-old earnestly wants to buy a new baseball glove, we remind him not to give in to the temptation to buy a lot of little things he cares less about, because he won't have enough left for the big-ticket item. If he fritters his savings away on "stuff," he'll be frustrated and have very little to show for his work and savings.

Leaders face a similar temptation, to fritter away their social credits with changes that bear little fruit. Then when they need to make significant withdrawals for large improvements, the people respond, "NSF." The social balance of a leader is always fluctuating. Savvy leaders have a feel for what their balance is at any given time and know when to make withdrawals and when to make deposits. Again, if you just want to make deposits, never calling for sacrifice or change, you'll not accomplish much as a leader and the Owner will be upset with your poor stewardship.

At the same time, you need to know when to stop pushing. After a significant withdrawal, take time off to build up more deposits. Care for people, minister to them personally, and rest. The cycle of adding and subtracting continues all the time you are building the ministry as well as kingdom assets. If you don't wisely track your spending and saving, you'll be surprised, frustrated, and ultimately defeated in your attempts to catalyze significant improvement.

How do you obtain social credits and raise your balance if you are new or if the challenge you want to "buy" is pricey? There are many sources of social credits. Some are granted, like a line of credit. These include perceived credibility, competence, reputation, experience, and charisma. Others you gain the old-fashioned way: You earn them. You do this by loving people and walking through life with them over time. The most common avenue for accruing social credits is by building on previous wins. Begin by creating and constructing on small changes. For example, you might set intentionally small, accomplishable goals so that you quickly stack up wins. Each victory adds a little bit to the total.

Just as an investor starts with a small amount, invests it well, and then takes the profits to invest in larger ventures, smart leaders do the same socially. They set attainable goals, then accomplish, celebrate, and reinvest them in larger challenges. All the time, the leader is increasing his balance until he has significant social credits to cash in on the really big-ticket items. If you try to bring about too much change too fast—before you have significant credits—the improvement process will have to file for Chapter 11. Many leaders do not understand why improvement processes fail, simply because they are not aware of how much they are able to charge against their leadership account.

MOTIVES

Whenever we talk about leadership and change, it is worthwhile to touch on motivation. When people distrust a leader's motives, the leader's social bank account will be emptier than he thinks. What is the leader's motive to bring about ministry improvement? Even the best of us, the most sincere Christian leaders, fall prey to subtle, human motives that stray from God's design. In days when the fastest-growing congregations and their leaders receive notoriety, pursuing changes to be recognized, working up the ministerial ladder, and grasping for more power are all temptations. When pastoral and lay leaders strategize to become the hottest church in town, the largest congregation in their denomination, or the latest gurus of church-growth techniques, they run the risk of pushing improvements for the wrong reasons.

Every church leader must soul-search and ask him- or herself, *Why do I want to pursue improvement and change in my church?* As we discussed in chapter 2, most of us suffer from blind spots, often ones of pride when we believe our motives to be worthy and pure. We must diligently keep our egos in check or else our motivations will become contaminated. Bad fuel messes up a carburetor, just as pride and ego foul ministerial pursuits. Leaders would do well to deepen their prayer and fasting during times of change, in part for their churches and in part for their own souls. Healthy churches usually grow, and growth can create a success syndrome that is dangerous, even for those of us leading God's people.

The success syndrome spawned in North America is not just a modern malady. You can find some of history's finest leaders struggling with it.

A dispute arose among them as to which of them was considered to be greatest. Jesus said to them, "The kings of the Gentiles lord it over them; and those who exercise authority over them call themselves Benefactors. But you are not to be like that. Instead, the greatest among you should be like the youngest, and the one who rules like the one who serves. For who is greater, the one who is at the table or the one who serves? Is it not the one who is at the table? But I am among you as one who serves." (Luke 22:24–27)

Then the mother of Zebedee's sons came to Jesus with her sons and, kneeling down, asked a favor of him.

"What is it you want?" he asked.

She said, "Grant that one of these two sons of mine may sit at your right and the other at your left in your kingdom."

"You don't know what you are asking," Jesus said to them. "Can you drink the cup I am going to drink?"

"We can," they answered.

Jesus said to them, "You will indeed drink from my cup, but to sit at my right or left is not for me to grant. These places belong to those for whom they have been prepared by my Father."

When the ten heard about this, they were indignant with the two brothers. Jesus called them together and said, "You know that the rulers of the Gentiles lord it over them, and their high officials exercise authority over them. Not so with you. Instead, whoever wants to become great among you must be your servant, and whoever wants to be first must be your slave— just as the Son of Man did not come to be served, but to serve, and to give his life as a ransom for many." (Matt. 20:20–28)

While we remind each other of the danger of wrong motives, we also need to encourage lay leaders and attendees not to assume that motives for growth and improvement are prideful or centered in the pastor's ego. Diagnosing self-centeredness is precarious. Only God reads people's hearts. Well-intentioned people in favor of the status quo often assume that well-intentioned people in favor of improvement have tainted motives. Leaders need to be very careful about perceptions, because perceptions are real. They are the stuff of influence. Careful word selection, giving verbal credit to God, and elevating biblical values are all crucial to how people perceive you, since they cannot truly know your heart.

A leader who seeks to reach the lost and renew a static church may be in it for all the right reasons. Outreach, growth, and renewal are biblical reasons for change and improvement. Some people hide their fears and stubbornness by blaming pastors for being wrongly driven. Change issues have a way of bringing out some of the best and worst of human motivations. We would all do well to emphasize an attitude of brokenness and obedience in such processes.

How-Tos: 10 Things Pastors Can Do to Get Going

1. Immerse yourself in books on leadership and organizational change. (See Appendix A.)
2. Develop an opinion-leader constellation for your church.
3. Form a Dream Team of four to ten people, consisting mostly of progressive opinion leaders who will brainstorm about improvement ideas and implementation strategies.
4. Take a leadership team to one or more conferences to experience a thriving church, such as Willow Creek Community Church (Illinois), Saddleback Community Church (California), Las Colinas Fellowship (Texas), or Ginghamsburg Community Church (Ohio).
5. Take a group of opinion leaders through a book like this (or others listed in Appendix A) and discuss it in a retreat setting or over a series of regular meeting settings.
6. Design a retreat that emphasizes prayer and seeking God's will, combined with brainstorming.
7. Bring in a consultant to talk to the church leaders about change. (This person should be a professional from the business world or a reflective pastor from a church that is effective.)
8. Take an honest look with statistical data at what is and is not happening in your church. List five things you're not doing at all that you would like to accomplish.
9. Prepare a Sunday morning series specifically on growth and improvement values, including themes on faith, facing your fears, and letting God do a new thing in your life.
10. Invite a group of opinion leaders to go through a two- to nine-month discipleship series with you on leadership and faith. (The nine months coincide with the school year, a natural time period.)

It is a terrible thing to look over your shoulder when you are trying to lead—and find no one there.

—FRANKLIN DELANO ROOSEVELT

QUESTIONS AND ANSWERS

Q: What are the most common weaknesses you see in terms of church leadership?

A: Probably the most common weakness that limits improvement measures is a lack of leadership gifts or abilities among pastors and those in roles of influence. We mean no disrespect to pastors, but most have grown up and been educated in systems that recruit and reinforce teacher, shepherd, and manager skills, not leadership. Many pastors are not wired to think and act like leaders. This is not their fault, just the natural result of a system that encouraged different gifts, along with a changing environment that seeks them.

In the past, when times were more stable and people seemed more naturally interested in going to church and in Christianity, we did not need pastor-leaders so much. But times have changed. We need leaders who respond to and create change.

The other weakness we see often is a lack of lay-leader development. Far too much potential is left on the table because we do not form leadership teams from the congregation: people who dream new dreams and plan strategies. God has provided more than enough leadership within most churches. Pastors need only to identify those people with leader gifts and then gather them to work together.

Q: What if we recognize the problem you mention: Our pastor is not gifted as a leader?

A: We know that this emphasis on the pastor acting as a leader can put a lot of pressure on pastor/lay-leader teams reading this book. Our intent is not to create conflict, but to catalyze improvement. A pastor can help stimulate improvement by working alongside people who *are* gifted as leaders. The key is to develop a team approach to ministry. In John 14:12 Jesus said, "You will do even greater things than these." We believe he referred to what the disciples could do as a team as opposed to what they could accomplish individually.

To empower staff and lay leaders who will in turn cast the vision for ministry change requires the pastor to be secure as a person. Ministers who are jealous of

or threatened by strong personalities are not apt to let go of control and will usually block change.

As well, a pastor needs to make sure, prior to and during the unleashing of a
strong leader team, that the members are adequately discipled. Jesus spent three
years investing in the spiritual formation of his team prior to releasing them to
lead. The New Testament teaches us that leaders must live up to higher standards
in their lives because of their influence. One of these standards requires that they
have a mature faith.

The role of the pastor or minister is to make sure people grow spiritually,
regardless of a pastor's gift mix. Thus, with the help of other gifted people, the pastor can see transforming change take place, even if he/she isn't gifted to bring it
about himself. The pastor's job is to prepare people for works of service. To recognize opinion leaders and to intentionally disciple them is a key to developing a
strong, trustworthy leadership base in a local church. Once the pastor can trust the
motives and character of those on the leadership team, he/she needs to trust their
insights, because leaders see things that others do not. They are able to develop
strategies and plans that can rally people and resources toward improvement.

*Q: What if there seems to be a potential power struggle in the opinion-
leader constellation?*

A: Once a pastor and leadership team understand the concept of varying
comfort with changes as well as who the opinion leaders are, they can build relationships with these influencers. Communicating dreams, fears, concerns, and
personal priorities builds trust. The main reason opinion leaders do not move a
certain direction is because they do not feel understood and connected.
Improvement is not apt to take place until a critical mass of your opinion leaders is either motivated to move toward the change or is at least neutral. As long
as a significant number of opinion leaders are against the improvement idea, the
idea will not happen without conflict or even division.

The natural human tendency when someone disagrees with us is to disengage
from him or her. Leaders must make every effort to get closer to opinion leaders,
especially those who are not warm to change, so that their thoughts are understood and they feel included. Spend time in fellowship, prayer, ministry, and
communicating. Nothing beats a good relationship to enhance understanding
and trust. Until that trust develops, leaders will need to slow the improvement
process to minimize alienating key social groups.

Q: We've heard stories of unsuccessful church-change attempts. How can we minimize the fear people feel because of this?

A: One large church we're familiar with "inherited" a number of disgruntled Foundationals from a neighboring congregation. These people left their original church because of a pastor's attempt to introduce contemporary music into the traditional worship service. Unfortunately, a certain amount of complaining and "sharing" about their frustrations resulted in their new congregation being tainted as it considered moving in that direction. The negative grapevine hampers many who seek ministry enhancement. The problem is that the grapevine always distorts the facts and does not take into account how each situation is different.

Fear is a significant ingredient in the trust relationship between leaders and those led. Perhaps the biggest reason for this is the short tenure of most pastorates. Trust is a matter of confidence based on competence, personality, proven track record, and mutual experiences. When pastors stay only three or four years in a church, they find it difficult to build an impressive achievement record. People need to feel secure in a leader's ability and motives, and sometimes this is time related.

In addition to a leader's having pure motives and making wise decisions is the need for a solid plan. To overcome change jitters requires education, building confidence through small victories, and frequent encouragement. A solid plan can deliver all of these benefits to your congregation.

One of the best ways to combat fear is to introduce your opinion leaders to models that have effectively implemented improvement ideas. Take them to a conference hosted by a thriving congregation. Let them experience services of fruitful ministries where they can catch the feeling. Facing our fears really is a venture of faith. Those of us in faith communities should be aware of what it means to trust God and not yesterday's tradition. Thus, a consistent menu of themes on faith, trusting God, and working together in unity are foundation builders for people who feel uncomfortable because of crash-and-burn stories on the grapevine.

> Leadership is defined in part by the ability to get people to agree both in present dangers and on a vision of the future that will enable them to overcome those dangers.
>
> —HARVEY ROBBINS AND MICHAEL FINLEY[8]

Discussion Starters

1. Do you agree or disagree that leadership is the key factor, good or bad, in a major improvement process within a church?
2. What did you learn about opinion leaders and their role in improvement processes?
3. How have you seen opinion leaders work for or against changes in past experiences?
4. Why is situational leading so important to overall leadership?
5. Is your pastor an L1, L2, or L3 type of leader? How will this affect how you develop your improvement strategy?
6. What can the pastoral staff do to unleash the leadership abilities within the laity?
7. What can lay leaders do to rally around the pastoral staff, to build trust, and to bring about change?
8. How do you determine "bad fuel" in yourself and others regarding church improvement motives?
9. Which of the ten "to do" ideas could you implement right away?
10. What kind of leadership-team training plan do you have in place?

An army of sheep led by a lion would defeat an army of lions led by a sheep.

—Arab Proverb

Contemplation

The Lord said to Moses and Aaron: "How long will this wicked community grumble against me? I have heard the complaints of these grumbling Israelites. So tell them, '. . . . In this desert your bodies will fall—every one of you . . . who has grumbled against me.'"

—Num. 14:26–29

Scripture

Read Numbers 14:20–45.

DEVOTIONAL THOUGHT

Oops! They blew it. The children of Israel had forgotten to trust God, who had just miraculously released them from generations of enslavement. And now, because of their arrogance and stubbornness, they missed the window of opportunity to go into the promised land.

How many times do we complain about changes in our lives, the transitions that take us from slavery to promised lands, that seem scary and unbearable? Well, most of these opportunities have windows. There are temporary options that, if missed, will never open again. Life is short. We may reap forgiveness, live long lives, and still enjoy heaven, but some ministry opportunities, if passed, will never come our way again.

When we buck the new vision, the improvement idea that stretches us, we inevitably pass up on new experiences—milk-and-honey experiences. The people who enjoyed the sights and sounds of what God intended were the ones willing to trust God in spite of the giants and unknown terrain. Entering into the unexplored is a frightful thing to do, but to stay where we are is more frightening in the long run. Imagine what we might miss!

What do you need to do to avoid repeating the history of wilderness wanderers?

Prayer

God, help us not to go the way of our forefathers, who considered stoning the prophets and chose to wander the rest of their lives. Free us from the unhealthy idea that staying where we are is better than moving forward where you want. Lead us, in spite of our fears. You are sufficient. Make up where we lack. We take you by the hand. A new promised land awaits. Amen.

CHAPTER 6
The Joshua Report: Developing a Vision That Compels

He that will not apply new remedies must expect new evils.

—FRANCIS BACON

No significant book on leadership or change can overlook the importance of vision. Entire books deal with the subject. George Barna writes, "In evaluating churches that are growing and healthy as well as those that are stagnant or in decline, one of the key distinctions that emerges between these categories is the existence of true vision for ministry."[1] Leadership expert Burt Nanus concurs: "There is no more powerful engine driving an organization toward excellence and long-range success than an attractive, worthwhile, and achievable vision of the future, widely shared."[2]

We must address the idea of vision because of its focal point in any nontrivial change/improvement process. A vision is a mental picture of a preferred future. Biblical accounts show us that God has ideas and plans for our lives. The ability to peek into the plans of God is a special skill, usually involving the gift of faith. Nanus writes, "A vision is a realistic, credible, attractive future for your organization. It is your articulation of a destination toward which your organization should aim, a future that in important ways is better, more successful, or more desirable for your organization than is the present."[3]

President Kennedy made famous the quote "Some men look at things as they are and ask 'why?' I look at things as they can become and ask, 'Why not?'" The first thing to understand about vision is that while it can and must be caught be a group of people, it is nearly always initially given and cast by individuals.

Throughout history, good and bad leaders have cast visions that have catalyzed people to bring about change. While vision is not everything, it is essential for significant improvement strategies. Writes Theodore Levitt, "No organization can achieve greatness without a vigorous leader who is driven onward by his own pulsating will to succeed. He has to have a vision of grandeur, a vision that can produce eager followers in vast numbers."[4]

CENTRAL CHRISTIAN CHURCH: OUR STORY

Casting the Vision

The vision began with my desire for reaching the lost. As I shared this ideal with key people in the church, we began to examine how to flesh it out. What does New Testament evangelism look like in southern Nevada in the late eighties? We studied the Great Commission, early church outreach, and the passion Jesus had for helping those outside the fold. We realized that we were not doing a good job of attracting pre-Christians to our Chrisitan family.

Key staff leaders and I began modifying our actions and attitudes within the existing system. We counted the number of people who were coming to Central from other churches as opposed to being unchurched. We tried to be more intentional in evangelism and discipleship without changing the ministry forms. Our initial strategy was not so much to dramatically change our worship services, but we used our current Bible-teaching times to cast a vision for reaching the lost at all costs. We tried to use what was already there.

Concurrently, I began casting more vision with staff and key lay leaders. I arranged times for us to hang out together, listen to tapes, have semiannual staff retreats, and just generally keep the issue alive. As a result, values and new dreams started to take root. In 1989, we had a staff, elder, and deacon retreat and I could tell we were in a new day. They talked about things they'd not discussed before, such as a possible Saturday night service and changing Sunday night service to Wednesday. There was a new freshness of ideas. Though Sunday school had always been the nurturing and discipling arm of the church, we discussed launching small groups to fill this role.

One critical time I remember was in the spring of 1989. Three of us went to a leadership conference at Willow Creek. There were only five hundred attending the annual church leadership conference then. Little did I know that we were a part of a groundswell that would engage hundreds of thousands of others in the next few years.

That experience was a defining moment for me as a leader and our staff. It was as if together we had an "a-ha" moment as we experienced the sessions as a team. The groundwork for dynamic change was laid during that conference. Our staff and lay leaders caught a new vision of what it meant to "do church" that reached a new generation. Our courage level rose sky-high because of that event, and we left it ready to lead Central through some major paradigm shifts. We were willing to do whatever it took to create a church that was effective at reaching the lost in Las Vegas.

Some of the results of this renewed vision included phasing out ministries and programs that were not effective toward that goal, and we began new ones. For example, that fall we changed the Sunday night service to a midweek believers' service and added a Saturday night service. When we initiated the Saturday evening service, we began to bring more contemporary changes, such as drama, creative visual aids, and thematic development through music. This opened the door for us to begin adding these to the Sunday morning service as well. By reducing our formal believers' services to one per week, we created better balance between outreach and inreach. We also launched small groups so that relationships could increase as well as discipleship. Contemporary people tend to stay with a church because of relationships, not programs. We also restructured our board system to make the decision-making process smoother and quicker.

We did away with a deacon board; we assigned former deacons ministry responsibilities. This helped us overcome the male/female issue, because "deacon" had become a term connoting male. By referring to these people as lay ministers, we ridded ourselves of a sexual bias and were able to better include women. We hired our first children's ministry staff person at that time as well. Since unchurched people value family resources, we wanted to make this a priority.

While all this was going on, we experienced the largest single year of growth in our history. We went from 900 in average Sunday attendance to 1,250. In 1991 we grew to 1,700. I think this was because people knew ours was a church that would accept people in their lowly states. We showed this by our willingness to let go of ministries and events that were not sensitive to the unchurched, and by letting the unchurched know that we understood their felt needs for relevance, love, and acceptance.

THE TOP 10 REASONS WHY VISIONS FAIL

1. *No vision exists.* "Vision? What vision?" Many people don't have it. Yet few transforming organizational accomplishments or revolutions have taken place in history without a vision. Unfortunately, vision designing is usually intuitive, requiring an innate blend of faith, God-inspired creativity, and a sense of destiny. The average person lacks the necessary ingredients for vision. That is why we have leaders.

Because most pastors are gifted as ministry managers and teachers, vision development often languishes. But gifted leaders ooze vision. The first responsibility of a leader is to provide a vision for an organization: headlamps into the future. If a nonleader is at the helm, vision casting will be very difficult. "Myth: If a pastor simply loves the Lord and does the things described in the Bible as the qualities of a good leader—teaching, preaching, praying, modeling forgiveness and love, and so forth—the church will grow, vision or no vision."[5]

2. *The vision isn't really a vision.* Leaders confuse goals and strategic plans with visions. Goals are milestones, end points, destinations. Strategic plans are links, how-tos, what to dos, but they lack passion and visual imagery. Vision is right-brained. It includes the head but aims for the heart, resulting in passion. Goals and plans are left-brained, stimulating thoughts but not necessarily emotions.

3. *The vision caster has poor communication skills.* A leader with a vision who lacks the means to communicate it is akin to a factory that produces wonderful widgets but has no transportation system to get the widgets to market. When the trains, trucks, and delivery systems are in ill repair, the factory will eventually shut down.

4. *The audience lacks passion or a sense of urgency.* Why did the chicken cross the road? To prove to the possum that it could be done. A swell idea these days has about the same chance of making it across the road as a possum. Information overload, fierce competition for our time and interests, and the speed of life itself make passion and urgency key to any vision success.

5. *The vision is too small.* "I'm not going to invest my life in something that has no hope of leaving a mark." People want to be part of something big, something

that requires God's power to be successful. Let's face it: If it isn't exciting, it won't draw a crowd's support.

6.   *The vision caster suffers from low credibility.* "Cool vision, but I don't think you can pull it off. I enjoy hearing you talk, but I'm not about to follow you. There's no way you can make this happen, based on what I've seen you do so far. Get real." The church historically applauds nice guys, but the nice-guy quality in itself does not muster leader credibility. During times of stress, people follow competence much more than cordiality.

7.   *The vision is unclear.* If it's cloudy in the pulpit, it's muddy in the pew. Vague generalities create random actions, helter-skelter planning, and frustration.

8.   *The vision caster has a great idea but no plan.* Some people are great at selling the sizzle but never go further. Many visions are like movie sets: beautifully detailed facades with nothing behind the storefronts, propped up by two-by-fours and nails. Visions without logical next steps and follow-through quickly lose support.

9.   *The vision isn't compelling.* The first assumption leaders make is that people will be interested in where they are headed. Enthusiasm isn't automatic; sometimes (often) leaders have to inspire, to build it.

10.   *The vision is too improbable.* Thinking big is one thing, but if a vision lacks a thread of possibility, like an untethered helium balloon it will float away. When too many people shake their heads and say, "No way," a leader has lost his opportunity.

A FRESH, OLD APPROACH

Because the term *vision* is so well worn, and because we all have the tendency to miss the meaning in overused terms, we want to use a different phrase for the concept of vision: *the Joshua Report.* By looking at the way Joshua (and Caleb) communicated the need to occupy the promised land, we can add some handles to the idea of visualizing a preferred future.

At the end of forty days they returned from exploring the land.

They came back to Moses and Aaron and the whole Israelite community at Kadesh in the Desert of Paran. There they reported to them and to the whole assembly and showed them the fruit of the land. They gave Moses this account: "We went into the land to which you sent us, and it does flow with milk and honey! Here is its fruit. But the people who live there are powerful, and the cities are fortified and very large. We even saw descendants of Anak there. The Amalekites live in the Negev; the Hittites, Jebusites and Amorites live in the hill country; and the Canaanites live near the sea and along the Jordan."

Then Caleb silenced the people before Moses and said, "We should go up and take possession of the land, for we can certainly do it."

. . . [Joshua] said to the entire Israelite assembly, "The land we passed through and explored is exceedingly good. If the LORD is pleased with us, he will lead us into that land, a land flowing with milk and honey, and will give it to us. Only do not rebel against the LORD. And do not be afraid of the people of the land, because we will swallow them up. Their protection is gone, but the LORD is with us." (Num. 13:25–30, 14:7–9)

A good Joshua Report has seven elements:

1. *Show them the fruit of the land.* By helping people see and experience the possible benefits of the change, you whet an appetite. Any salesperson knows that you don't start with the sticker price, you begin with the need and then provide the solution. You can show people fruit by talking about it, sharing personal experiences, introducing them to books, tapes, and consultants, and taking them to another church that is experiencing great fruitfulness.

2. *Emphasize the benefits.* If you consider going to college in light of all the costs, hours of research, tests, writing, tuition, and work that go into obtaining a degree, you probably won't go. Instead you focus on the degree, what you can do and earn with it, and the opportunities it affords. You must outweigh the pain and cost for the wonderful, positive potential.

3. *Do not deny the giants.* Caleb, Joshua's positive partner, silenced the detractors, but he did not deny the existence of giants in the land. If he had, the people would have been ill-prepared to face the challenges ahead. Instead he brought their focus back to the benefits they would be losing if they did not take the land.

4. *Affirm success in the journey.* Caleb went on and said, "We can do it!" During times of potential change, people need encouragement. They need to know that obtaining these benefits is within their reach. Dangling a carrot in front of a person without suggesting that it is obtainable is cruel and irresponsible leadership. Cheer short-term wins. Keep people moving.

5. *Communicate passion.* "I have a dream," cried Martin Luther King Jr. in one

of the most dynamic speeches of the last century. This speech oozed with the sort of passion and commitment that Joshua demonstrated when he tore his clothes. In that culture, tearing one's clothes expressed intense emotions. The difference between a Joshua Report and a goal is that a goal is focused on logical conclusion; a vision is centered around passion, enthusiasm, and urgency. Without passion and drama, few significant changes will occur in the life of any organization. Remember, the primary resistance to change is emotional, not logical. Thus, the primary element in a Joshua Report focuses on the heart, not the head.

6. *Repeat the benefits with increasing emphasis.* Joshua repeated what Caleb said, but he called the land "exceedingly" good. In nearly all improvement processes, the outcomes will outweigh the previous expectations because realized dreams are not diluted by fear of the unknown.

7. *Acknowledge people's fears, but build their faith.* Joshua understood that the people were grumbling and resisting because they were afraid, not because they were bad people. The antidote to fear is faith. God is on our side. We can do all things through Christ who strengthens us. We all need to be reminded that our Creator is bigger than any giants we might face. Build your people's faith in God.

While the Joshua Report we just read is a great example of how to cast vision for a group of people, history shows us that this particular report was ineffective. The people chose instead to wander for four decades. When they refused to go into the promised land, they had no idea what the repercussions would be. We nearly always turn down change because the cost-for-return ratio does not seem right. But what we fail to measure, because it is often immeasurable, is the high cost of not making the change. When we say no to sensible but faith-stretching improvements in life and ministry, we never fully understand how expensive they are. No doubt, most of the Israelites would have reconsidered if they knew they would die in the wilderness without ever glimpsing the land of milk and honey. Life does not afford us unlimited time and opportunities, so we must seriously consider the high cost of change versus no change. Even Moses, Caleb, Joshua, and others could not convince the majority to move, and so they wandered.

THE TOP SEVEN REASONS WHY VISIONS WORK

1. *A vision is made of heart.* Vision touches both the head and the heart. People are much more emotional and spiritual than they are intellectual, even

though most of us like to think of ourselves as primarily logical beings. The best way to move people is by touching their hearts, which is what vision is about. The most memorable events in life are primarily emotive, not intellectual.

2. *A vision provides a picture of a desire.* Aristotle said, "The soul never thinks without a picture." Most people think in pictures but lack the ability to see what can be, focusing rather on what is. A clearly communicated Joshua Report is key because it paints a visual picture of a preferred outcome, whether it is a new church, a growing ministry, an excellent program, or transformed lives. Leaders are social artists who paint mental landscapes reflecting a potential outcome. The best communicators are storytellers, mental image-makers.

3. *A vision highlights a way out of today's discomfort.* Vision paints a preferred future, which creates hope for tomorrow and disappointment for today. People tend to change for two reasons: pain or gain. The most powerful motive for changing is pain, to get rid of an uncomfortable situation. The difference between what can be and what is, often creates enough frustration to motivate people out of comfort zones. The basis of any "change from" has to do with a "change to."

4. *A vision is full of hope.* For emotional health, people want and need to hope. Because vision is a preferred future as opposed to a dreaded tomorrow, people are naturally drawn to visions; we function best when hope is high. A lack of hope in our lives results in pessimism, ill health, fear, and insecure faith. "Faith is being sure of what we hope for and certain of what we do not see" (Heb. 11:1). "For in this hope we were saved. But hope that is seen is no hope at all. Who hopes for what he already has? But if we hope for what we do not yet have, we wait for it patiently" (Rom. 8:24–25). Do not underestimate the importance of hope! The pursuit of the dream is often more important than its accomplishment.

5. *A vision provides a reason for unity.* A singularly communicated vision allows a group of people to unify around a cause. The result is synergy, where people working together create a sum total that exceeds what individuals could produce. It is equivalent to 2 + 2 = 5. A vision that is clear can be understood; a vision that is strong can be shared among a group of people.

6. *A vision often provides God's direction.* Visions are usually how God reveals his will among groups regarding direction and change. This is not to suggest that every vision is God-given, but when God does reveal a plan for a people, it is usually via a divinely appointed vision.

7. *A vision is powerful.* When you analyze significant goals and improvement

endeavors that fail, one of the missing elements is a clear, strong vision. While vision alone is not enough to create an improvement cause, a lack of vision is enough to sink well-intended people. Nearly all effective improvement endeavors reflect clear, strong visions from individuals who grasp the heart and resources of participants and other team members.

MEASURING A VISION

The most difficult thing about making a good Joshua Report is that the concept is so difficult to translate into skills, or how-tos. You know it when you see and hear it, but otherwise, vision is difficult to quantify, like the concepts of love, faith, and hope.

Analyzing a good Joshua Report is much like inspecting facets of a diamond. A diamond is often measured by color, clarity (brilliance), and weight (karats). In a similar fashion, there are three primary characteristics for grading the quality of a Joshua Report: intensity, clarity, and size. Following are some ideas on how to actually measure and analyze a Joshua Report for your congregation.

Intensity

First, the strength of a Joshua Report is reflected in its intensity. Just as vivid, deep, primary colors stand out more than pastels, visions with intensity emerge from the blurred lifescape of busyness and marketing. Now more than ever, Joshua Reports that lack intensity tend to get lost in the array of messages bombarding us daily. Intensity consists of two elements, importance and urgency.

You can test the importance of a vision by asking: *Why do we need to pursue this change? What good thing do we have to gain from this?* List the positive possibilities. *Who will gain from these improvements? How much do we have to gain?* Because motivation comes primarily via two avenues, the hope of gain or the hurt of pain, a better consideration might be to list the things that will happen if you do not pursue the intended change. What will happen if we stay the way we are for five more years? What will we miss by staying the same? Who will be hurt by our lack of improvement? How much ground or how many opportunities might we lose? "Vision, then, becomes a bold reason for living. It is a badge of purpose that the bearer wears proudly and courageously. Vision is not vision if it is not inspiring."[6]

While importance measures gravity, impact, and weight, urgency considers timing. Every improvement issue has time considerations. When a vision is deemed important but not urgent, the natural tendency is to put it off. When we procrastinate on an improvement, we are apt to occupy ourselves with matters that are less important but more urgent. Our lives are filled with squeaky wheels, calls and e-mails, and instant opportunities that scream for attention. Most of us function like a MASH triage unit that must prioritize the gravity of wounds and place the direst situations ahead of the rest. Unfortunately, our culture has consciously or subconsciously picked up on these cues, so that most people can make you believe that their message is urgent. If we believe them, we busy ourselves with urgent tasks that lack importance, thus the phrase "the tyranny of the urgent."

Clarity

Now that we've examined the first measurement of a vision, intensity, we can tackle the second: clarity. "If the trumpet does not sound a clear call, who will get ready for battle?" (1 Cor. 14:8). If intensity measures importance and urgency, clarity looks at how clearly a vision is understood. I (Alan) spoke in West Virginia the week following college finals and before commencement exercises. After that Sunday night service, we had to drive through the night to make a Monday morning graduation exercise near Chicago. The problem was that we got lost in the fog on the back roads of West Virginia and almost missed our commencement procession.

Striving toward unclear change organizationally is akin to driving a car in foggy, foreign country. When the vision is foggy, the ministry team and congregation tend to wander. While many leaders claim to have a vision, some are unable to articulate it well. Unless the preferred future is clear and well defined, a haze will exist in the minds of the followers. When directions are muddy, we tend to plan diverse and sometimes contradictory strategies to get there. Vision vacuum is a common phenomenon in organizations where the leader either does not have a vision or is too fearful to risk verbalizing it well.

Admittedly, communication is difficult. Taking an abstract concept like a vision and turning it into a compelling mental picture is no easy task. If a leader does not have the ability to communicate what he visualizes, he may select a spokesperson. Moses did that. Make sure the speaker understands the vision clearly, and let him or her cast the vision to the people.

You can also resort to an array of creative means to help people feel the vision. When Jesus' early disciples were striving to tell their friends about the Messiah, sometimes they would simply say, "Come and see." This may be the most powerful process, because it allows the would-be follower to experience the vision individually instead of through another person. As we have said, a pastor or improvement team can take people to a model ministry that is thriving in order to let them "come and see." By hearing, seeing, and feeling the sort of church you see yourselves becoming, you can begin to plot out the strategies. Take advantage of any number of books, tapes, and church conferences in order to sow the seed of a new thing in your church. Unleash people who are gifted at vision casting, communicating, and strategic planning to craft the vision once they have gained a sense of where the church should go.

Three years into Scottsdale Family Church, we did an analysis to see why our rate of growth was tapering off around the five-hundred mark. One thing we noticed was that our leadership team was not able to articulate well the specific reasons why we did what we did. So we spent time talking about why we were in business and created graphic illustrations to reflect our ministry purpose. This process has helped us become a more unified leadership team and thus communicate more effectively to others in the congregation.

A team approach to vision casting is a great tool for leaders who are unable to communicate well personally, or who want to increase the impact of their personal voice. The vision must be lit by the leader (pastoral or lay), but a team can fan the flames. When team members understand what an improvement movement is designed to accomplish, they are able to multiply the individual impact and clarification to their peers. As in our case at Scottsdale Family Church, providing graphic illustrations and charts as visual aids can do a lot as well, since a picture paints a thousand words. The synergistic effect of an entire group of people delivering the message of hope, direction, and purpose can be powerful.

In addition to clear vision in the mind of the leader and the leader's communication skills, three other characteristics are key to clarity. First, variety is essential. Some people are visual learners, others audio, and some experiential. Providing vision via an array of methods and styles is important to connect with a variety of people. Visual aids such as schematics, artwork, graphics, three-dimensional models, video and audio presentations with music, banners, and brochures are all means to effective communication.

The second vital characteristic is frequency. Over the course of days and weeks, vision leaks out of us. The sheer number of messages that our brain receives daily is enough to make us feel overwhelmed. What was a clear vision for ministry slowly becomes a foggy idea in comparison to more recent messages. Since the media world is vying for the attention of our team members, keeping the vision visible is more important than ever. Again, use a variety of means. Relying on the same mode to communicate vision will quickly bore people and thus reduce your effectiveness. While leaders often feel they frequently talk about a vision, members quickly forget. A fresh vision cast every couple of months is a minimum these days.

The third characteristic essential to clarity is feedback measurement. Effective communication is two-way. Leaders inevitably believe they are doing a better job than they are because they do not gather feedback. If you ask the people of your ministry and congregation to write down the vision of the church or its various characteristics, how many different ideas would you glean? Know that there will be inequity between what the leader thinks he has communicated and what others understand. One study noted that nearly 66 percent of its respondents said their company's leadership failed to ensure a clear understanding of a corporate vision, mission, and goal in its workforce.[7]

Consider individual interviews, quick surveys, and small-group forums in order to listen to what people are hearing. Never assume people understand the vision of your church just because a leader has spoken on it. Gather feedback and try to measure it as tangibly as possible. Writing exacts ones thoughts, so written feedback is often more valuable than just verbal. Ask open-ended questions. Use the feedback to rearticulate the vision more effectively. Then measure again.

Size

Extreme sports, huge conglomerates, and bigger-than-life architecture and media are examples of what make attention-grabbing visions and goals more difficult to spotlight. Because people are inundated with bigger-and-better homes, toys, and electronics, they are also desensitized to visions that lack grandeur. Facts and figures that used to amaze us now seem to produce yawns. We must think in terms of supernatural expectations if we are to raise eyebrows as well as the excitement level of people we want on our teams. The difference between a slam-dunk, no-nonsense change and a risky, exciting one that requires prayer and God, is faith.

When Joshua and Caleb suggested the Israelites take on the giants occupying their land of promise, they were stretching the slave-minded nation beyond what it could imagine. "One of the most popular and devastating barriers to true vision is the notion that God would never cause you to do something different from what you've always done before."[8] Notice the wording in the doubtful spies' report: "We seemed like grasshoppers in our own eyes, and we looked the same to them" (Num. 13:33). The problem with fear is that it distorts thinking; we can see this in the spies' belief that they knew what the enemies thought of them. It's true that we must carefully weigh the inherent risks with the size of the dream. But when we choose against risk, we nearly always choose against great benefit and fruitfulness as well.

Here is a visual representation of how risk and payoff work together.

6A
Risk vs. Payoff

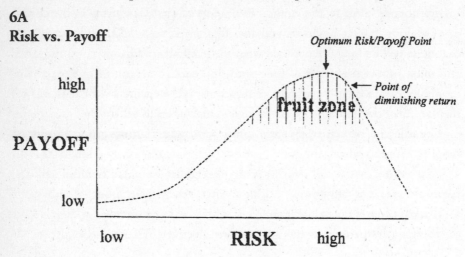

The vertical axis (left side) measures the size of payoff and fruitfulness. The horizontal axis (bottom line) measures the level of risk. No risk, representing no faith required, is on the far left. Foolishness, taking illegitimate risks, is on the far right. The higher the shaded area, the greater the effectiveness.

The problem of determining the amount of risk worth taking is that it is subjective, or open to debate. The human tendency is to fear, not to exercise faith. Still, increasing the size of the dream is wiser than decreasing it. There are countless examples of congregations that sold off adjacent land because they felt they would not need it or built tiny buildings, eventually boxing in the church from future growth.

The good thing about faith communities is that we share a common belief in the Bible, with its historical evidences of God at work in risky projects, and we teach the virtue of faith, which addresses the invisible, unobservable. But various people in any congregation have differing degrees of faith, experience, and fear of risk. People with the gift of faith find it quite easy to dream big and trust for big things. They are tempted to see others as low-faith people. Low-faith people tend to see faith-gifted people as foolish.

Visions can also be too large for people to swallow. While most visions suffer from dwarfism, some die from elephantitis. As the risk/payoff chart portrays, there is a point of diminishing returns, when the risk suggested is beyond enlarged reason and realistic faith. This may be due to a leader's inability to lead the charge, environmental problems such as a recession or industry change, or any number of other factors. Visionary leaders can get caught up in the excitement of doing great things for God, so that they "over-hear" God's leading and venture onto thin ice. When they fall through, everyone suffers.

Finding that optimum risk/payoff point is usually subjective and often elusive. History is laden with stories of huge dreams gone awry because leaders bit off more than they could handle. Having said that, let us affirm that the grosser sin by far is that of underestimating what God and a group of faith-oriented people can achieve.

Throughout Scripture, God frequently brings his people to points where the size of the idea is intimidating. Abram did not believe he and Sara could bear a son, thus he took Hagar illegitimately. Jesus faced the doubts of many people, including his hometown folk:

> They took offense at him.
>
> But Jesus said to them, "Only in his hometown and in his own house is a prophet without honor."
>
> And he did not do many miracles there because of their lack of faith. (Matt. 13:57–58)

> Later Jesus appeared to the Eleven as they were eating; he rebuked them for their lack of faith and their stubborn refusal to believe those who had seen him after he had risen.
>
> He said to them, "Go into all the world and preach the good news to all creation. Whoever believes and is baptized will be saved, but whoever does not believe will be condemned." (Mark 16:14–16)

What if some did not have faith? Will their lack of faith nullify God's faithfulness? Not at all! (Rom. 3:3–4)

As has just been said:

> "Today, if you hear his voice,
> do not harden your hearts
> as you did in the rebellion."

Who were they who heard and rebelled? Were they not all those Moses led out of Egypt? And with whom was he angry for forty years? Was it not with those who sinned, whose bodies fell in the desert? And to whom did God swear that they would never enter his rest if not to those who disobeyed? So we see that they were not able to enter, because of their unbelief. (Heb. 3:15–19)

The challenge is to find *God*'s dream for your ministry and congregation. Human nature causes us to doubt when we are stretched. On the other hand, it takes only a few humanly inflated visions to jade would-be followers, providing war stories to substantiate naysayers' cautions.

A HOOK TO HANG YOUR HAT ON

D. L. Moody said, "Give me a man who says 'This one thing I do' and not 'These fifty things I dabble in.'" Just as a title and subtitle of a book give you an idea of the topic and an illustration creates a word picture in a sermon, a vision statement provides a mental hook on which you can hang the improvement concept. A vision statement may be for the entire church or it may be specifically for the proposed change. Developing a vision statement is a very useful tool for succinctly and clearly communicating a vision. Burt Nanus gives us eight criteria on which we can evaluate a vision statement:

1. To what extent is it future oriented?
2. To what extent is it utopian—that is, is it likely to lead to a clearly better future for the organization?
3. To what extent is it appropriate for the organization—that is, does it fit in with the organization's history, culture, and values?

4. To what extent does it set standards of excellence and reflect high ideals?
5. To what extent does it clarify purpose and direction?
6. To what extent is it likely to inspire enthusiasm and encourage commitment?
7. To what extent does it reflect the uniqueness of the organization, its distinctive competence, and what it stands for?
8. Is it ambitious enough?[29]

One way to apply these criteria is to answer each of the eight questions on a scale of one to five, with five representing the highest degree of compliance possible. You can see what aspects of the vision statement are weak and also come up with an average to see how well it is formulated. You may want to gather a variety of vision statements and evaluate each one. Let your Dream Team provide the feedback. Pick the one that has the highest rating to communicate publicly.

APPLICATION TOOLBOX

Although it's subjective, the vision factor is involved every day in the life of a church. Establishing a way of measuring such a nebulous concept will help you better communicate what needs to happen. Ask a group of people such as staff, the Dream Team, the church board, or others to rate the church or improvement vision on the following criteria.

Rate how you perceive the urgency of the vision:

1. Not urgent. We need it someday.
2. Somewhat urgent. We need it soon.
3. Very urgent. We need it now.

Rate how you perceive the importance of the vision:

1. This will not make a significant impact on our church/community.
2. This vision will make a significant impact.
3. This vision will transform our congregation and potentially our community.

Rate how clear the vision seems to you:

1. Clear as mud. It is very foggy and unclear; views on it are diverse.
2. Some of it makes sense. I see it in black and white but not in color. A minority of people are convinced it should happen.
3. Crystal clear. I see it in full color. A majority are unified on where we're headed.

Rate the size this vision seems to have:

1. This is a small vision—no biggie.
2. This is significant and would take some doing to pull off.
3. This would be nothing short of a miracle, requiring faith in a big God.

Plug the estimated numbers into this formula:

Urgency _____ x Importance _____ + Clarity _____ + Size _____ = _____ (V-factor)

The V-factor will range from 3 to 15. Use the following range categories to describe the V-factor of your church.

3–6: Vision is weak or practically nonexistent. Pray hard and select an emergent leader who will carry the ball.

7–11: Figure out where you are weak and what you need to do to make the vision stronger, more motivating.

12–15: Vision is strong—go for it! Work out the details and pursue the plan so long as God is in it.

> Not much happens without a dream. And for something great to happen, there must be a great dream. Behind every great achievement is a dreamer of great dreams.
>
> —Robert Greenleaf

Crash-and-Burn Story

The church was located in a very affluent, fast-growing area in Texas. The average age of people living in the area was thirty-two, and the community consisted primarily of technological and white-collar professionals. The church was about twenty years old at the time. I would categorize the worship style of the church when I arrived as modified traditional. While it was very much a Baptist church service, the staff was doing some things differently, such as projecting worship songs on a large screen and using praise choruses and a band.

The senior pastor was a sixty-five-year-old Bible scholar whose main strength was teaching. The people really enjoyed his ability to communicate the Bible with clarity and simplicity. The church averaged about nine hundred in Sunday attendance when I came on staff.

The senior pastor had a passion for evangelism and was known throughout our denomination for leading churches to reach lost people. The problem was that he was having a difficult time understanding and connecting with the fast-paced culture and young members of the community. In other words, he did not seem to have a vision for being able to transition our church into the present culture. The pastoral staff and key church leaders understood this better than the pastor. After evaluating the church and the community, they realized that the church was growing mainly from transfers from other churches. There was very little personal evangelism on the part of the members.

I had been studying the Willow Creek model for about a year prior to coming on staff. As a part of my interview process with the senior and associate pastor, I was asked what I believed would be the best strategy for leading the church to reach unchurched people. I introduced them to Willow Creek's seven-step strategy and was asked to come on staff for the purpose of educating the pastoral staff and church leaders on the strategy and leading the transition to this strategy.

We began the process with pastoral staff retreats and weekly staff meetings. We also brought approximately seventy-five church leaders to Willow's church leadership conferences. We held weekend retreats and monthly meetings with our key leaders to educate them on the whys and hows of becoming a seeker church. Later we established a transition strategy and a time line for implementation.

During this time we brought on pastoral staff to complement the change in strategy. We created a transition team of church leaders to assist in the planning, communications, and implementation. We held several small-group meetings of various age and affinity groups to discuss the strategy and change as well as several churchwide forums for question-and-answer periods. We led people to begin identifying, praying for, and developing relationships with their unchurched friends.

We established drama teams, technical teams, bands, and vocal teams for the new services. Because there was already a move to changing the existing Sunday services to a contemporary-style service, we continued gradual changes during this two-year period of planning. The plan was to make the first Sunday morning service a contemporary-believer service and the second a seeker service.

After some analysis, it became obvious to the leadership that the senior pastor would not be best equipped to speak at the seeker service because of his age, presentation style, and difficulty communicating and relating to the age group of the community. Although he was allowing some of these changes to percolate, he was not able to articulate the vision of how and why we needed to make them. The staff and key church leaders discussed this with the senior pastor and he initially affirmed the assessment; he agreed to allow two of the other staff pastors to carry the speaking responsibilities of the second service. But as the days approached to initiate the change, the senior pastor began having second thoughts about "giving up" the 11:00 A.M. "prime time" service. When he approached the staff and church leaders concerning his reconsideration, we decided to place the transition on hold. This in effect began a chain reaction that led to the senior pastor's retirement. After he retired, the church leaders asked the staff to continue the transition.

As seems to exist with every transition, we had an opposition group. What we didn't know was that previously, the senior pastor had held this small group in check. There was a strong value that the senior pastor was holy and set apart and that no one in the church should openly challenge him. This was not the belief regarding other staff pastors.

Upon the departure of the senior pastor, this group began to undermine the church's direction. Its members successfully created enough strife and conflict in the church that the tension became obvious to anyone who attended a service. The church then had to turn inward to deal with internal problems instead of focusing outward to reach the unchurched. The members committed to the transition did not feel comfortable inviting their unchurched friends to services full of unhappiness.

It became painfully clear that we would have to put the seeker services on hold until the problem was resolved. Meanwhile, members of this opposing group strategically positioned themselves on the pastoral search and interim church leadership committee and continued attempts to sabotage the pastoral staff's leadership. Over time, the pastoral staff left the church for other ministry opportunities. When I left, the church had lost about two hundred members.

Today the church has grown again to about its original size, primarily through transfers from other churches. As I understand, the church has incorporated many of the styles of a contemporary church but has not made the leadership and seeker-church-values transition.

Crash-and-Burn Lessons:

- When the senior pastor does not have a vision for the desired/recommended improvements, it is difficult to make them happen. Permission granting is significantly different from vision driving.
- Vision is important, but implementing the vision into a potentially barren or even hostile setting can preclude it from becoming reality.
- Spend a great deal more time teaching and modeling the values behind a seeker-church model than focusing on the "cosmetics" of a seeker church. Changing the way you do things without a clear understanding of why you do what you do does not produce the results you're looking for.
- Identify the key influencers of the church and establish relationships with them. Then enlist their commitment to the church's direction.
- Celebrate the church's past successes. Don't bash the past in order to obtain commitment to the future. Grieve with those who are missing "the way we used to do it" and celebrate the small victories that reflect the new values. Be patient with those who are struggling to "buy in." Our staff spent virtually eight hours a day for months learning and assimilating the biblical basis for building a seeker church, but we spent only an hour or two a week trying to teach what we had learned to our church. As a result we became frustrated and even short-tempered with those who "didn't get it" as fast as we wanted them to. We mistook this as resistance, selfishness, or spiritual immaturity.
- Do not assume that "if you build it, they (seekers) will come." Without a strong vision and commitment from church members to build relationships with their unchurched friends, to share a verbal witness, and to invite them to attend church, seeker services will not work. What happened for us was that when we changed to weekly seeker services, the large number of churched people who regularly visited our church

stopped coming—they enjoyed the service as it was—and since we were not bringing our unchurched friends, it looked like the plan was a bad idea, creating even more resistance to the changes.

QUESTIONS AND ANSWERS

Q: Help me better understand the difference between goal setting and vision casting.

A: Managers set goals. Leaders cast vision. You can set goals without a vision, but every good vision becomes the foundation for establishing measurable and strategic goals. Vision has more to do with passion and answers the "why" question. Goals are more about logical thinking and answer the "what" question. There is a lot of confusion between the two concepts, but the most common misperception is that pastors think they have established a vision when they set a goal, whether it be attendance, a building, a new worship service, or something else. Any significant improvement issue must begin with vision, a preferred future. From that point, we can begin to plan strategies and measurable steps toward accomplishing this vision. Goals are both intermediary bench marks as well as long-term criteria established to measure vision accomplishment. Goals are a subset of vision but can and often do occur where there is little to no vision. Vision moves the heart. Goals tend to move the mind. Vision is big picture. Goals are smaller picture.

When President John Kennedy announced that by the end of the sixties we would land a man on the moon, that was a dream, a vision. That singular announcement riveted a nation that empowered NASA to begin a huge strategic plan consisting of countless goals, bench marks, and time lines. Because people are primarily emotional beings, the heart and emotions control the will to action. The motivation button is located in the heart, not the mind, so when you want to push it, you have to appeal to emotion. In church settings, year-end budget and attendance goals in and of themselves lack energy. The "wow" factor must be present for a vision to motivate.

Q: What is the difference between a mission statement and a vision statement?

A: Mission statements are not unimportant, but they tend to represent somewhat generic biblical fundamentals that are easily transferable from congregation to congregation. They usually refer to the Great Commission, discipleship, evangelism, worship, care, and so forth. While being important value expressions, mission statements rarely have the teeth in them to compel allegiance and lack the clarity to hone in on specific actions and strategies. Very few mission statements transform congregations. They are neat worship-folder bylines or web-site slogans, but they rarely distinguish one church from another.

A vision statement, on the other hand, reflects what we believe is important. It is the incarnation, the tangible record, of what we value. Discerning between the mission statement and the vision statement is a bit like loving children in general and loving your kids specifically. A vision is "our kid." It reflects our church's DNA.

If you're not sure which you have, George Barna provides ideas for testing the difference between a vision statement and a mission statement. If all or most of the answers to the following questions are "no," what you have is probably a definition of your mission rather than a statement of God's vision for your ministry.

- If someone talked to you about getting involved in a good-sounding ministry opportunity, is the statement specific enough to help you lovingly say, "Thanks, but no thanks," and explain the reasoning for rejection?
- When comparing your statement with those of other nearby churches, does it provide information that sets your church apart from them?
- Does the statement identify a target audience whom you hope to impact through the ministry?
- Does the statement lead to a clear direction in the future, including precise understanding of strategies and tactics?
- Does the statement prevent the church from seeking to be all things to all people?
- Have any inactive people in the church become excited about ministry prospects after being exposed to the statement?[10]

Here is an example:

The mission of Scottsdale Family Church is to help people develop a relationship with God and continually grow via relevant worship and Bible study, use of their gifts for service, and loving community with each other.

The vision of Scottsdale Family Church is to be a premier provider of soul-growth resources in the northeast valley (Phoenix metro).

Notice how the vision statement explains our business and reason for existence and targets the primary demographics of a geographical area. While it is not perfect, it provides a pithy foundation from which to elaborate a full color vision. Measurable goals can be created from further defining of elements within this statement. Note that since our vision includes reaching the unchurched, we avoid using terms in our vision statement that offend pre-Christians, such as *irreligious, lost,* or *unchurched.*

> **Q: If we do not have a clear-cut, leader-cast vision, can we develop a group vision? Why do you say a vision has to be cast by an individual?**

A: The first answer to that is in one word: hierarchy. People are created socially, so that certain individuals influence others. Even in a group where it appears that no hierarchical positions exist, influence is never dispersed evenly. Thus, groups will rely on ideas and articulations from certain individuals more than others. That's in a scenario where all of the individuals are somewhat equal in motivation and competence. In short, one person's vision will inevitably win over the group. So it is impossible to create a "group" vision.

When you look at history, especially biblical history, you will find that individuals are the key to catalyzing dreams and changes. Leaders never bring about change alone, otherwise they would not be leaders. But they are the stewards of vision. God entrusts his plans into the hands of individuals. Therefore he holds them more responsible than anyone else. Pop quiz: Name a single social movement that cannot be traced to the vision of a single individual!

Catching a vision as a group is feasible and may for a while appear to be a group process, but the true catalyzing of a vision is via an individual. The bottom line is that the leader is responsible for laying the vision egg, and the group's role is to incubate it.

> **Q: Visions are fine, but I've seen so many great ideas cast with little to no follow-through. How do you make sure a vision becomes grounded in the fabric of planning and day-to-day ministry?**

A: Visions require significant amounts of energy to get them up and running. When a rocket blasts off, the initial going is slow and expensive because of gravity and lack of momentum. It consumes more fuel in its early stages than in any other time in its life. The same is true of a vision. Most people underestimate what it takes to get an innovation going. The learning curve can be significant. All the while, you are busy taking care of the old machinery and its squeaks.

In the context of a local church, one of the benefits of a Dream Team is that its primary responsibility is to keep the improvement on target and to lovingly hold people responsible to make sure the plan is implemented. The Dream Team members should not be burdened with other significant matters so that they can devote their best skills to keeping the vision on target. We will talk about this more in the next two chapters, but if you're concerned about too much talk and too little follow-up, you are wise. Every time a vision is hyped, sold, and not completed, it makes it more difficult to get people excited and committed to the next one.

Discussion Starters

1. Why is vision so important to an improvement process?
2. Why is the vision idea so difficult to nail down in tangible terms?
3. Can you think of examples of effective and ineffective vision casting? What made the difference?
4. From the Top 10 Reasons Why Visions Fail, which do you think are the most common two or three?
5. Can you think of any examples of risky ventures that paid off well and risky ventures that did poorly, personally and churchwise?
6. What do you think your church needs to do to develop a vision as a whole or for an improvement in particular?
7. Take a stab at drafting a possible vision statement for the proposed improvement.
8. Does your church have a mission statement? Does it have a vision statement? If you have the latter, how would you rate it according to Barna's criteria?

> If people don't get it, don't fix the people—fix the process.
>
> —W. Edwards Deming

Contemplation

Then Caleb silenced the people before Moses and said, "We should go up and take possession of the land, for we can certainly do it."

. . . But the men who had gone up with him said, "We can't attack those people; they are stronger than we are."

. . . All the Israelites grumbled against Moses and Aaron.

—Numbers 13:30–31, 14:2

Scripture

Read Numbers 13:17–14:12.

DEVOTIONAL THOUGHT

Every one of us has twelve spies inside our heads. Ten strive to convince us why we need to stay put, rally the wagons, and avoid any new vista. But two mental spies tell us about greener pastures, fruitful horizons, and impressive skylines. Whom do we trust? Whom should we listen to? Who is speaking truth? Could it be that they all are?

God created our minds to fulfill what we choose to place in them. When we place fear in our thoughts, our minds quickly seek to substantiate our worries. We find tangible reasons for why we should stay right where we are. But when we focus on the possibilities, our minds equally race toward faith and how our dreams might come true. The question is not whether you have positive or negative spies inside your head, but to whom you are listening.

History repeats itself daily, for people never change. Our basic nature is to avoid the unknown and emphasize the giants, the barriers. We multiply our fears by sharing them with others, until an entire group is placing faith in its doubts. But God calls us to live beyond ourselves. Faith forces us to consider the unknown possibilities.

Are you going to be a believer or a murmurer? Do you believe that God is able to do a new thing in your midst, that the best is yet to be?

Why is it important that you verbalize hope to others instead of complaining? How can you be a part of the faithful minority instead of the more skeptical majority regarding change and improvement?

Prayer

Dear God, today I choose to place my faith in the possibilities, not to complain. Help me to continue this choice. Empower me to activate my belief that you're not done with us yet and that you have a preferred place for us that flows with milk and honey. The giants we can tame, with your help. Go with us. Take our hands as we pursue your promise. Amen.

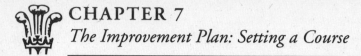

CHAPTER 7
The Improvement Plan: Setting a Course

There is much talk of slaying sacred cows. Few are slain; most die of old age. The mandate for change is seldom bold enough to overcome entrenched obstacles to change.

—PRICE WATERHOUSE CHANGE INTEGRATION TEAM

Up to this point, we have focused on understanding the different elements in the change process, how people process innovation, and how God wants us to respond to something new. Once you've synthesized all of that, you are ready to decide what needs to actually change in your church situation. That is what we will begin to do in this chapter.

If you are on an improvement team, take your time on this one. Spend adequate energy in prayer, contemplation, discussion, and writing. The fruit of your labor will be significant. "Plans fail for lack of counsel, but with many advisers they succeed" (Prov. 15:22).

A THEOLOGY OF PLANNING

In the church realm, we see two opposing trends. There are some who suggest that life in the Spirit is not a matter of planning, but of living spontaneously. In the other corner, we have the very methodical and plan-obsessive folks, who pretty much wring out the Holy Spirit and anything even appearing to be faith oriented. Neither method is perfect. Too little planning tends to make faith a mockery, and too much often squeezes God out of the equation.

Temperaments affect our passion for detail and forethought. You can see varying temperaments within a congregation and within Dream Teams. But in issues of church change, we advocate good planning because it reduces the risk. Planning increases the potential and improves effectiveness. Although God is sovereign and can do what he wants when he wants, we need to realize that he does have a place for plans in his work.

Thanks to God, Joseph came up with a plan to save Egypt and ultimately Israel from starvation (Gen. 41). God showed Moses the specific plan for the tabernacle (Exod. 26), not to mention a plan to free Israel from slavery. David had a God-given plan for the construction of the temple (1 Chron. 28).

Consider these:

> Commit to the LORD whatever you do,
>> and your plans will succeed. (Prov. 16:3)

> In his heart a man plans his course,
>> but the LORD determines his steps. (Prov. 16:9)

> Many are the plans in a man's heart,
>> but it is the LORD's purpose that prevails. (Prov. 19:21)

> Make plans by seeking advice;
>> if you wage war, obtain guidance. (Prov. 20:18)

> The plans of the diligent lead to profit
>> as surely as haste leads to poverty. (Prov. 21:5)

> Woe to those who go to great depths
>> to hide their plans from the LORD,
> who do their work in darkness and think,
>> "Who sees us? Who will know?"
> You turn things upside down,
>> as if the potter were thought
>>> to be like the clay!
> Shall what is formed say to him who formed it,
>> "He did not make me"?

Can the pot say of the potter,
    "He knows nothing"? (Isa. 29:15–16)

"Woe to the obstinate children,"
    declares the Lord,
"to those who carry out plans
        that are not mine,
    forming an alliance, but not by my Spirit,
heaping sin upon sin." (Isa. 30:1)

But the noble man makes noble plans,
    and by noble deeds he stands. (Isa. 32:8)

"For I know the plans I have for you," declares the Lord, "plans to prosper
you and not to harm you, plans to give you hope and a future. Then you will
call upon me and come and pray to me, and I will listen to you. You will
seek me and find me when you seek me with all your heart. I will be found
by you," declares the Lord. (Jer. 29:11–14)

May he give you the desire of your heart
    and make all your plans succeed. (Ps. 20:4)

But the plans of the Lord stand firm forever,
    the purposes of his heart through all generations. (Ps. 33:11)

Perhaps we have overstated our point, but your goal is to maintain a delicate balance between thorough planning and a flexible, inclusive attitude about God's involvement. When improvement plans go awry, it is nearly always because leaders did not adequately consider significant factors.

Working as a team is vital here. Chances are that you may think some factors are important or clear-cut but others on the team will not. Working as a team enhances the likelihood that you will cover the bases. Jesus taught, "Suppose one of you wants to build a tower. Will he not first sit down and estimate the cost to see if he has enough money to complete it? For if he lays the foundation and is not able to finish it, everyone who sees it will ridicule him, saying, 'This fellow began to build and was not able to finish'" (Luke 14:28–30).

THE NEED FOR TWO PLANS

In chapter 3, we pointed out that the hardest part of change is the transition. In order to minimize the pain and stress of change, it is important to have two distinct plans, an improvement plan and a transition plan.

The first issue to resolve in strategic planning is *what* needs to improve, not *how* you will go about it. In this chapter we will help you thoroughly consider what needs to be changed in your church to bring improvement and how to formulate a plan for implementation. In chapter 8, we will bring these and other elements together to form a transition plan, which involves timing, amount of change, leadership, readiness, communication, and going public with the improvement ideas.

When considering improvement, there are at least five areas we need to consider. We have adapted these from a book called *Better Change:*[1]

1. *Customer groups:* While this term may sound coolly corporate, we are all customers of our churches in some respect. We receive services and benefits from them. The questions we need to ask, then, are: *Whom are we serving? Are they from the neighboring community or do they drive in from other areas? Do we want to keep serving Christians or do we want to begin ministering to those outside the church? Can we do both at the same time? Can we do both at different times? Are we in a changing community, where the people we are now serving are moving away and the people moving in have different needs (perceived or real)?* When you seek a change in customers, chances are high that you will need to bring about significant changes in terms of what you have to offer and how you offer it.

2. *Services and resources:* As we said, if you want to attract different customer groups or just expand the variety of ministry opportunities, you will need to change services and resources. When Gene cast the vision for Central Christian to reach the unchurched, it meant modifying their worship format and eventually adding a midweek service for believers. When Alan cast a vision for discipling the new believers at Scottsdale Family Church, it meant developing discipling groups and spiritual assessment tools.

3. *Ministry/administrative processes:* How we accomplish ministry is at times more important than what we accomplish. For example, if we want to create community in our ministry teams and not just get people to do their jobs, we'll need to train ministry directors in how to care for their people

and schedule huddle time into their ministry meetings. We'll want to establish accountability systems to monitor and measure community building. When we change how ministry gets done, it will inevitably impact multiple areas, such as people, resources, training, and even items like facilities and technology. Do not underestimate the importance of process issues when it comes to improvement results.

4. *People and reward systems:* If a church begins to go a different direction or change services and resources, it will obviously need staffing changes as well. Reallocating funds to reflect these priorities and even changing staff roles or members may occur. If a church wants to begin engaging the laity in active ministry, putting a ministry involvement director on staff may be required. After that takes place, you will need to maintain for a few months or years; then you may be able to let some paid positions go and hire support help for lay directors who donate their time and energies. If you begin prioritizing leadership development as opposed to paid staff doing the ministry themselves, you will want to give raises and bonuses on that criteria. As a general rule, what gets rewarded gets done.

5. *Structure/Facilities/Technology:* We are all affected by tools and physical manifestations of ministry. *If we decide to begin a seeker-sensitive service, where will it take place? Will we use the present sanctuary, the fellowship hall, the gym, or an off-site location? Do we need to purchase new equipment, software, furnishings, and décor?* If we bring new staff on board, they will need office space, supplies, and furnishings. Turf battles are sometimes financial, sometimes spatial, and sometimes control oriented, but always emotional. *How will this improvement plan affect what we have now in terms of facilities and tools?*

As you consider these ramifications of change, realize that one-dimensional change is rarely enough to significantly impact your church. For example, getting all the staff on a local computer network with shared database software is not going to significantly impact how you do ministry. But when you talk about reaching a new customer group (pre-Christians) or changing the way you process ministry (for example, teams versus committees, or lay-driven versus staff-driven), you are talking about significant impact that will affect many aspects of church life as you now know it.

APPLICATION TOOLBOX

A man was arrested one day for peddling Fountain of Youth pills. The prosecutor said to the judge, "Your honor, I think you ought to throw the book at him. This is just about enough. This same man was arrested on these same charges in 1980, 1941, 1903, and 1869."

There comes a time when we have to take a deeper look at something *because* it's working. That is what we've tried to do as we've studied Central Christian Church in Las Vegas and several other congregations. While we need to analyze what works, we also need to realize that there is no perfectly transferable improvement template for your ministry context. PricewaterhouseCoopers is a consulting firm for some of the strongest corporations in the world. Its members knowledgeably confirm:

> The circumstances surrounding your change projects are unique to your situation. What you must do to transform your organization cannot be detailed precisely by any book. This is one of the challenges of change: There is no explicit calculus, no prescriptive outline of the steps you must hazard to drive change in your organization. However, our experience, drawn from hundreds of client assignments, points to a finite set of principles to which one can securely look to achieve better change.[2]

Through experience, PricewaterhouseCoopers has developed a list of fifteen guiding principles.[3] We have translated this list into a church context and consolidated it into twelve principles.

Why twelve? Throughout the Bible, the number twelve occurs with significance. God divided his nation into twelve tribes. Jesus selected twelve men to be his disciples, to become the foundation for the church. When Joshua was leading the people of Israel into the promised land, God instructed him to have twelve stones taken out of the Jordan river bottom:

> The LORD said to Joshua, "Choose twelve men from among the people, one from each tribe, and tell them to take up twelve stones from the middle of the Jordan from right where the priests stood and to carry them over with you and put them down at the place where you stay tonight."
>
> So Joshua called together the twelve men he had appointed from the Israelites, one from each tribe, and said to them, "Go over before the ark of

the LORD your God into the middle of the Jordan. Each of you is to take up a stone on his shoulder, according to the number of the tribes of the Israelites, to serve as a sign among you. In the future, when your children ask you, 'What do these stones mean?' tell them that the flow of the Jordan was cut off before the ark of the covenant of the LORD. When it crossed the Jordan, the waters of the Jordan were cut off. These stones are to be a memorial to the people of Israel forever." (Josh. 4:1–7)

In this way, the number twelve is also symbolic of the transition of God's people into their new home. Every church is on a journey. There are other promised lands, with giants as well as milk and honey for us to experience. As God leads us and our churches through change to a promised land, there are twelve "stones" essential for us to consider.

We have placed them in a journal format so you can respond to them in writing. Forget what your parents said about writing in books. This isn't a book; it's an inexpensive, consultant-in-the-box tool. Feel free to write on these pages and margins.

The following section is designed as a notepad for you to jot down your ideas and thoughts in response to the questions listed. The blank space is where you can respond informally, creatively, and thoughtfully. Use it as a draft, not a finished work. Invest sufficient time, concentration, and brainstorming to make this exercise substantive. The paper and ink that went into the next dozen pages is minimal in cost compared to the invaluable ideas that you will write. As you finish each page, consider any large white spots remaining as potential gaping holes in your improvement plan. When you finish the journal draft, use it as a discussion tool with your improvement team; synthesize your answers toward a master improvement plan. You will soon see a synergistic effect as the team process outperforms individual efforts.

STONE 1: CONFRONT REALITY

We all want to believe that we have invested our energies into a church that will be successful, effective, and enduring. But what are our blind spots? What do the statistics say about our growth patterns? What are the trends? Are we accomplishing the Great Commission in our community? Does our church match its surrounding area? What do we need to take an honest look at?

STONE 2: IDENTIFY AND FOCUS ON STRATEGIC LEVERS

A good mechanic investigates what is causing a car to run poorly. If 20 percent of improvement possibilities result in 80 percent of the fruit, what are the areas of improvement that will result in significant payoff? Where do we need to invest in change? Where do we need to see improved performance? Where are the key points of application that will be fruitful? How can we coordinate various levers for a whole, unified change instead of piecemeal improvement?

STONE 3: BUILD A POWERFUL MANDATE FOR CHANGE

How are we going to communicate the importance and urgency of our need to improve? Are the people aware of our need? How can we turn up the heat of concern? Does our leadership team buy into the need for change? "Without a strong and consistent mandate, you may double the cost of change and halve the impact."[4] How can we build a case for change and work toward consensus?

STONE 4: ESTABLISH A REASONABLE SCOPE

How far-reaching will this improvement process be? Is it realistic to think in terms of a total church transformation? Are we talking about a single ministry transformation? Are we adding to or deleting from our current ministry portfolio? Are we healthy enough to sustain significant change? Is our situation critical, requiring drastic action? What is appropriate for our situation? How will we know if we've made progress, and how much?

STONE 5: LET THE TARGET GROUP(S) DETERMINE THE CHANGE

Who are our ministry target groups now? Whom do we want to reach tomorrow? Describe these groups. Our customers are our allies. How can they help us determine what we need? How do we know what they need, think, feel? Whom are we talking to who represents that target group? What can we do to better minister to these people? What do we need to start, delete, or change?

STONE 6: WHO ARE OUR STAKEHOLDERS?

Who are the opinion leaders? Who are the people who stand to lose or gain from any changes we propose? Who has the power, the money, the invested time and talent? If the church were a publicly owned company, who are the primary stockholders? Are these people willing to let the improvement process happen in their church? What do we need to do to get their permission and/or include them in the process?

STONE 7: COMMUNICATE WELL

Good communication is consistent, variable, and creative. It considers different kinds of interests and learning preferences. How can we communicate our values, motives, and ideas for improvement? Who could be spokespeople for the changes? What methods can we use to communicate? Whom do we need to communicate with and what angle should we take with each group? Who can help design these messages?

STONE 8: INSPECT THE FRUIT

No matter how well we roll out the improvement, it can be ruined if we have inadequate ways of measuring the results. What are we trying to achieve and how can we tell if we're making progress? What are we looking for? How can we measure it? Who will measure it? How will we communicate the results? What will we do with the information we gain from measuring? What levels of fruit do we need to warrant changes?

STONE 9: FAITHINK

How can we add faith in a big God to the way we think and plan? How can we think "out of the box"? What is limiting our thinking? Do we believe God is in this process? What are we doing to prepare ourselves spiritually? Do we believe God is "able to do immeasurably more than all we ask or imagine, according to his power that is at work within us" (Eph. 3:20)? Where have we limited God in our planning? What would be a grand dream to come from this improvement?

STONE 10: SKILL TRAIN

We cannot expect different results from the same actions. How do we need to invest in people? Whom do we need to train, hire, let go, motivate, or retrain? How are we going to develop people at all levels in ministry? Whom can we bring in to train? Where should we send people to learn new skills? What is it going to cost us? How can we make skill building a key performance measure in all our staff, paid and unpaid?

STONE 11: PLAN YOUR WORK AND WORK YOUR PLAN

How are we going to document the ideas and conversations that are being generated from this process? Who will put these plans in written form? Who needs to know what the plan says and how it will work? Who will hold the implementation people accountable, if not the improvement team? Do we have both a strategic plan as well as a transition plan?

STONE 12: ROLLIN', ROLLIN', ROLLIN'

How would we outline the improvement process right now? How fast should we take it? How far should we go? What concerns do we have? What contingency plans have we developed if things do not go as planned? How much money and time will we invest? How will we obtain it? What is it going to take to begin acting on the plan?

Part of deciding on changes involves measuring our current progress. When we establish measurement types and levels, we do more than just provide feedback on how we are doing. We prioritize what is important. If we have multiple tasks to perform, we are apt to do what gets measured and rewarded. Therefore, we need to carefully think through what we want to see happen and legitimately come up with adequate measuring instruments.

These measuring standards can and should change with the ministry, to strengthen areas that are weak. Just as an athlete will work on certain muscle groups at various times, leaders can adjust priorities by applying measurements to these areas. That is a challenge in church work, because much of what we do is relational, spiritual, and intangible. But fruit inspecting and numbers counting are biblical concepts that we can articulate and expand in our local congregations.

No single form of measurement is going to adequately describe the health and progress of a ministry. That is why a set of measurements is important. Pastors are often stressed over the two big numbers: worship attendance and offerings, but we need a broader variety of measurements. If we are serious about creating mature believers, we need to figure out what one looks like and then incorporate offerings in our church that help create the appropriate attitudes and actions. Jesus said, "By their fruit you will recognize them. Do people pick grapes from thornbushes, or figs from thistles? Likewise every good tree bears good fruit, but a bad tree bears bad fruit. A good tree cannot bear bad fruit, and a bad tree cannot bear good fruit" (Matt. 7:16–18).

More of us need to brainstorm ways of measuring internal growth. Measurements should be developed along four lines:

1. *Relevance:* How does this measurement reflect the improvement plan we are trying to implement? New programs and goals require new measurements. For example, many denominations ask their churches for Sunday school statistics, while most new-paradigm congregations disciple primarily through midweek small groups.

2. *Reliability:* Will the measurement help me know the strengths and weaknesses of what we are striving to do? In other words, can I trust this feedback or is it skewed because of who responded, how it was presented, or how it was tabulated? The answers we get are only as good as the questions we ask.

3. *Availability:* Are we able to gather the information we need? The best

measurement ideas are useless unless we can effectively gather sufficient data for reliable feedback. How can we adequately harvest the information we seek? If we mail out two hundred surveys but have only five returned, we cannot base decisions on this response.

4. *Accountability:* Who will gather the information, process it, debrief the appropriate people, and take action to implement appropriate changes? The last thing we need is a plethora of unused information. People who administrate the measurements will be frustrated, and so will those who respond to the surveys/interviews/questionnaires. Obtaining data without doing anything about it is self-deceiving. Information is not the same as wisdom.

For example, perhaps one of your strategic plans is to significantly improve the quality of the services provided by the subministries of the church. Let's say you choose to grade each ministry according to a five-point scale: one—poor, two—fair, three—good, four—very good, five—excellent. On a quarterly or semiannual survey of the ministry users/customers, you rate a variety of items that pertain to that ministry. If you set a bench mark of a minimum of a four average, you can get an idea of where you may need to improve. If you raise the average, you can know that reward and celebration are in order.

Let's say that you are interested in starting a new service that would cater to the unchurched in your community. You would have to measure more than the total attendance in your church—you might be filling the seats but failing the objectives. You probably need to ask how many of those attending were not active in another church within the last year: 25 percent, 45 percent, 65 percent? How many known decisions for Christ have been registered? Since a part of spiritual formation is finding a small group for care and accountability, how many new people are involved in a small group and/or ministry after their first year? If your measuring reveals that you're missing the marks, then you need to reevaluate what you're doing in order to make appropriate changes.

Let's say that you decide to move toward a lay-ministry paradigm, believing that ministry to the body of Christ by the body of Christ is a fundamental spiritual growth principle. How do we know if we're making progress toward these ends? We could measure what percentage of active people are attending our gift-discovery class. How many new people per month is the ministry involvement team placing? What percentage of our active attendees are currently involved in a ministry?

Besides measuring processes like these, we can also look at outcomes such as Bible knowledge, spiritual fruit as revealed in attitudes and behaviors noticed by others, giving records, and self-assessed testimonials.

WHO AND WHAT TO MEASURE

Nearly every church ministry has both internal and external participants. Visitors and people who aren't part of the ministry team have different needs and perspectives from those who are workers and in leadership. If you survey only one group, your feedback will miss potential insights from the other perspectives. For example, if a church is doing strategic planning to figure out how it can engage pre-Christians more effectively, it is silly to survey the ministry leaders to see what it should do. Church leadership views do not reflect those of pre-Christians and those who are outside of the church. Their felt needs differ; so do their opinions about the church. If you want to design ministries for certain people, you need to survey and interview them directly. The same is true for measuring effectiveness of current ministries: if you want to know how valuable a ministry is, ask its recipients for feedback.

Results are physical outcomes. But church life is about family, relationships, and personal growth via those relationships. The completion of the task is just part of the story. How we complete it is the other part. If we accomplish the goals we set out to achieve but do it haphazardly, use people in the process, and frustrate participants, is it worth it?

When we measure our current effectiveness, we should look at processes as well as results. We should examine the training, communication, resourcing, timing, meeting structures, leadership demeanor, and how we get things done in general. Good processes usually result in good results, but not always. Process is itself a product that those of us in the people-growing business want to consider. You can monitor process issues by talking to team members and those associated with them, such as family and friends.

REWARD WHAT YOU MEASURE

A friend of ours works for an insurance company. The company leadership noticed a high turnover in customers and began to motivate the agents to retain existing accounts as opposed to focusing on new business. Our friend, an agent, said, "The problem is that they want us to service existing customers and emphasize retention, but we get commissions only on new business that we sign." In other words, what the company said was important was not what they rewarded. When retention continued to be a problem, management began paying commissions on existing customers, not just new ones.

Measurements should be tied to what gets rewarded. What a joke for us to go through the hassle of setting measurements and elevating certain values while we celebrate and esteem people for other matters. Rewards in ministry are often not financial, so do not let the word *reward* intimidate you. There are many ways to reward ministry progress, such as minicelebrations, public notice, plaques and donated gift certificates, as well as personal "thanks" from church leaders.

APPLICATION TOOLBOX

The improvement-plan exercise you completed earlier in the chapter should help you think through the multiple aspects of significant church improvement. Take your responses from the Twelve Stones journaling exercise and summarize them in less than ten sentences. What specific changes does this exercise suggest?

Begin to lay out a plan for implementing these changes. Remember to work as a team. For example, as you look at the Twelve Stones journaling by your team, what themes emerge? You can't do everything all at once, so creating a priority sequence is important. What are three to five areas for improvement that your team would like to work on first? After you have a short list of agreed-upon priorities, ask what sort of changes need to be made to fulfill those priorities. How will these take place? When should they be done? Who will carry them out? What will need to give way for this to happen?

For example, say your improvement team decides that your church needs a worship service to which your current attendees can invite their unchurched guests without embarrassment. Ask and answer:

Where are we now?

What needs to happen to get us to the goal?

Who, when, where, how is this going to happen?

What measurements will we set to see how we are doing?

Or say you decide you want to create a system that will educate, motivate, train, and track people in roles of service to each other. Ask:

What do we presently have in place for ministry involvement?

How many people are currently "employed" in ministry?

What needs to happen to get to where we want to be? Who models this well?

Who, when, where, how is this going to happen?

What level of ministry involvement do we want to see in the next year; two years; three years? Who will monitor this progress?

QUESTIONS AND ANSWERS

Q: What if we can't agree on what we want to accomplish in an improvement plan?

A: The process can be as important as the product or outcome. Do not underestimate how you decide what will and will not be changed. Hopefully, the people who are developing the improvement plan elements are primarily Dream Team members. These people should consist of progressive influencers, people who welcome change. If this is the makeup of your Dream Team, then you may want to spend more time discussing what you want your church to become. Read another book together, attend a conference as a team, and talk to experts. The more you can share experiences together, the more refined your focus will become.

If your Dream Team does not consist of people who are unified in their outlook, you will need to ask why. Are there people on board who were invited for other reasons than their progressive wiring? Did you taint the process by including people who are going different directions and appear to be holding on to vestiges of the past? Philosophical differences split churches far more than theological ones. Seek consensus—but don't assume that a consensus agreement means everyone is completely on board. It merely means that everyone is basically in support of the plan. At this point, don't get hung up on agreeing on how to get there as much as the end result.

Q: The process of getting to a final, formal improvement plan seems messy, involving a lot of subjective analysis. Isn't there a neater way to achieve an improvement plan?

A: The process *is* messy, no matter how refined your finished product is. The fact that you're dealing with a majority of unpaid servants in a faith community that is very relational and tradition filled means it is not going to be simple. But don't let the messiness intimidate your work. Move forward. Whether it's marital counseling or spring cleaning, you know that with improvement, things tend to look worse before they get better.

Our goal is to provide you with the basic areas you should consider in developing a church-improvement plan. We are not strategic planning experts, but you probably do not need one to develop your own plan. If you think you do, you may find someone in your church, hire an outside consultant, or resort to other books and software programs that will enable you to get the refinement you need and want.

Q: Improvement looks so time consuming. How do we maintain what we are doing while we legitimately focus on the improvement plan?

A: Someone compared organizational change to changing the tire on your car with the car still moving. If you do not have one team of people dedicated primarily to the task of improvement and another team focused on day-to-day ministry, chances are slim that you will be able to prioritize the time to carry out the plan. If improvement issues are a priority, then certain staff and team members will need the freedom to put other things on the back burner while they work on the improvement plan.

If you are an existing church, you must keep the ship fueled and running as you transition. Only a church plant or a church in crisis mode can pull off a sudden, complete direction change. Relax existing demands as you funnel more time and energy toward the improvement efforts. Set up regular meetings and put time expectations on tasks, so that accountability can keep you moving forward. The stress of change itself is significant enough. If you expect people to maintain what they have been doing while adding more changes, the cumulative stress can burn out people and create unnecessary negative energy. Smart planning means freeing people up to focus primarily or solely on improvement issues.

> Every organization has to prepare for the abandonment of everything it does.
>
> —Peter Drucker

Discussion Starters

1. Why is it important to differentiate between the improvement plan and the transition plan?

2. How are they related?
3. How are they different?
4. Which of the twelve-stone issues were the most fun and fulfilling to complete?
5. Which of the twelve-stone issues were the most difficult?
6. What areas have you possibly missed? What stones do you still need to turn over?
7. How can you measure what you want to see happen through your improvements?

> At the end of every day of every year, two things remain unshakable: our constancy of purpose and our continuous discontent with the immediate present.
>
> —ROBERTO GOIZUETA, Chairman and CEO of Coca-Cola

Contemplation

> See, the former things have taken place,
>   and new things I declare;
> before they spring into being
>   I announce them to you.
> Sing to the LORD a new song,
>   his praise from the ends of the earth.
>
>   —Isa. 42:9–10

Scripture

Read Isaiah 42:1–14.

DEVOTIONAL THOUGHT

Do you ever get tired of the same routine every day: shower, shave, apply deodorant, brush your teeth, and so on? What if you had tacos for every meal of the day, every day of the year? After a while, even gourmet tacos would make you nauseous. What is not new eventually becomes stale.

Change is good. Change is healthy. And most things need to change—

including our songs to God. It is not that God was not happy with yesterday's songs—yesterday. But a part of growth is being able to turn over a new leaf, a new branch, and bear new fruit. Former things were good in their time, but God has new things for us.

Ironically, this new thing he has for us will eventually become a former thing, and he'll do something new again. So it would seem that our job as followers of Christ is to stay flexible, responsive, and supple. God will tire of our old songs, and if we get too attached to them, we'll miss the new thing he's doing. Life is too short to have regrets. So how can you sing a new song for him today, one whose words or notes you may not yet know?

Do you think people sometimes perpetuate the old and familiar in order to avoid the new? Why do they do that? How do you try to control your life and even God by sustaining the former things?

Prayer

God, you never change, but you're always new. Sometimes, I admit, I fall in love with the routine, and I expect you to work the same way tomorrow as you did yesterday. I am wrong. Forgive me. Help me to stay vibrant, alive, dynamic, and new in my response to you. Help me to mature, and not grow old and set in my ways. Today, may I sing a new and better song to you. May you be pleased by what you hear. Amen.

CHAPTER 8
The Transition Plan: Getting from Point A to Point B

Every exit is an entry somewhere else.

—TOM STOPPARD

In the last chapter, we talked about the need to analyze what you want to do in your improvement process. We now want to bring together the various elements to develop a transition plan for your improvement plan. As you can see, well-constructed improvement and transition plans are a lot more complex than merely returning from a church growth conference, standing up the next Sunday, and proclaiming, "Let's change!"

In chapter 5, we created an influence constellation. You (leadership), the improvement team, your surrounding community, your heritage, theology, and organizational structure, and your opinion leaders all create a unique ministry chemistry. Now that you know how people work together, you are ready to put all the ingredients together to determine how far and how fast you will roll out your improvement plan. Four important factors will determine the effectiveness of the change process in your church. Determining a number value for each of these factors and working the equation, which we call the Nelson Change Formula, will help you predict the effectiveness level of the transition plan. These are how long the change will take to implement, the amount of change, the capabilities of leadership, and the readiness within the organization. The result is the Delta Factor.

NELSON CHANGE FORMULA

Time x (Leadership Capacity + Congregational Readiness) = Delta Factor
Change Impact

Change Impact

1.   *Time:* As the amount of time required to implement the change increases, the better our chances are to implement change at a natural, appropriate rate. When time is limited, change becomes a very stressful process and can be barred by a critical mass that opposes the change for whatever reason. People do not like to feel pushed. The natural reaction is to push back in the opposite direction. When the high-pressure salesman says, "The deal is off unless you sign today," most of us turn down the contract.

One reason that time is an asset is because communication/feedback loops do not happen readily. People generally need time to process the proposed change and think it through. Often, though not always, the longer a habit has been functioning, the longer it takes to change. At Central Christian Church, Gene wisely took two to four years to teach, build relationships, and establish credibility before casting a vision for significant change. Even then, many people did not like the proposed ideas, but because of the foundation laid, the transition toward a relevant, outreach-oriented church could begin. Before a new change is implemented, an old way must usually be put to death. Mourning the loss of an old tradition, practice, or process can take some time.

An exception to the basic time rule is that some changes have windows of opportunity. If a new leader or ready core of team members are seeking the recommended changes, taking too long to implement them can backfire and result in further entrenchment.

Another time issue is the size of the organization. Larger organizations usually require longer time to change because the communication factors and reorganization issues are more complex. A mom-and-pop store can transform a business overnight, but a huge conglomerate needs months or years.

Robbins and Finley offer these wise words:

> Organizations that have had the best success with change take major steps
> in short time frames, with the end product carefully described up front.
> With this information under their belts, people tolerate the short-term pain

for the longer-term payoff. The "dribble" or incremental change method only heightens the sense of mistrust of management that many employees already have.[1]

Another way to look at time of change is with a cooking word-picture. Change recipes cook at different speeds. Certain foods and dishes, like improvement issues, need to be prepared differently.

Level 1: Microwave 0–6 months

Level 2: Stovetop 6–12 months

Level 3: Conventional Oven 12–24 months

Level 4: Crock pot 24–36 months

Level 5: Thaw in the Sun 36–60 months

2. *Change Impact:* As the amount of change increases, we reduce our effectiveness when we have limited amounts of time. It is an inverse relationship. In general, the larger the change, the longer it will take to process the change effectively. Obviously, change is happening all the time whether we like it or not. But most of the changes tend to be minute and managerial. You need to look at how deep and far-reaching the proposed change is. Improvement that affects the entire church versus one that varies a specific ministry is more stressful and more time consuming.

People view changes differently. The amount of perceived and real stress varies from person to person, making total impact more difficult to estimate than merely doing a structural or cost-benefit analysis. A word picture for looking at church-change impact is to compare it to trauma on the human body. While improvement is positive, remedies to illness and disease in themselves can create stress. Try to convince a child getting a shot that the sickness is worse than the vaccination. It is possible to die from a remedy. Your improvement team needs to determine the impact of both the illness and the remedy on your local congregation.

Level 1. Common cold: over-the-counter medication sufficient

Level 2. Cut/sprain/flu: first aid/ prescription drug

Level 3. Minor surgery: outpatient

Level 4. Major surgery: hospitalization

Level 5. Heart transplant: transformational

Every congregation has its unique health condition. Some are very healthy and hardy. Others are weak and feeble. When a church is strong, it can withstand a significant operation. The same operation on a weaker congregation could kill it. Just as doctors will defer an operation when a patient may not survive it, leaders need to estimate the resilience of a congregation to the sort of change they are pursuing. Some churches are not strong enough to sustain a significant change remedy, even though they are deathly ill.

3. *Leadership Capacity:* When capable leaders who are passionate for the new thing exist, you increase your chances for effectiveness. That is one of the main reasons for developing quality leadership in a church: Strong leaders can greatly enhance the effectiveness of change as well as decrease the time required, even with larger change issues. Change involves risks, giving up familiar practices, and going into uncharted areas. When leaders are trusted, loved, and embraced for their vision and communication skills, change can happen a lot faster than when leaders are perceived as uncaring, incompetent, and untrustworthy. The job of the senior pastor in most churches is to develop these leaders as a team.

Leadership teams quickly influence and communicate with various spheres of influence within the church, while a single pastor tries to rally support from the entire congregation. Leaders must be aware of opinion leaders, networks, and social circles. The more confident and competent the leadership, the faster change can happen and the better chance for change effectiveness.

4. *Congregational Readiness:* Readiness varies from person to person and is based on how much the person stands to lose or gain with the proposed improvement. If you simply survey people to find out who is for or against a change, the feedback can be deceptive. The key is not *how* many but *who* many. Improvement issues affect people in different degrees. A better strategy than surveying is to look at who will be impacted most by the changes and whether or not they support the improvement. Because most of us look at churches in terms of what we get out of them, we must not overlook the importance of individual perceptions. Let's look at readiness in terms of Impact Camps:

8A
Impact Camps

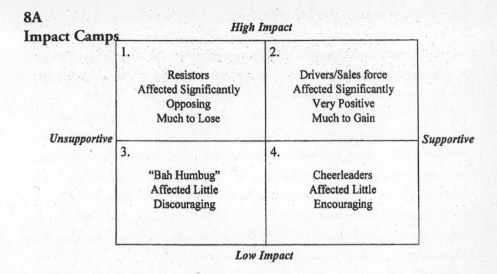

Camp 4: (We will work backward in our explanation.) If a group of people will be impacted very little by an improvement issue, they may support it. They do not have much at stake in the issue, as reflected in Camp 4. This is a cheerleader group, willing to encourage the improvement process, even though it will affect them very little. For example, if a church is considering adding a contemporary worship service to the current traditional service, a grandparent may be in favor of the improvement for his grandson's sake. He wants him to get involved in church and thinks his grandson will appreciate the new style. Since the new service does not conflict with the grandfather's Sunday habits, he is in favor of it.

Camp 3: Conversely, people in Camp 3 will be impacted only slightly by the improvement but do not support it. These people may be antichange regardless of what it is, because they fear what it will do to their current church or what it may cost financially. They may have friends who will be impacted significantly who are against the improvement. If a group of people will not be interrupted by a new style of service, they may oppose it merely for what it represents, a new and different idea that could eventually encroach on their personal preferences. The question with this group is whether they are truly concerned about the doctrinal values reflected in the improvements or if they are merely obstinate.

Camp 2: The people in Camp 2 will be impacted heavily, but they are for the improvement. These people will likely be the drivers and sales force to see the improvement implemented. In terms of our example, this group may include a large class of young marrieds who have been pushing hard to see a worship service that better reflects their tastes and also provides an opportunity for them to invite their unchurched friends. Up to now, they've not felt that freedom, so they are motivated to see the new service happen; they stand to gain a lot from the new format.

Camp 1: Camp 1 people are against the change because they will be impacted heavily. They are most apt to campaign against it either because of what they stand to lose or because of what it might cost them to make it happen. Let's suppose that an outreach service will bump up the time of the traditional service, as well as force the senior adult class to give up its Sunday school room. These people will be forced to find a new location and change their longtime habits, and the new service may divide friends and family. These people do not see the change as an improvement and so they oppose it.

What do you do with this information after you've looked at who will be impacted and who will support the idea? If you appear to have a large contingency in a quadrant not supporting the activity, you know you need to do some communication, education, and negotiation. If you have a large group of people who will be impacted lightly but who are adamantly against the improvement, you might want to look at deeper issues such as control, bad attitudes, or divisiveness. Confronting these issues with Scripture and tough love may be the best prescription. Looking at these differences lets an improvement team know how to go about presenting the improvement plan as it factors into the effectiveness formula.

In Matthew 13:3–8, Jesus told the parable of the seeds that are sown in the various soil conditions. The biblical story helps us understand why some people accept the life-changing gospel and thrive while others resist it. Some people allow it to sprout but not root, and others nurture it for a while only to be distracted by other worries and priorities. The change effect in this parable is similar to the change effect in churches. Some climates welcome improvement while others reject it. Other churches catch a vision but never see it to completion because there is no plan behind it or structure for growth. Still others add improvement items to their already full plate of ministry activities and wonder why they never see the fruit of what they start. The seed of improvement may be the same for each situation, but the soil conditions vary, resulting in different outcomes.

A miniformula to discern the readiness of a congregation looks like this:

Discomfort with Status Quo + Vision + Doable Next Steps = Resistance to change[2]

A leader's responsibility in the improvement process is to make sure there is adequate dissatisfaction regarding the present situation. This runs against the grain of many leaders, who are perpetually "selling" the benefits of the church to the congregation (sales team) and the community (potential customers). People who are comfortable with the way things are will not pursue improvement, period.

As we said before, people will make adjustments for two main reasons: to alleviate pain and to pursue gain. Throughout the Bible, leaders and prophets reminded people of the difference between where they were and where they needed to be. Leadership sometimes involves creating a sense of discomfort in staying the same. One way to illustrate this is with a rubber band. Hold the band in front of you in one hand and with the other, pull it down. The top is where you want or need to get. The bottom is where you are. The tension is what creates the motivation to seek improvement. Too much tension will break the rubber band and damage the church. Too little tension and the motivation to pursue the improvement will not exist.

The easiest organization in which to bring transformational change is the one in crisis. The ease is not in terms of work, but in the ability to gather support for an improvement plan. Pain has a way of moving us quickly to solutions without the need for significant political correctness. People take drastic measures when the pain level becomes intense. Throughout Scripture, God allows people to go through times of breaking in order to tenderize their hearts and make them pliable for the new thing he wants to do in and through them.

Once a certain degree of discomfort with status quo emerges, doable next steps are vital. This is where development of a vision comes in. As we have described, a vision must be clearly communicated and should dictate necessary actions for a church to take. When you create an atmosphere of dissatisfaction without next steps, you'll see an increase in discouragement and frustration with church leaders. Many churches that experience high turnover and membership decline either do not recognize the high level of discomfort with the status quo or do not know what to do next. As a leadership team, before you raise the level of discontent with status quo, make sure you have an idea of how to get where you want to go. People want to know there is a possible solution to their discomfort, that things can get better. Hope is created when there is a plan for things to get better. It is diminished when there isn't.

Finally, then, when you combine discomfort with the status quo with a clearly developed and communicated vision that dictates doable next steps, you decrease resistance to change.

And when a congregation is ready to improve, the chances for effective change significantly increase. In situations where the congregation is not ready for change but still needs it, a more capable leader is required to offset the lack of readiness. When a congregation is ready for change, the amount of change can increase and the amount of time needed can decrease without affecting effectiveness. Leaders who take too long to pursue change issues in ripe congregations run the risk of being overrun by lay leaders and perceived to be incompetent.

We have seen more congregations with a core of ready lay leaders than those with pastors primed to lead. Readiness looks at who is ready, since all parishioners are not the same in influence. It also analyzes what circumstances created the desire to change and what it will cost to make the needed improvement.

CENTRAL CHRISTIAN CHURCH: OUR STORY

Getting Through Transitions

In retrospect, though our changes went over fairly smoothly, I have some regrets. Not the changes themselves—they were and are essential to our effectiveness as a church. But if I could do it all over again, I would do things a little differently. For example, I would work harder at keeping open lines of communication with the disenchanted. I should have had a cup of coffee with a few key players and followed up better. To this day I don't even know why some people left because we never had conversations about what bothered them. I might have prevented that.

On a personal level, I also regret that I was not balanced. Change initiatives require extra work and in devoting my energy to the church, I sometimes neglected family and friends. During our significant change processes, added meetings, conflict resolutions, and planning meetings swallowed even more time than usual ministry did.

During times of change, a leader would do well to maintain minimums of prayer, exercise, and family time, almost as a legalistic regimen. Otherwise, these tend to be the first to go. If you are big enough to have paid staff, work hard at delegating ongoing tasks to lighten your load and/or give up some of the things in your normal schedule. Use gifted lay people if possible to maintain existing ministries, so that you can give your best energy to where it is needed most, the improvement process. Also make sure to keep other key leaders informed. By improving communication, you avoid the hassles of unnecessary meetings to iron out questions and conflicts. Leadership teams can lighten the load of a leader, helping him or her avoid burnout.

The transition process is always somewhat difficult. A man I'll call Jim wanted the church to grow—he was passionate about reaching people but struggled with the methodology that we were adopting. He dragged his feet and battled with me and with others. You could see the tug of war going on in his life in that he liked seeing the progress but wondered about the methods.

I admire the fact that even during his questioning, he didn't give up. He didn't run. All the time he was serving in key positions at the church as a layperson, but he didn't bad-mouth our efforts.

The real turning point for Jim came when I invited him and another man to a leadership conference sponsored by the Willow Creek Association. The atmosphere created a sense that what we were doing was happening in other churches and it also gave him an opportunity to tell our story and celebrate the growth and changes. He realized that the people we were trying to emulate had solid, trustworthy methods. That trip alone gained Jim's enthusiasm and influence to promote our values and methods.

The transition process can also be costly. We had an affluent husband and wife who had been longtime leaders in the church. In the process of seeing changes implemented, they decided that Central couldn't do anything right and they shared their opinions freely in circles of friends and with leaders. Some people suggested that we not make this couple unhappy because the church needed their tithe. At the same time, this couple hinted at "really trying to help out" if we did things their way, but they were actually not big givers. The staff and elder board felt that Central needed to stick with its values and methods and so we did. The couple left. God always has a way to provide for resources lost if he's in it.

APPLICATION TOOLBOX

The Nelson Change Formula can be a useful tool for predicting transition effectiveness. By establishing numerical values and plugging them into the formula, you can estimate how well the transition phase will go and make appropriate changes as needed. Obviously, this does not base effectiveness on the quality of communication, the improvement ideas themselves, or the talent involved. The formula does weigh the four main factors of time, change impact, leadership, and readiness to establish a reasonable transition success estimate.

$$\frac{\text{Time x (Leadership Capacity + Congregational Readiness)}}{\text{Change Impact}} = \text{Delta Factor}$$

CHANGE IMPACT

Time

How long do you plan to take to fully implement this new idea? Place the appropriate number (1 to 5) in the space below, which corresponds to your time goal.

1. 0–6 months (Immediate)
2. 6–12 months (Fast)
3. 12–24 months (Assertive)
4. 24–48 months (Modest)
5. 5 years or more (Cautious)

Your improvement plan time factor: _____

(Pastor's) Leadership Capacity

These questions pertain to the specific role of leading and should not be confused with competence in any number of other pastoral areas. Pastors can rate themselves, and improvement team members can rate their pastor. Respond to each of the ten questions with "yes" if it represents a strong majority of the people's perceptions as opposed to a doubtful minority. Try not to answer as you believe you should, but answer the way you actually think. Give 1/2 point for each "Yes" answer to the questions below. Place the numerical sum in the space supplied at the end of the questions.

1. Do you have the *gift* of leadership specifically (versus the *role* as leader)? (Change is a leadership role and most pastors are nurturers/teachers by nature; they are often ministry managers rather than leaders.)
2. Have you been at the church less than three years? (Although much is to be said about longevity and earned respect over time, the longer you are in an organization without representing significant change, the more difficult

change becomes, because people/structures do not consider you to be a change agent.)

3. Do you plan to stay at this church more than ten years? (The long view is important to enduring change, because it influences both the way you plan and people's perception that you are someone they can trust.)

4. Are you willing to risk failure? (If you factor out all the risk and therefore avoid significant change, chances are the change will not be bold enough in size or scope. Managers hate risk and therefore avoid significant change. Faith requires the real possibility of failure.)

5. Are you willing and able to handle conflict well? (Change will create miscommunication, hurt feelings, and a degree of conflict, which is why many avoid change at all costs. If you have effective tools to respond to resistance, you need not fear it.)

6. Do you have a clear idea of what you want the church to become? (Only certain improvements are significant. Do you have a clear mental picture of where you're headed, and have you thought through why these changes are needed?)

7. Are you an effective communicator? (Casting vision, resolving conflict, and preparing the environment for change rely heavily on effective communication in various forms.)

8. Are you intentionally developing leaders around you? (Leaders demonstrate their gifts by identifying other influencers and discipling, recruiting, training, and preparing them for leading subministries.)

9. Have you started any new ministries in the last year? (Leaders tend to see needs and respond to them by creating new ministry roles and structures.)

10. Do you have the ability to staff the needed changes once they're made? (Once you help implement the improved ministry, do you have what it takes to staff the ministry or to recruit someone adequately gifted to fill that role?)

Add the "Yes" answers at 1/2 point each. Total leadership capacity factor:

_____

Congregational Readiness

For every one hundred active people in your church, write a confidential list of the five most influential, people to whom others look for answers and opinion formation. While position is not unimportant, emphasize informal influence, the ability to sway beyond formal roles. Beside each person's name, assign a number based on the following response scale.

How will this person respond to the improvement you are recommending?

1. Will resist/sabotage the idea
2. Will discourage/not support the idea
3. Will allow the idea (neutral)
4. Will encourage/support the idea
5. Will drive/promote the idea

Total all the values and come up with an average by dividing the sum total by the number of influencers considered. Place the numerical average in the space below.

Your congregation's readiness factor: _____

If you find that considering the 5 percent most influential is insufficient, feel free to increase the number to 10 percent. Larger churches will tend to have lower percentages; more established, smaller congregations may have more, due to official roles and ministry positions.

If you are not satisfied with the accuracy of this number, here is a slightly more involved approach to determining congregational readiness. Since everyone on your influencer list does not have the same size of influence, take your list of influencers and assign an "influence level indicator" to each. The indicator is an estimate of the amount of influence a person has: light, medium, or heavy.

Influence level indicators:

1= low influence
2= medium influence
3= heavy influence

Multiply each influencer's response estimate (value 1–5, whether they are for or against an improvement) by the influence indicator (value 1–3, degree of influence weight).

Add the totals.

Then divide the sum total by the number of influence units.

This added process helps avoid skewing the average by considering all leaders' influence the same, which of course it never is.

For example:

Jane Doe is a high influencer (3 influence units) who might discourage a new idea (2 on the response scale). Her total influence value is 6.

John Smith is a light influencer (1 influence unit) who would encourage a new idea (4 on the response scale). His total influence value is 4.

Bill Farland is a medium influencer (2 influence units) who'll drive a new idea (5 on the response scale). His total influence value is 10.

By adding the three totals (6, 4, 10), you get a sum of 20. Divide this by the total number of influence units (6). You get a readiness average of 3.67.

Natural leaders calculate these factors more intuitively, measuring the potential support and resistance of a new idea. At the same time, even good leaders are sometimes hamstrung because they overlook a person's resistance or underestimate the cumulative effect of influencers working together. Quantifying congregational readiness provides a bench mark with which you can mold a transition plan, develop communication, and reconsider time and impact factors.

Your congregation's more exact readiness factor: _____

Change Impact

Establishing this factor is vital, because it becomes the denominator in the equation. Although all of these factors are somewhat subjective, consultants, doctors, scientists, and businesspeople make these sort of determinations daily in their work. Since ministry often deals with difficult-to-quantify issues such as faith, hope, and love, most church improvement teams should be able to establish an estimate on how much a certain improvement will impact their church.

1. Level 1: Cosmetic. This may be something as simple as redecorating, adding an age-group ministry, or changing church names. While Level 1 changes can still create some friction, they are rarely sufficient to catalyze growth. This tends to be a managerial, maintenance, incremental sort of impact.

2. Level 2: Modest. This is more than cosmetic but will not significantly impact anyone. Depending on what the change is, many people may not even be aware of it. Major overhaul of facilities, making subministry program changes, and staff expansions are all within the Level 2 boundaries.

3. Level 3: Minor. If you leave what you have in place while adding new styles or ministries, you're probably looking at Level 3, primarily because you're not really asking people to give up much. You are seeking permission for them to allow new ideas to take root in the church.

4. Level 4: Significant. People are bound to notice this impact because it will change the feel, look, sound, and self-image of the congregation. People will have to give up something for these new ideas to be born. This improvement is sufficient to transform the congregation over time while being built upon the foundation of the past. Starting a seeker-type service, rearranging the current worship format, and replacing Sunday evening service with small groups are usually significant changes.

5. Level 5: Major overhaul. This can be viewed as transformational or even a restart. In other words, soon after the change is made, the primary essence of the church will be different. People who visit after the improvement will not recognize the church as the same one they attended prior to the change, other than possible physical features (building, location, people).

Your improvement/change impact estimate: _____

DELTA FACTOR: TRANSITION EFFECTIVENESS

Now that you have estimated the four transition factor levels, you can plug them into the formula to determine the Delta Factor. Your answer should fall within the range of .4 to 50.

$$\frac{\text{Time}\_\_\_\_ \times (\text{Leadership Capacity}\_\_\_\_ + \text{Congregational Readiness}\_\_\_\_)}{\text{Change Impact}} = \text{Delta Factor}$$

Delta (the physics symbol for change based on the Greek letter D) represents a synthesis of the primary improvement elements that help predict how effective the transition process will be. This does not predict how effective the improvement plan itself will be, since that is more of a strategic issue based on what you're trying to accomplish.

Following is a graph that categorizes various effectiveness levels. None of these categories is necessarily a reason to abort the pursuit of an improvement strategy. Rather, they are to help you in planning the transition phase, much like a physician observing a patient who is about to deliver a baby. Birthing new improvement ideas is a delicate procedure. Effective leaders accurately gauge the crucial transition phase, which will affect the life of a new idea and the health of an organization.

These numeric categories are somewhat subjective, but if you decide to implement an improvement plan in spite of less-than-optimum conditions, have good reasons to substantiate that decision and be ready to compensate appropriately if you run into snags.

8B
Delta Factor

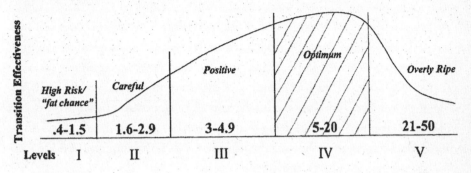

Level I: (0.4–1.5) High Risk. Extreme, elaborate care will need to be taken in the transition process. Expect tension. Reconsider the benefits as well as the reasons behind the time and new-idea impact factors. Plan on a bumpy ride with fallout if you choose to implement improvements at this effectiveness level.

Level II: (1.6–2.9) Careful. The fruit is still green. Significant planning and strategic thought should go into the transition process to reduce the pain. Realize there will be some who may not make the transition, but if it is needed, pursue the change with God-led confidence.

Level III: (3.0–4.9) Positive. You should do well at this level. Make sure you do a thorough job in the transition plan as it still could go either way, depending on the momentum created. Heighten communication, social networking, and creating a positive movement whose flames you can fan.

Level IV: (5.0–20.0) Optimum. Thumbs up. Avoid carelessness or smugness during the transition, but emphasize the positives and cover the necessary bases. This level is prime for pursuing well-planned improvement ideas. If you've picked the right improvement strategy, success should follow.

Level V: (21.0–50.0) Overly Ripe. Little care is needed above the normal communication and planning factors. You probably have waited a bit long to pursue improvements and have left some potential on the table. Proceed without hesitance, and next time, proceed sooner with the improvements.

For example, First Rapture Church has analyzed the factors regarding their transition plan. They decide to add an outreach, seeker-sensitive service to their Sunday morning format. The change impact is estimated at 3, significant but not displacing regulars from their normal worship habits. The church has a very kind, loving pastor, but he is not a strong leader or visionary (2). The congregation is open and ready for this kind of improvement, so long as it does not take programs away from the people who are already happy. A progressive group of lay leaders has driven the improvement process, and they feel confident and supportive of the ideas. They have averaged the opinion leaders' readiness at 3.8. The improvement team wants to implement the changes over a one- to two-year process, beginning by emphasizing outreach values and then developing a communication campaign to thoroughly inform and train the congregation (2). Let's plug these numbers into the change formula.

$$\frac{\text{Time (2) x (Leadership Capacity (2) + Congregational Readiness 3.8))}}{\text{Change Impact (3)}} = \text{Delta Factor (3.9)}$$

Summary: The math looks like this:
A. 2 (Capacity) + 3.8 (Readiness) = 5.8
B. 2 (Time) x 5.8 = 11.6
C. 11.6 / 3 (Impact) = 3.9

The 3.9 Delta Factor places the transition plan in the middle of Level III, the positive range. The congregational readiness is a strong factor, as well as the idea that the change impact will be minor to significant, but not huge. While the leadership factor is not apt to change long term, the pastor can raise his leading over the short term by working through natural influencers and intentionally developing the team. The improvement team could make the situation more optimum through raising the level of readiness by sufficiently preparing the opinion leaders. They could also increase the transition period by a few months, thus raising the Delta Factor.

THE POWER OF THE PILOT

Up to now, we have been talking about change and improvement in terms of developing an optimum transition plan. We have talked about the need for improvement teams to do their homework, to make sure that what they are proposing has the best chance possible of surviving. One of the most effective tools for improvement teams that are still leery as to how their churches will respond to an improvement idea is to develop a pilot program. Be warned: A pilot program can often be a cheap shortcut to introduce change without going through adequate analysis. Let us introduce the idea and then explain its limitations.

Because most people naturally are against what they have not experienced, the idea is to let them become familiar with the new idea with no strings attached. The idea is akin to test-driving a car, eating a free sample of food at a grocery store, or getting a ninety-day, money-back guarantee on something you purchase. Because we are all fearful of buying something that we will not like, resulting in buyer's remorse, we sometimes avoid the possible sale altogether.

Churches that want to introduce a new program, service, or ministry idea can often roll out a sample that they call an experiment, pilot, or trial. The idea implies that it is for gathering feedback, a short-term option. If people do not like it, no big deal, because no one has really bought into it yet. You are not truly marketing the new idea, because it's not ready for sale. This is merely a model, a prototype, a taste test. Legitimate taste tests include surveys for gathering feedback. They will be communicated beforehand so people can know what to expect, and they are performed in a low-key manner, so people do not feel threatened by a "sell."

The power of the pilot can be huge. Many churches find this a nonthreatening way to introduce new ideas to their congregations without all the low-level anxiety, gossip, and conflict that can surround an unknown quantity. When a pilot program is introduced as a no-strings-attached idea, people can easily experience it, provide feedback, and over the course of a few weeks and months, get used to the idea. Then the program can be reformulated to better fit the congregation in its initial state and later be introduced on a more permanent basis. The power of the pilot is that it can often avoid a lot of miscommunication that creates false fears and convoluted expectations and potentially kills a new idea even before it has a chance to be born.

While there is great potential in a pilot program, there are also some downsides to this idea. Obviously, if you try to load your improvement plan in a Trojan horse, hoping to roll the whole thing into the church without people noticing—to actually inject a change without preparing anyone—the congregation is apt to feel manipulated and betrayed. The improvement plan can backfire. This is a high-risk venture for an improvement team and leadership and will likely inoculate the church against an improvement plan for years to come. Stewardship teaches us to be as wise as serpents but as harmless as doves. We need to count the costs of using the pilot idea and to what extent.

Another downside to a short-term experiment is that if it is poorly executed, if the congregation has a bad first impression, you may not have an opportunity to bring the idea back. "We tried that before and didn't like it." It's the equivalent of a bad experience the first time you golf, ski, or fly. You're not going to want to do it again. Sometimes it takes a few times to enjoy a new experience. If people know that a program is going to be ongoing, they are often more understanding, allowing forgiveness for a less-than-optimum first experience, hoping it will improve as they learn.

For example, one church with which we are familiar felt the need to develop an outreach ministry. The pastor led the staff and leaders through a process of studying congregations that were effectively reaching the unchurched. The findings pointed toward the need for a relevant, contemporary Sunday morning worship service. But because the church had a long, traditional heritage within the community, there was sufficient fear that the new style of ministry would alienate long-time members. The grapevine stories of split congregations and critical comments about contemporary, "liberal" methods also created concern among the leaders. The pastor felt strongly that much of the fear was based on unfounded hearsay and that if the people could experience the new ideas, they would welcome them. Therefore, he and the leadership planned to promote a trial service that emphasized community outreach. The service would run each Sunday for three months.

The church had worship services at 9:30 and 11:00 A.M. Both were equally attended, with more young families coming to the first service and slightly older and single adults attending the second. While the numbers were sufficient to support the two services, neither one was full. The pastor preached a series of messages on evangelism, reaching the lost, and doing whatever it takes to share the good news. He then announced the idea of a ninety-day trial period in which Sunday morning services would be significantly different from the current ones, and the congregation was to invite unsaved friends and neighbors. "This is a ministry designed for the unchurched, not for you," he instructed. "Our plans at this point are to treat this much like the revival services of the past, where unchurched people come to church and find God. The difference is that we are doing it in a style that is proven to be most effective in reaching the unchurched." Informal surveys were taken as to which service should do the outreach. The more traditional folks attended the later service, so it was decided that the early service would be outreach oriented. Anyone who did not feel comfortable with the more upbeat music, creative arts, and seeker-friendly messages was encouraged to attend the 11:00 A.M. service, where nothing would be changed.

The pastor emphasized that this was a test of a new idea that would last three months. If the outreach proved effective, however, and the people wanted to continue a ministry for their unsaved friends, the church would then discuss the pros and cons.

Publicity and equipment changes took place. Ministry teams were formed. The event created a lot of excitement within the church. Those involved began the program with confidence and enthusiasm, even though they knew it was a temporary change. The outreach service attracted a significant number of newcomers, and testimonies from these new people filtered into the newsletters and traditional service highlights. Traditional members with children and grandchildren in the church heard how their kids and grandkids loved the new format. The result was that the service became palatable among the long-term members because once familiar with it, they felt less fear about the new style—and they appreciated the positive feedback the service earned. Although many did not want to attend the service themselves, they could not deny the visible benefits. They voted with those involved in the new service to allow it to become an ongoing feature of the church. The long-term benefit was that a sleepy church was awakened and became a hub of excitement.

> It is easier to get forgiveness than it is to secure permission.
>
> —JESUIT SAYING

Improvement Story: Olivet College Church, Bourbannais, Illinois

In the fall of 1991, Olivet College Church was very traditional, running about 850 in Sunday services and incorporating various elements of formal worship including a robed choir, a pipe organ, and hymns. *Stoic* and *respectable* were good adjectives to describe the church.

Like many congregations associated with denominational colleges, the church was a mix of university faculty, staff, and students. Less than 10 percent had non-denominational ties. The pastor began to cast the vision for an approach to ministry that would be more outreach oriented. He sent a few people to a Willow Creek conference and hired a consultant to analyze Olivet's community influence. The evening the consultant's report came back, some of the elders went home and wept over the lack of impact the church was having on the surrounding neighborhoods. The idea was spawned to begin a church that would be designed for outreach, but the pastor was then elected college president and left the church.

The church board was sold on the need to change the way the church had been operating. They were honest about the difficulty but felt that since there were so many young people nearby at the college, they needed to make the transition and not just plant another church off-campus. They sought a pastor who was willing to help them with the change. The church called Dan Boone.

"None of my friends thought I should take the church," Dan reports. "They said, 'There is no way that church is ever going to change.' But I felt the hand of God leading me to that congregation, to help them make the transition, even though we believed the transition would be bloody.

"We decided to leave a traditional Sunday school/worship service track for those who wanted to continue, while starting an additional service that was seeker sensitive. Very quickly, the traditional service fell from about six hundred to two hundred in attendance on good Sundays. Those attending said we had also changed their service, so we went back and repeated some of the service orders exactly from the eighties. But what they were feeling was sociological in nature. Even though the traditional folks had their style of service, they felt alone and left behind.

"Our board and staff supported the changes; in fact, the staff bonded during the friction. I was very impressed with one of the more traditional board members who disagreed with us behind closed doors based on his personal preferences but who publicly supported the changes based on the rest of the staff's and board's feelings.

"For about eighteen months after we began the new services, I wanted to die. It was hell. There is no other word for it. Nearly 150 people left. I cringed coming to the office each week because another family or two would announce their exit. Some of them left quietly. Others made their opinions very public, criticizing my motives and the motives of our staff. But while we lost members, we gained in attendance—the plan to reach outsiders was working. Those leaving were replaced by newcomers, plus another two hundred over the course of the year. Offerings went up, not down. After people quit leaving, we asked the staff and board to make contact with those who had left, asking them if they'd been heard, thanking them for their gifts of time and money, and seeing if they'd found a new church home. The goal was not to bring them back, but to express appreciation and concern.

"One of the most memorable events in my ministry was the first Sunday we introduced our contemporary service. Instead of the choir chairs there was a row of green trees. Our worship leader came onto the platform without a tie and jacket. And then the guitarist began with a loud, driving introduction to a contemporary song. The first couple of minutes, you could see looks of shock and terror on the faces of the congregation, who were used to very solemn pipe-organ music. You could imagine them thinking, *What is happening to my church?* But after three or four minutes, smiles began breaking on the same faces. It was as if you could hear the people thinking, *I'm home! This is the church I want to belong to!* I'll never forget that day.

"Our church is now running 1,450 in three Sunday morning services. While we continue our traditional service and have invested in it, most of our new Christians have come from our outreach service. We are now contemplating what we should do regarding a new building for expansion. People now consider us a community church, not just a college church."

Improvement Lessons:

- Make sure you are motivated by biblical motives to reach the lost. It may be the only thing that keeps you focused and going during the tough times.
- Be up-front with your board and leadership team that "we all go or we don't." When the team comes unglued, it is difficult. Invest in your core leadership. Some of the board members preferred to keep things as they were, but they handled their conflict biblically, discussing the issues in private with me, not publicly. That unity was all I had at times during the difficult times.

- Don't quit in the middle. In the years following the transition, ministry has been a sheer joy. A character development takes place in the soul of a church when it guts out something God has challenged it to do. There is a team feel that allows us to face future difficulties, united and with optimism.
- Get ready to lose 10 percent of your congregation. That seems normal. I was naïve to think we could keep all on board. You can't make everyone happy.

> The world fears a new experience more than it fears anything. Because a new experience displaces so many old experiences. . . . The world doesn't fear a new idea. It can pigeon-hole any idea. But it can't pigeon-hole a real new experience.
>
> —D. H. LAWRENCE

TIME FOR REVIEW: THE ROLLOUT CHECKLIST

Right about now, many of you may feel overwhelmed. There is so much to consider in a well-orchestrated improvement strategy. Now that we have gone deep into transition issues, it may be helpful to pull back a bit and provide an overview of the big picture. There is much talk these days about seeking church health as opposed to numerical growth. This seems to be a wiser emphasis, one that looks at churches more holistically. A naturalistic approach to ministry and specifically change should result in the fruit we are seeking as a by-product of health and vibrancy.

Jesus used agricultural word pictures a lot in his teaching, primarily because the people to whom he was speaking related to them. Even though most of us are city slickers, the farming metaphor is still a good one to represent the church-change process. Creating a significant improvement plan in a church is much like planting a new idea, nurturing it, and seeing it bear fruit. If you have worked through this book as a team, you should now have a good sense of what you want to do and how you will be most effective at doing it. You are now nearly ready to implement your plans, what is commonly referred to as the "rollout." We will use this planting metaphor as an outline to illustrate the rollout sequence. The purpose of this outline is to make sure that you have adequately covered the bases in terms of process and sequence. The rollout plan is designed to combine the improvement plan with the transition plan, resulting in a fruitful harvest. You may find it helpful to use this outline as a discussion tool for your improvement team: Is there anything you have missed?

Soil Preparation

Assess the Readiness
Create a Change-Receptive Culture
Confront Reality/Sell the Problem
Teach Values Underlying Improvements
Make Spiritual Preparation
Pray
Nurture
Develop the Improvement Team and Plan

Plant

Celebrate the Past; Say Good-Bye
Cast the Vision for the Future; Communicate Well
Count Down to the Kickoff; Start

Cultivate

Weeding; Insecticide; Dealing with Conflict
Fertilizing; Persevering; Troubleshooting
Watering; Testimonials; Early Success Stories

Harvest

Adopting the New Thing
Celebrating Victories; Using Momentum
Doing It Again; The Learning Church

SOIL PREPARATION

Creating a receptive environment for change is the essential starting place for any improvement plan. Jesus talked about soil conditions and their impact on fruitfulness. Just as a farmer invests a lot of time, money, and energy into plowing, fertilizing, and chemical analysis of fields prior to planting, leaders need to check and prepare the congregational soil prior to advocating change. Improper soil preparation results in limiting or even nullifying the proposed improvements.

> Then he told them many things in parables, saying: "A farmer went out to sow his seed. As he was scattering the seed, some fell along the path, and the birds came and ate it up. Some fell on rocky places, where it did not have much soil. It sprang up quickly, because the soil was shallow. But when the sun came up, the plants were scorched, and they withered because they had no root. Other seed fell among thorns, which grew up and choked the plants. Still other seed fell on good soil, where it produced a crop—a hundred, sixty or thirty times what was sown. He who has ears, let him hear." (Matt. 13:3–9)

An article from *Harvard Business Review* states:

> Most change programs don't work because they are guided by a theory of change that is fundamentally flawed. The common belief is that the place to begin is with the knowledge and attitudes of individuals. Change in attitudes, the theory goes, lead to changes in individual behavior. And changes in individual behavior, repeated by many people, will result in organizational change. According to this model, change is like a conversion experience. Once people "get religion," changes in their behavior will surely follow.
>
> This theory gets the change process exactly backward. In fact, individual behavior is powerfully shaped by the organizational roles that people play. The most effective way to change behavior, therefore, is to put people into a new organizational context, which imposes new roles, responsibilities, and relationships on them. This creates a situation that, in a sense, "forces" new attitudes and behaviors on people.[3]

All of this makes sense, especially when you consider that the leader's primary responsibility is to serve as the organizational culture nurturer. In the context of the local church, the pastor or leadership team are the ones who must help create the congregational culture. They can make improvements in the existing culture by preparing the "soil," or the congregation, for growth.

Assess the Readiness

While we have invested quite a bit of time talking about both the importance and the assessment of a congregation's receptivity to an improvement plan, we do not want to overlook this ingredient in the context of the rollout. Here is a helpful checklist that will give you another angle on how ready your people are for the proposed improvement. In *Making Change Irresistible,* the author provides an eight-reason list for why people support change.[4]

Respond to each of the eight items with a numeric value of 1–5 (1—No, 2—Doubtful, 3—Unsure, 4—Some, 5—Definitely).

1. People believe their needs are *not* currently being met. They are dissatisfied with the status quo. They either don't believe we're getting ahead or they believe we're going backward. _____

2. People believe the change will make it easier for them to meet their needs. (To test this area, some people need to be presented with the new idea so you can gather feedback. Use your opinion leader list to do this. Do they think the recommended idea will make the church healthier and more productive?) _____

3. People believe the benefits outweigh the risks. They believe the risks are worth taking because they and/or others will benefit from incorporating the new ministry approach. _____

4. People believe the improvement is necessary to avoid or escape a harmful condition. If we are losing people or finances or not keeping up with the surrounding community, then we need to make the changes. _____

5. People believe the improvement process will be handled well. (Are people feeling like they are treated fairly? Do they trust those who are in charge? Have they been given an opportunity to participate in the planning? If the change affects them, will they be included in the discussion?) _____

6. People believe the change will work. This is the right time for the change and we have the right staff, resources, and facilities to accommodate it, let alone a plan. _____

7. People believe the improvement is consistent with their values. (Have we clarified why we are doing this and tied it to an accepted, biblical value? Do we hold this value as a priority?) _____

8. The people responsible for the improvement can be trusted. If people are in favor of the change but lack trust in leadership, they may balk. If people are unsure of the innovation but have confidence in the leaders, they are apt to comply. People are suspicious of those they do not trust. _____

Now average the total. If you are in the 4–5 range, you can be confident that there is a receptivity to the proposed improvement. If not, then you need to spend more time in readiness preparation. Sometimes fruit rots when it is picked too green.

Create a Change-Receptive Culture

Confront Reality/Sell the Problem. If the numerical average on your readiness estimate (which you figured in the Application Toolbox a few pages ago) is below four, you'll want to invest more time and energy into creating a hunger for the improvement. Adult learning is significantly different from kids'—adults are not motivated to learn just because someone says they need to know something. Adults desire to make the connection between need and solution. If there is no perceived need, people are not in the market for a solution. As we mentioned in chapter 3, the key is to sell problems, not solutions. "Most managers and leaders put 10% of their energy into selling the problem and 90% into selling the solution to the problem. People aren't in the market for solutions to problems they don't see, acknowledge, and understand. They might even come up with a better solution than yours, and then you won't have to sell it—it will be theirs."[5]

There are four reasons why selling problems is beneficial.

1. People who realize there is a need within the church are ready for a solution and require less information and education.

2. If the improvement team recognizes the need for the improvement but the people do not, this creates a polarity. If everyone understands the same problem, it puts them on the same team to find a solution.

3. If everyone recognizes the problem, it is quicker to solve as well. If the improvement does not address the perceived need, then people will not adopt it.

4. When you sell problems, everyone is implicated in the solution. You create an atmosphere that says, "If you want to be part of the solution, get involved. If you don't, don't complain."[6]

Teach Values Underlying Improvements. One of the most common suggestions made by leaders we interviewed, both of effective as well as crash-and-burn improvement plans, is that going back to the biblical fundamentals behind the changes is essential. Gene invested the first few years of his teaching at Central Christian in covering the fundamentals of the faith, including the Great Commission and the need for relevant and effective outreach evangelism. While our for-profit counterparts have clear bottom lines in terms of profit and growth, we have clear bottom lines in terms of obeying biblical mandates. Church leaders have the opportunity to use God's Word as a legitimate and practical motivational tool.

If your emphasis is on evangelism, you can craft messages around the theme of the Great Commission, Paul's missionary journeys, and Jesus' purpose in coming. Illustrate these teachings with current community and church growth trends, outreach statistics, and models of health and vibrancy. The Holy Spirit, through the Scriptures, can begin to soften the hearts of the congregation toward obedience at all costs. If that cost is leaving ineffective practices, so be it. Using our tools at hand, namely Scripture and rich church history, we can cultivate a receptivity to methods that pursue the tasks God has called us to fulfill.

The more entrenched your people are in traditions and opposing new ideas, the more time you will need to design messages, Bible studies, discipleship, small-group curricula, and everyday conversations around these biblical fundamentals. If you get the cart before the horse, you'll end up selling methods and stylistic forms that are void of the power you need to accomplish the improvement. Again, our goal is not change for change's sake. If it's not broken, don't fix it. Stewardship demands that we change only what is not bearing fruit. But the average church in America does not have far to look to find several broken ministries that are not producing.

Make Spiritual Preparation. This involves two ingredients: *prayer* and *nurturing*. A faith community should never overlook the powerful tool of prayer during any times of stress and transition. This is a valuable resource that our secular counterparts do not employ, at least in obvious ways. If leaders truly believe that the improvements are based on obedience to God, then they should boldly incorporate prayer prior to rolling out the plan. By creating an atmosphere of faith, seeking God, and experiencing the presence of the Holy Spirit, people are far more apt to deal with the transitions smoothly.

Prayer seems like an obvious ingredient, so much so that you may wonder why we even mention it, but in the context of potential conflict, fighting giants, and crossing Jordan rivers, it's a remarkable tool. Do not underestimate the spiritual warfare that goes on when churches get serious about doing whatever it takes to expand the kingdom and occupy territory held by the enemy. The best weapon is nothing more and nothing less than the most overlooked spiritual discipline of concentrated prayer. The result of concerted prayer is the increased presence of God's Spirit.

> The fruit of the Spirit is love, joy, peace, patience, kindness, goodness, faithfulness, gentleness and self-control. Against such things there is no law. Those who belong to Christ Jesus have crucified the sinful nature with its passions and desires. Since we live by the Spirit, let us keep in step with the Spirit. Let us not become conceited, provoking and envying each other. (Gal. 5:22–26)

The other essential ingredient is *nurturing*. Change creates stress and usually temporarily drains a church of emotional energy. In order to prepare for improvements, intentionally raise the level of nurturing. Strengthen relationships. Make sure leaders are perceived as visible, loving people, not aloof change agents huddled in a war room scheming over battle plans. Be sure there are sufficient pastoral care and verbal expressions of endearment and commitment. Help people connect with each other through small groups and socials. By raising the level of love and care, you are storing up reserves for leaner times and helping people know your motives when they are tempted to question them.

Develop the Improvement Team and Plan

By now you probably have your improvement team established and on board. When it comes to rolling out the transition plan, it is important that you double check—make sure you have who you need on board. If necessary bring on new team members who can add to the plan, especially during the transition phase.

Make sure the improvement plan is refined and somewhat detailed. The plan needs to be flexible, but people want to know that the improvement team has thought through who is going to do what, when, where, and how.

PLANT

Celebrate the Past; Say Good-Bye

As a farmer drives down the barren fields about to be planted, he imagines the previous season's harvest. At one time, the empty field looked just like it does now. But then he planted, and the seeds germinated, and young shoots reached for the sky, eventually filling the field with tall, green plants that yielded a bountiful crop. As the farmer contemplates this new start, he remembers the past rewards and celebrates.

Another idea we brought up in chapter 3 is that an important predecessor to starting is saying good-bye. To do this effectively, you need to clearly define what is over and what is not. Confusion is a common denominator in the transition, and being as exact as possible as to what will and will not change reduces this anxiety.

Many churches that effectively initiate transitions take special effort to create activities and events that dramatize them. Oliver Wendell Holmes said, "Historic continuity with the past is not a duty, it is only a necessity." Honor your members by honoring the traditions that have been meaningful to them.

> Never denigrate the past. Many leaders, in their enthusiasm for a future that is going to be better than the past, ridicule or talk slightingly of the old way of doing things. In doing so they consolidate the resistance against the transition because people identify with the way things used to be and thus feel that their self-worth is at stake when the past is attacked. Rather than attacking the old functional organization as inefficient and archaic ("Nobody in his right mind would run a business that way!"), he credits it for bringing the organization to the point where it now stands: on the brink of an important development.[7]

One church we discovered among our case studies actually transitioned to a whole new style of service by throwing a celebration. They played it up big. On a specific Sunday, the leaders announced, First Church was going to officially close. The entire service was a nonstop walk down memory lane, applauding past leaders, remembering milestones, and doing a big "Yeah, God" for all he'd done over the years. The final ceremony concluded with a procession outside to the front of the church. At the end, the doors were chained and padlocked. During the week, the signs were changed and a new name was given to the church, and the next Sunday, the congregation came back to the "start" of a wonderful new service and ministry format that is now thriving. People are still talking about the honor and dignity given to that congregation, and how the transition went so smoothly. "More beginnings abort because they were not preceded by well-managed endings and neutral zones than for any other reason."[8]

If the improvement plan involves physical changes in facilities or décor, you may want to let people take a piece of the old way with them. Take plenty of creative effort into celebrating the past. Realize that we all have selective memories when it comes to the past. We remember certain things, forget others, and modify our experiences.

William Bridges provides a checklist to consider regarding managing endings. Answer yes or no:

_____ Have we studied the change carefully and identified who is likely to lose what—including what I myself am likely to lose?

_____ Do we understand the subjective realities of these losses to the people who experience them, even those that seem like an overreaction to me?

_____ Have we acknowledged these losses with sympathy?

_____ Have we permitted people to grieve, and have I publicly expressed my own sense of loss?

_____ Have we found ways to compensate people for their losses?

_____ Are we giving people accurate information and doing it again and again?

_____ Have we defined clearly what is over and what isn't?

_____ Have we found ways to "mark the ending"?

_____ Are we being careful not to denigrate the past but, when possible, to find ways to honor it?

_____ Have we made a plan for giving people a piece of the past to take with them?

_____ Have we made it clear how the ending we are making is necessary to protect the continuity of the church or conditions on which the church depends?

_____ Is the ending we are making big enough to get the job done in one step?[9]

Cast the Vision for the Future; Communicate Well

As we have said, communication is a key element to any effective transition plan: communicate, communicate, communicate. Two German professors developed a model called the Resistance Pyramid that helps us understand why people resist a new idea. It also shows how we can intelligently and compassionately respond to people based on reasons for their resistance. Similar to Maslow's hier-

8C
Resistance Pyramid

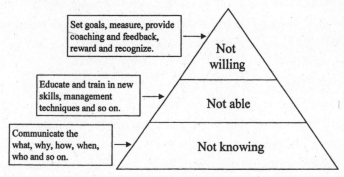

From: Timothy J. Galpin, *The Human Side of Change: A Practical Guide to Organization Design* © 1996 Timothy J. Galpin. Reprinted by permission of John Wiley & Sons, Inc.

archy of needs, it shows that we tend to have certain needs regarding adopting a new idea. Note that unless the preceding level is fulfilled, we will not move on to the next level.

While it is tempting to conclude that people who are not in favor of a new idea are unwilling to make a change, that is often an incorrect assumption. The most common reason for resisting an idea is a lack of knowledge or understanding. When we have effectively educated and informed, many people will allow a change, if not support it.

The next level of resistance pertains to an individual's perception of the church's ability to make a change or accomplish the proposed task. If we show that with adequate money, training, staffing, planning, and resourcing we can accomplish the new idea, still more people will allow or support the improvement. Only after we have informed and resourced people can we conclude that they are unwilling to make the change.

The final level of resistance is when people are simply not willing. There are some things we can do to help improve the response to improvement. By establishing benefits, rewards, and recognition tied to achievable goals and measurements, we increase the odds that people will pursue or allow a change to be made.

As we have said, one of the most important issues for an effective transition is the level and degree of communication. Some leaders think that it is best to keep information about improvement issues secretive. They think that the less people know, the better. Actually, the opposite is true. The issue is more a matter of timing than extent. If you prematurely discuss end goals, methods, or improvement details, you run the risk of having them rejected. After you have prepared the soil for improvement, then redundant, detailed communication becomes an asset.

There are five Cs regarding effective communication plans.[10]

1. Be *candid.* Tell the truth. Be honest. While that would seem to be a no-brainer for church people, politics and the proverbial grapevine can filter details. There is no need to disguise what you are trying to do. If people feel they are not being dealt with fairly, you will reduce trust in the church leadership, thus decreasing the hope of effectiveness. Help all who stand to lose or gain understand what it is they have to lose or gain.

2. Use *context.* Show stakeholders why this improvement plan is relevant to the church. Why does it relate to why we exist?

3. Be *constructive*. Talk team. Build people up to focus on the unity of the church and the excitement of the improvement. Guard against words or arguments that pit people against each other or create a sense of debate.

4. Be *consistent*. Make sure that what you say and what you do are compatible. Keep the messages the same. When you change the content along the way, people begin to question the credibility and/or competence of the improvement team.

5. Be *continuous*. We learn by repetition. With so many messages bombarding people daily, we must repeat our cause and plans over and over. Let people know that the leadership is committed to the new ideas. If you communicate sporadically, you leave room for doubts to develop.

As you create your communication plan, consider some of these elements:

- Who are the stakeholders? Who needs to be hearing this information?
- What are our objectives? Why are we planning to do what we claim?
- How do these tasks break down into actions? Who will do what?
- How many and how often will we communicate?
- What will be the tone of the messages: urgent, hopeful, dramatic?
- What media will we use (newsletters, sermons, video, audiocassettes, special brochures, Town Hall meetings, home-group meetings)?
- Who will be the spokesperson or spokespeople?
- What are the expected outcomes? How will we measure the outcomes?

Publicly and privately presenting the case for improvement should include a combination of logic and passion. The logical side includes the reason behind the change, why the improvement plan is a viable solution, how the improvement will be implemented, and what to expect. The passion element must include biblical grounds for obedience, persuasiveness minus manipulation, and a very positive outlook on the future: "Imagine the potential benefits." Strive to avoid getting too muddy or vague. The case for improvement should be brief, clear, well articulated, logical, qualitatively and quantitatively documented, and compelling.[11]

Count Down to the Kickoff: Start

Part of the countdown involves double checking to make sure everyone has what they need to accomplish the launch. Consider the four Ps:[12]

1. Explain the *purpose* behind the outcome you seek. People have to understand the logic of it before they turn their minds to work on it.

2. Paint a *picture* of how the outcome will look and feel. People need to experience it imaginatively before they can give their hearts to it.

3. Lay out a step-by-step *plan* for phasing in the outcome. People need a clear idea of how they can get where they need to go.

4. Give each person a *part* to play in both the plan and the outcome itself. People need a tangible way to contribute and participate.

Remember that we all have selective memory when it comes to past pain and joy. Time has a funny way of changing our perspectives on change. "Whenever something that is viewed as a controversial and dangerous break with the past turns out successfully, people forget the loss they felt when the change happened and begin to celebrate it as a tradition. Yesterday's ending launched today's success, and today will have to end if tomorrow's changes are to take place."[13]

CULTIVATE

Weeding; Insecticide; Dealing with Conflict

Like any garden, some weeds will spring up. No improvement plan is perfect and no transition plan will reduce all of the problems that will arise. At the same time, problems and conflicts need not be fatal. Expect some heat. The better you are at establishing a good plan and rolling it out when the congregation is ready, the fewer issues you will have to address. Try to postpone extra changes that are either not necessary now or do not add to the productive outcome you are pursuing. Don't buy into the idea that since you're making some changes, you may as well make them all. Stress has a cumulative effect, so you want to reduce it where you're able so that all your energies can go into the improvement processes that count most. The next chapter deals with this element in more detail.

Fertilizing; Persevering; Troubleshooting

The key to any effective plan is flexibility, especially when you are in the people business. Certain aspects will happen prematurely, others late. Some of the results will be less than hoped for and resources may not be as available as desired. After the launch begins, you will need to respond to any number of communication, resource, training, and morale issues. Obviously, the better plan you have, the fewer surprises there will be. Chapter 10 deals with this issue in more detail.

Watering; Testimonials; Early Success Stories

People need to see fruit as early as possible. Whenever there are positive results from the improvement plan, make sure they are communicated. The stress of change can be disconcerting. Even the best of us have doubts at times, so whenever you can proclaim a success story, do it. The best form is a testimonial. When a new family starts attending because of outreach efforts, or a child or teen finds Christ, or a person gets involved in a ministry that changes his or her life, tell the story. Nothing creates excitement more than a changed life. When enough of these stories are told, publicly and privately, positive momentum builds. Momentum is an incredible anesthesia that dead-ends the pain change can bring. Chapter 11 addresses this issue in more detail.

Adopting the New Thing

Everyone who has been married for long understands the difference between deciding to get married and deciding to stay married. "You can tell a young man in love, but you can't tell him much" sums up a lot of premarital counseling. Introducing change and getting used to change are two different concepts. One of the most common reasons that improvement never takes deep root in a church is that initial victories are celebrated quickly and everyone assumes that they have now experienced transformation. New ideas are a bit like bungee jumping. You leap. The cord stretches. You survive the jump. That's it. But the natural resiliency of the cord, like the purpose behind organizations themselves, is to return the cord/church to its existing condition. If you do not do something to fix the new idea to the existing programs and self-image, the ministry improvement will not stick. The improvement idea is not secure until it has become a part of your church culture.

There is a point of no return, when the old ways no longer overpower the new ways. When a gardener cultivates a new plant, he waters and nurtures it until it has developed its own root systems. When the plant is young, it can be easily overtaken by winds and weeds. The improvement team's responsibility is to make sure the improvement plan is not only implemented, but becomes a part of the ongoing life of the church. The rooting process is part of the transition plan. Even after an improvement is put into practice, it takes a while to become familiar with it. When there is a feel that "we wouldn't be the same without this improvement; we can't go back," you know the improvement has entered the self-image of your church.

There are many stories of congregations that began a new idea only to see it fade into oblivion. Other stories include pastors who champion a new idea then leave, followed by a person who returns the congregation to the former ways. Just as a tree takes time to adopt a branch that is grafted into the trunk, improvement adoption is far more than merely initiating the change.

How long does this take? In the Bible there are two Greek words for time: *chronos* and *kairos*. One refers to quantitative time: minutes, hours, days, months, years (Matt. 24:48, 25:19). The other refers to qualitative time (Matt. 13:30, 21:34). As the winemaker advertised, "We will sell no wine before its time." Jesus used this term to communicate rightness and ripeness. For example, in preparation for the Last Supper, Jesus told his disciples, "Go into the city to a certain man and tell him, 'The Teacher says: My appointed time is near'" (Matt. 26:18).

Qualitative time varies from church to church. Congregations that are more ready for improvement and that have prepared themselves for the new idea are far quicker to adopt the innovation. Stymied churches are more apt to reject the initial idea and may require years to change their self-identity. God "provided" the children of Israel four decades, the equivalent of an entire generation, to accept the idea of occupying Canaan. Wilderness churches abound in America.

There are three primary factors that affect the speed of innovation seasoning. One has to do with the percentage of new advocates. When enough new people begin attending, people who know the church only as it is with the improvement, a critical mass will shift the center of gravity and secure the improvement. Sociologists vary in their ideas on when a new habit becomes a part of the culture. Some say it only takes 5 percent of society to bring about a change. But in terms of adopting (versus initiating) a change within a congregational context, our estimate is 20 to 35 percent. That is why churches growing quickly from an implemented improvement can endure significant resistance: The positive momentum keeps them moving forward. A church that strives to include a new idea for years with little growth may never experience a change as part of its culture.

A second factor is time in terms of quantity. Familiarity breeds acceptance. As time passes, we no longer see the improvement as a threat, even if we are not excited about it. When a piece of furniture in your home doesn't quite seem to fit the rest, it becomes less obvious and more acceptable over time. Plan on one to two years after the improvement plan is implemented to see the new idea fully adopted.

A third element that affects the speed of an improvement adoption is visibility. Familiarity is a product of time and visibility. When the improvement is off-site, out of sight, or behind the scenes, adopting will take longer. When budget, building, publicity, and staffing are behind the improvement, people buy in faster. Churches in rented facilities are perceived as less permanent within a community than when they have their own facility. Portachurches virtually disappear during the week in the eyes of the community. That is why many churches grow significantly when they move into a new building, even though their programs and ministries change little. People equate what they see with what is real and accepted.

Celebrating Victories; Using Momentum

Just as we celebrate the past as part of launching the new, it is important to celebrate the wins so that we reward our people for stepping out on faith. There is a difference between "Yeah, God" stories and tooting our own horn. There is nothing that perpetuates momentum as much as feeling victorious. Be careful not to create division by telling the stories in the context of, "See, we told you so. The Progressives won. We showed you up." You want to communicate a team approach, an "us" victory. Even though the improvement team and supporters drove the improvement plan, many others gave at least marginal permission to let it happen.

Gene says that one of the assets at Central Christian is the baptismal ceremony during midweek service, where people can see and hear about changed lives. When a person experiences a transformed marriage; when kids make a commitment to Christ; when a lifelong skeptic suddenly confronts the reality of God in a personal way, heads turn. Don't let up on storytelling. Throw improvement parties. Create weekly kudos for those who have helped perpetuate the new idea and implemented change in his/her area of ministry. Create multimedia presentations that tug at the heart and visually tell the story of what the new wine and wineskin are producing. Let the glory go to God while you create more energy for further growth and improvement.

Momentum is highly underestimated. In terms of what it can do for a church, when the tide of momentum is low, changes and ministry in general are difficult matters. When momentum is high, things such as conflict, challenges, and the wear of everyday monotony seem mild. Momentum to a church is what adrenaline is to the body. We jump higher, feel less pain, and enjoy the process far more when positive momentum exists. Leaders seem better than they are. Life appears more wonderful than it is. People buzz about good news and naysayers have a hard time finding a sympathetic ear when things are going well. When the tide comes in, all the boats rise.

The key to momentum is to maximize it. Make additional changes and strategic decisions when momentum is high. Like ocean tides, momentum usually comes and goes. In the average church, it goes more than comes. The temptation is to sit back and relax when the tide starts to come in because it feels so good. But like the old farm adage says, "Make hay in the sunshine." Take advantage of this positive energy, which is often a by-product of improvement plans that begin to be fruitful.

> If you have always done it that way, it is probably wrong.
> —Charles Kettering

Doing It Again; The Learning Church

No transition plan is complete until you consider how the improved plan will let you make subsequent changes in the future. Take advantage of the process. Once a congregation has learned to implement new ideas, it is easier to do it again. Peter Senge, an MIT professor, made famous the term "the learning organization" in his bestselling book *The Fifth Discipline*. Learning organizations are those that make learning an ongoing process so that they are tradition resistant and more flexible for ongoing improvement.[14] A learning church realizes that it must stay responsive to a changing society if it is to be effective in impacting that society for Christ. What works today is not what will work tomorrow. While the basic human need for forgiveness, salvation, love, and discipleship is not likely to change, personal perceptions and tools do evolve. When we fail to stay in touch, we grow out of touch.

Many of us talk about the significant difference between old-paradigm and new-paradigm churches. I (Alan) find much more affinity within my Willow Creek and Leadership Network associations than with my own denomination. The reason is one of philosophy and mindset, not theology and doctrine. One of the big differences between old- and new-paradigm congregations is that the latter have the built-in element of change. They are able to implement change on an ongoing basis much more easily than old-paradigm churches. For the latter, change and improvement are big deals. This does not mean the new-paradigm churches change automatically or avoid the difficult processes we discuss in this book. But their congregations neither fear change nor avoid it as a foreign concept. In many new churches that have high percentages of either Progressives and/or Baby Busters, a lack of change is perceived as dangerous. "If we do the same things the way we did them three years ago, something must be wrong. Let's fix it." This way of thinking is quite alien to the traditional church.

Once a church has broken out of its entrenchment, it is much easier to implement future improvements, so long as the congregation stays flexible. Old-paradigm thinking suggests that we find a single model that works for us, and then ride that model into the ground. Enduring models have shorter and shorter shelf lives as society changes at an increasing rate. Developing a learning-church attitude is akin to staying in shape once you're fit. Most of us understand how things that are used moderately stay in better shape than those that go unused. Houses fall apart faster when they are vacant for long. While old thinking tempts us to preserve the innovation, savvy leaders recognize the need to keep learning, growing, thinking, and implementing improvements. Once you've paved the way to do this once, you can more easily keep perpetual improvement as a ministry lifestyle, not a once-a-decade major surgery. *The law of stewardship teaches us to make sure we take advantage of this improvement for the sake of future change.* A learning church keeps looking at cutting-edge ministries and seeks to employ new ideas into everyday ministry. After a while, people begin to expect change instead of being shocked by it.

> Entrepreneurs see change as the norm and as healthy. Usually they do not bring about the change themselves. But—and this defines entrepreneur and entrepreneurship—the entrepreneur always searches for change, responds to it, and exploits it as opportunity.
>
> —Peter Drucker[15]

QUESTIONS AND ANSWERS

Q: Why is the transition plan so complicated?

A: Organizational change in the context of the local congregation is a complex matter. If it were easy to do, the church would not be losing ground these days and there would be little need for books like this. You have embarked on one of the most challenging processes know to modern civilization: the intentional transformation of an organization. The goal of this book is to dismantle the improvement process so that teams can cover the necessary bases and maximize gain. There are times when the complexity may be overwhelming. The transition plan is more complicated than the improvement (strategic) plan because it is loaded with the emotional stuff that makes change difficult to begin with. Transition plans must consider the improvement plan elements, but they must also consider cultural idiosyncracies and relational issues. People respond to innovations differently. There is no simple way to make a congregational change. If we oversimplify, the process is likely to implode. The bottom line is, change is messy, but it need not be negative or impossible.

Q: How do we know when we're through planning and ready to start?

A: Actually, you have started your improvement process by planning. A worship service starts in the hearts and minds of the staff long before the first note is played on the organ or piano. Most improvement plans fail because of underplanning in terms of leaving out vital considerations.

Planning is vital, but it can also become a way of avoiding the real work of implementing the plan. There comes a time when you have to start. Varying temperaments will approach this differently. Plan-happy members will want to kill the program by overplanning, presuming there is some perfect plan out there. There is no perfect plan. Plan-frustrated people will want to forego the group discussions and process issues and shoot from the hip. These valiant warriors are heralded as heroes if they succeed. They become early victims if they fail. The stakes are too high for us to haphazardly run into battle.

Use the Nelson Change Formula to estimate the optimum time for effectiveness and then set time dates beside the plan items and empower the improvement team to hold people accountable. Since this has been designed as a team project, the bottom line is to let the team determine when it is right to start. Consensus and unity among the improvement team members are vital for effectiveness.

Q: What if we begin only to realize we miscalculated the change formula?

A: The chances that you will significantly over- or underestimate church conditions are slim if you have done your homework. Leaders who shoot from the hip and rely almost solely on intuition are far more likely to miscalculate. If your improvement team has included the analysis of opinion leaders and the change formula, you have significantly reduced the chance of miscalculation.

If after you begin you realize that people have withheld information or misperceived proposed improvements, then you have the option of reformulating the plan. Improvement and transition plans that are not flexible are worthless. Most pilots will tell you that they are off course at least 90 percent of the way to any destination. The lunar lander was off track most of the way to the moon's surface, but NASA made corrections along the route. The key is to constantly observe, respond, and stay the course.

The question, of course, is how much have you miscalculated. If the answer is significantly, ask the question, *How did we miss so much?* Most of the time, you are able to backtrack a bit and recalculate. This may mean further education. It may mean pinning back the size or speed of the improvement. While someone may have to eat crow and admit wrong, the overall concern is for the improvement plan as a whole. Do what you need to do to make corrections and try again. If the miscalculation is minor, do what is necessary to correct it and stay the course. Perfection does not exist. Do not let the early awareness of imperfection intimidate you to pull back or lose confidence.

Q: What if in celebrating the past we go too far and create an atmosphere where people don't want to leave it?

A: Human nature can be funny. The story is told of a man who wanted to sell his house. A real estate broker designed the ad to read: "Beautiful, two-story, white-colonial home, located in a beautiful, tree-lined neighborhood with picket fences. Large green yard, flowerbeds, spacious living and dining areas, and immaculate bedrooms; a must-see." After reading the ad, the owner took the house off the market, explaining, "I never knew I had it so good."

We as humans have an uncanny ability to forget about past pains and create "good ol' day" feelings that are not realistic. Remember when the children of Israel began suggesting that instead of going into the promised land they return to slavery? How quickly they forgot how terrible enslavement was and how much God had done for them to bring them out of Egypt. Such is human nature.

Although it sounds humorous at first, there is the possibility that in celebrating the past, we create a feeling that we should go back or not move ahead. The key is doing this all in the context of an improvement, move-ahead plan. In other words, keep in front of the people that the reason you are celebrating and honoring the past is because you are building on what you've done. To not celebrate and honor the past can result in a greater danger of alienating people. You want to thank previous pastors and members for what they've done without camping in yesterday. Explain how values in the past are being translated into present and future actions. Don't spend an inordinate amount of time on reflection, but when you do, tie it to the future.

> Faced with the choice between changing one's mind and proving that there is no need to do so, almost everybody gets busy on the proof.
>
> —JOHN KENNETH GALBRAITH

Discussion Starters

1. What have we done to assess our congregation's readiness for the proposed improvement?
2. What can we do to better prepare ourselves for the improvement plan?
3. How can we make prayer a more intentional part of our congregation?
4. Have we sufficiently connected the improvement ideas with the biblical fundamentals?
5. Have we adequately sold ourselves on the problem and the solution?

6. Having gotten this far in our planning process, what have we learned in this chapter that will enhance our rollout process?
7. What are we still missing?
8. Who is going to develop a written transition plan, to make sure we're all on the same page in terms of who, what, when, where, and how?
9. When should we begin?
10. How often will the improvement team meet to make sure we're progressing as planned?

> Confusion is a word we have invented for an order which is not yet understood.
>
> —HENRY MILLER

Contemplation

Forget the former things; do not dwell on the past. See, I am doing a new thing! Now it springs up; do you not perceive it? I am making a way in the desert and streams in the wasteland.

—Isa. 43:18–19

Scripture

Read Genesis 12:1–8.

DEVOTIONAL THOUGHT

God called a seventy-five-year-old man to leave his family and venture into a foreign land, where there was no established road, home, city, or business. He went on the promise from a God he hardly knew. The man's name was Abram and he became the father of a great people called Israel.

We can track God's plan for all of us back to this one man who dared to trust God with his future. All great ministries can be traced back to individuals and groups who dared to venture into deserts, vast wastelands where nothing else existed. Abandoning comfort zones is not a job for the easily intimidated. But it's the way God has always built great nations, and in the process, built great people. Never underestimate the personal benefit of stepping out on faith. God calls all of us from time to time to give up the familiar and follow him into new lands. To do this means pulling up stakes, saying good-bye to the past, and embarking into the unknown. History repeats itself. Every generation has its Abrams, people whom God has called to follow him in spite of the reasons and rationale to stay put.

Prayer

Dear God, I think you may be calling me into new areas. I'm tempted to remember the former things of the past. But I know you want to do something new. I don't know how you're going to do it, but I trust you to make a way in the desert. I'm counting on you to bring refreshing waters to us as we make this trek into the unknown and unproven. You are God. I trust you. Amen.

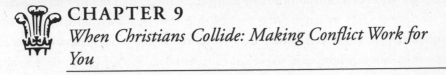

CHAPTER 9
When Christians Collide: Making Conflict Work for You

I don't know the key to success, but the key to failure is trying to please everybody.

—BILL COSBY, *Comedian*

The single biggest fear and pain that church change produces is conflict. We know that we would accomplish little in the kingdom of God alone; teamwork multiplies our efforts. But togetherness also cramps our style. The word *conflict* has a Latin root that refers to striking together. A Boy Scout creates a fire, potentially a wonderful or harmful substance, by actively rubbing two sticks together. When you strike two rocks together, you often get sparks. When hardheaded people bump heads, sparks ignite. When soft-hearted people collide, communication, give-and-take, and ultimately strength result.

I (Alan) like to take the Truman saying "If you can't stand the heat, get out of the kitchen" and give it a twist: "If you can't create some heat, get out of the kitchen." Where there's smoke, there's fire, and where there's a leader, there's heat. Because leaders are by nature change agents, they will create opportunities for people to confront new ideas, the status quo, and the need to progress and change. If you want to keep peace at all costs, you'll rarely accomplish more than maintenance. You can care for people, teach, and even build buildings without accomplishing what God wants in terms of relevance and evangelistic effectiveness. But beware the person who enjoys conflict. This is an unhealthy neurosis. Good leaders respect conflict but do not kindle it for conflict's sake. Managers and nurturers tend to fear it and thus avoid creating, even if that means letting productivity slide. When maintaining the ship is all you need, a manager will do perfectly. But when you need to improve, move, and bring about significant transformation, you need a leader.

> For every action, there is an equal and opposite criticism.
>
> —ANONYMOUS

CONFLICT: FERTILIZER FOR GROWTH

Conflict between God's people is not new. Look at this passage:

> That night all the people of the community raised their voices and wept aloud. All the Israelites grumbled against Moses and Aaron, and the whole assembly said to them, "If only we had died in Egypt! Or in this desert! Why is the LORD bringing us to this land only to let us fall by the sword? Our wives and children will be taken as plunder. Wouldn't it be better for us to go back to Egypt?" And they said to each other, "We should choose a leader and go back to Egypt."
>
> Then Moses and Aaron fell facedown in front of the whole Israelite assembly gathered there. Joshua son of Nun and Caleb son of Jephunneh, who were among those who had explored the land, tore their clothes and said to the entire Israelite assembly, "The land we passed through and explored is exceedingly good. If the LORD is pleased with us, he will lead us into that land, a land flowing with milk and honey, and will give it to us. Only do not rebel against the LORD. And do not be afraid of the people of the land, because we will swallow them up. Their protection is gone, but the LORD is with us. Do not be afraid of them."
>
> But the whole assembly talked about stoning them. (Num. 14:1–10)

Conflict existed even before the murmuring Israelites. The first obvious worship contention dates back to Cain and Abel, feuding over sacrifices: "My worship is as good as your worship." As Solomon said, "There's nothing new under the sun," and that includes the way Christians experience differences.

Any significant change initiative in a church is going to create conflict, bottom line. You can hope it won't, pray it won't, and deny it, but reality tells us that you can plan on it. If a church is so ready for improvement that no conflict emerges, it means that significant fruit has been lost. Because people respond to innovations at different speeds, you can count on at least some, if not a lot of, low-level conflict. Transition plans that are adequately deployed reduce the risk of significant blowups.

Church splits and intense combustion are nearly always reserved for congregations that have not considered the elements of timing, readiness, leadership, and size of change. If you have made it this far, the chances are slim you are going to have the kind of divisive conflict that makes the front pages of the grapevine news.

Throughout this book, we have encouraged you not to overlook the process for the outcome. In other words, don't miss opportunities to grow in character as you pursue improved ministry fruit. How you handle anger and disagreements as a church family is a huge lesson on life and spiritual growth. We encourage you to consider the possibilities of growing in love, appreciation, and your relationship with God as you progress through the waters of conflict. This is a time to experience brokenness and restitution, to seek and give forgiveness, and to model a Christlike attitude.

In *Broken in the Right Place*, I (Alan) wrote about the idea of other people bringing out the worst in us. If we did not have the worst in us to begin with, they couldn't bring it out, could they? Our hot buttons are targets for maturation. Anger and disagreement are perhaps the most effective emotions to reveal how we love in difficult situations. Do we model God's unconditional love or do we allow personal preferences to alienate us from our spiritual siblings? Seize this opportunity to not only get through the conflict, but to grow because of conflict over improvement issues. "The key to capitalizing on change lies in understanding and utilizing the cycle of challenge and response. As historian Arnold J. Toynbee demonstrated in his book *A Study of History*, the great civilizations have risen to power not because of their advantages but because they treated their disadvantages as challenges to which they discovered creative responses."[1]

CENTRAL CHRISTIAN CHURCH: OUR STORY

Sifting Through the Inevitable

In a church-improvement process, conflict at some level is a given. While the staff was excited about being led, from time to time different persons expressed resistance to change. At other times people expressed not resistance but varying visions. One time a difficulty arose with a staff member. It was not his work ethic, integrity, or character; he simply did not reflect the type of church God was wanting us to become. While being committed to the values, he was not able to flesh it out. There can be a big difference between buying into a value or philosophy and being able to live it out in ministry actions. A growing number of people are able to articulate new ideas through their reading and conference attending, but translating these ideas into the local church is still a foreign matter to them. The unfortunate result is that we had to let go of the staff member.

In the congregation, some of the most vehement reactions came in response to what seemed like the most insignificant changes. One such incident took place when a longtime member requested a meeting with the elders to voice his displeasure with the way things were going. Two elders were asked to hear his complaints. Not knowing exactly what to expect, they sat down with the man, who was barely able to control his anger. He asked, "Why are we no longer singing the *Doxology* at the end of the Sunday service?" That was it.

Some months after moving from the padded pews of our former worship center to folding chairs in the larger activity center, the elders received a lengthy letter from a former elder about the move. The new location was not "worshipful," he stated. "God is not honored. Attending services in the activity center is not like going to church."

Two elders met with the man and said, "Tell us why and how the new location is not worshipful. In what way does it not honor God?"

The man dodged. "A worshipful atmosphere can't always be put into words," he said. "Some things can be experienced more easily than they can be explained."

The elders pressed for details and dislodged them, one at a time. As it turned out, the new location was not worshipful, did not honor God, and did not offer a churchlike setting because the folding chairs were close together and the seats were too hard.

For years, our church didn't allow women to participate in certain ministries, such as ushering and passing out Communion elements. When we allowed a woman to do it one time, it isn't too much of an exaggeration to say that she barely escaped with her life.

Changing the invitation was particularly stressful for some. One longtime Christian was downright traumatized when the seekers were no longer required to walk to the front of the room but advised to go to a separate room after the service where they could ask questions in a relaxed, nonthreatening atmosphere. Some weeks later, the complainer left the church and found a congregation where they still did things "God's way."

Sometimes Christians rationalize in order to make petty complaints sound noble and to make matters of personal opinion seem like biblical doctrine. Never assume longtime members are immune to such temptations.

WHEN BAGGAGE EXPLODES

When you travel, airlines allow you two pieces of carry-on luggage. Imagine every church being an airplane. Everyone has some sort of personal baggage. Some of us are able to keep ours in a small pouch. Others have briefcases. And some are what the airlines refer to as "bin hogs."

Character, as well as emotional and spiritual baggage, is revealed during times of stress. Squeezing a bottle shows what's inside; the way people handle the tension of change and conflict reveals much. Some people pull away and withdraw. Others engage, lash out, and try to overpower their "opponents" with their bank account or heavy-duty network. Controller types emerge quickly during conflict. Some people go underground and initiate rumor mills and covert division. Still others step up to the plate, keep peace, exude a humble attitude, and display incredible Christian character.

Leaders need to realize that *not* all of the conflict that an improvement plan can manifest is created by the change itself. People are prone to transfer their anger and frustrations onto moving objects. They attach their baggage to current affairs, even though they may be totally unrelated.

If you have tried fasting for more than a couple of meals, you've probably experienced the minor headaches, nausea, and gray attitude that often occur when your body detoxifies. The state of transitioning in itself tends to create a setting where church toxins are released, which tends to complicate already complicated situations.

> Transition is like a low-pressure area on the organizational weather map. It attracts all the storms and conflicts in the area, past and present. This is because transition "decompresses" an organization. Many of the barriers that held things in check come down. Old grievances resurface. Old scars start to

ache. Old skeletons come tumbling out of closets. Every transition is an opportunity to heal the old wounds that have been undermining activity.[2]

Feelings are feelings, so you have to accept them. But church members with gifts of wisdom and discernment can be great assets during this time, as you distinguish between current losses and old wounds.

A THEOLOGY OF CONFLICT RESOLUTION

What happens when you disagree with the official leadership of a church? What is the pastor's responsibility and what is that of the members? The New Testament is vague in terms of church policy, because the early church was just getting established as the Bible books end. Organizationally speaking, it was still experiencing significant growth in its S-curve. Management was just starting to provide structure and order. Yet no doubt the early Christians experienced one of the most difficult situations within any congregation: when the senior pastor is at odds with the values and feelings of others. Both sides may have legitimate concerns.

Many churches have groups of dedicated, progressive lay leaders who long to be led well and taken into new promised lands. Unfortunately, pastors who are unprepared to lead occupy the primary positions to create such change in many congregations. Should lay leaders take charge? Should they risk being seen as power-hungry and controlling when they see their home church languishing? They know that the average pastoral tenure is often only a few years, whereas they have invested many more years of money, time, and emotion into their church. Pastors have come and gone over the years, so why should they leave the health of their congregation up to the abilities of a virtual outsider?

Conversely, what if the pastor starts taking you down what seems to be the wrong road? Do you jump on board without challenging the values and methods? Should your response be: "He doesn't understand us. He's too new. He'll be gone in just a few months or years, and what will be left of our church when he goes? Our job as lay leaders is to preserve what we've worked for years to accomplish. No one or nothing is going to ruin that. We'll do whatever it takes to resist changes, no matter how well they are pitched or planned." Laypeople know the frustrations of dealing with pastors who seem to be going in a different direction than they are.

Likewise, pastors understand the irritation of power-hungry lay leaders who block progress, innovations, and improvement ideas. Power struggles, disrespectful comments, gossip, backbiting, manipulation, and malicious actions cut pastors to the core. The bloodletting in some churches is nothing short of the historical Holy Wars on a smaller scale, where marauders justify their ungodly actions with the cause of Christ. Travel awhile and you can compile a tall stack of stories of well-intended lay leaders sabotaging improvement processes, resulting in divided congregations, clergy burnout, and people who have given up on formal Christianity for lack of a positive model. Much like marriage counseling, you can build empathetic cases for and against each party in conflict, depending on whom you're listening to.

So what do you do when you disagree? What should happen when Christians collide? The problem with anger in the church is that we have not learned how to deal with it in a Christian manner. Some of us pursue unhealthy expressions such as denial or passive-aggressive tactics. Others of us resort to pre-Christian behaviors of blatant disregard for the command to love others.

> Surely you heard of him and were taught in him in accordance with the truth that is in Jesus. You were taught, with regard to your former way of life, to put off your old self, which is being corrupted by its deceitful desires; to be made new in the attitude of your minds; and to put on the new self, created to be like God in true righteousness and holiness.
>
> Therefore each of you must put off falsehood and speak truthfully to his neighbor, for we are all members of one body. "In your anger do not sin": Do not let the sun go down while you are still angry, and do not give the devil a foothold. (Eph. 4:21–27)

God our Father has given us some powerful tools for conflict resolution. They go unused because we are either ignorant or too stubborn to obey them. Because anger is a normal, natural emotion during times of stress and transition, we want to specifically deal with how to handle it in social settings. If individuals learn how to address this emotion constructively, they will have far less chance of experiencing the negative effects of conflict that so many fear.

Following are biblical guidelines that are clear-cut instructions for how we should live within a faith community.

Work Hard at Living in Harmony

> Make every effort to live in peace with all men and to be holy; without
> holiness no one will see the Lord. See to it that no one misses the grace of
> God and that no bitter root grows up to cause trouble and defile many.
> (Heb. 12:14–15)

> Finally, all of you, live in harmony with one another; be sympathetic, love as
> brothers, be compassionate and humble. (1 Pet. 3:8)

Reflect the Mercy of God

C. S. Lewis said the most significant difference between Christianity and other
world religions is God's grace or unmerited favor. The God of mercy expects those
of us who have received grace and mercy to pass them on to others. The only people
to whom Jesus was not merciful were those who did not exude mercy to others.
Jesus told the story of an unmerciful servant who had forgotten how much he had
been forgiven (Matt. 18). Pride leads us to the conclusion that others are far more
in need of judgment and criticism than we are. Jesus' parable reveals his attitude:

> "Shouldn't you have had mercy on your fellow servant just as I had on you?"
> In anger his master turned him over to the jailers to be tortured, until he
> should pay back all he owed.
>   "This is how my heavenly Father will treat each of you unless you for-
> give your brother or sister from your heart." (Matt. 18:33–35)

Ask Divisive People to Leave

> Remind the people to be subject to rulers and authorities, to be obedient, to
> be ready to do whatever is good, to slander no one, to be peaceable and con-
> siderate, and to show true humility toward all men.
>   At one time we too were foolish, disobedient, deceived and enslaved by
> all kinds of passions and pleasures. We lived in malice and envy, being hated
> and hating one another. But when the kindness and love of God our Savior
> appeared, he saved us, not because of righteous things we had done, but
> because of his mercy.
>   . . . Avoid foolish controversies and genealogies and arguments and

quarrels about the law, because these are unprofitable and useless. Warn a divisive person once, and then warn him a second time. After that, have nothing to do with him. You may be sure that such a man is warped and sinful; he is self-condemned. (Titus 3:1–5, 9–11)

Respect the Position of Authority, No Matter What

Obey your leaders and submit to their authority. They keep watch over you as men who must give an account. Obey them so that their work will be a joy, not a burden, for that would be of no advantage to you. (Heb. 13:17)

Everyone must submit himself to the governing authorities, for there is no authority except that which God has established. The authorities that exist have been established by God. Consequently, he who rebels against the authority is rebelling against what God has instituted, and those who do so will bring judgment on themselves. For rulers hold no terror for those who do right, but for those who do wrong. Do you want to be free from fear of the one in authority? Then do what is right and he will commend you. For he is God's servant to do you good. But if you do wrong, be afraid, for he does not bear the sword for nothing. He is God's servant, an agent of wrath to bring punishment on the wrongdoer. Therefore, it is necessary to submit to the authorities, not only because of possible punishment but also because of conscience. (Rom. 13:1–5)

The Bible tells us that people within a church, good or bad, right or wrong, need to respect and honor those in positions of authority. While you may not agree with a pastor/leader and have the right to lovingly disagree, you do not have biblical grounds to be divisive or promote negativity. The bottom line is, if you can't honor those in authority at your church, find a faith community where you can. You do not enhance the kingdom by staying where you are and initiating conflict.

Don't Gossip

While the temptation to talk to others who have listening ears and similar values is very tempting, to wage verbal wars is not conducive to a loving faith community.

> Without wood a fire goes out;
>> without gossip a quarrel dies down.
> As charcoal to embers and as wood to fire,
>> so is a quarrelsome man for kindling strife.
> The words of a gossip are like choice morsels;
>> they go down to a man's inmost parts. (Prov. 26:20–22)

Be Blameless: Stars Shine Brightest When It's Darkest

When we complain and argue with each other, we run the strong risk of hurting the faith of others, or even keeping people out of the kingdom because all they see is our negativity toward each other.

> Do everything without complaining or arguing, so that you may become blameless and pure, children of God without fault in a crooked and depraved generation, in which you shine like stars in the universe. (Phil. 2:14–15)

Be Careful; Others Are Watching

> Live such good lives among the pagans that, though they accuse you of doing wrong, they may see your good deeds and glorify God on the day he visits us.
>
> Submit yourselves for the Lord's sake to every authority instituted among men: whether to the king, as the supreme authority, or to governors, who are sent by him to punish those who do wrong and to commend those who do right. For it is God's will that by doing good you should silence the ignorant talk of foolish people. Live as free people, but do not use your freedom as a cover-up for evil; live as servants of God. Show proper respect to everyone: Love the brotherhood of believers, fear God, honor the king. (1 Pet. 2:12–17)

If You Have a Beef with Someone, Go to Him or Her

> If your brother sins against you, go and show him his fault, just between the two of you. If he listens to you, you have won your brother over. But if he

will not listen, take one or two others along, so that every matter may be established by the testimony of two or three witnesses. If he refuses to listen to them, tell it to the church; and if he refuses to listen even to the church, treat him as you would a pagan or a tax collector. (Matt. 18:15–17)

Do All You Can to Reach a Win-Win Position

Live in harmony with one another. Do not be proud, but be willing to associate with people of low position. Do not be conceited.

Do not repay anyone evil for evil. Be careful to do what is right in the eyes of everybody. If it is possible, as far as it depends on you, live at peace with everyone. (Rom. 12:16–18)

CHURCH CONFLICT MYTHS

There are three common myths regarding conflict in the local church.

Myth 1: *A lack of conflict is good.* In marriage counseling, when spouses claim that they never argue and always get along, you can count on something being awry. All healthy relationships have times of disagreement. People collide. The key is to work through the conflict toward growth. When people are angry and pretend that things are fine, it is a sign that there is a coercive or authoritarian personality who is intimidating the other into silence.

When a person represses feelings for fear of punishment or undue stress, negative side effects will emerge. People may become passive-aggressive, dragging their feet in ministry or actually sabotaging it as a means of expressing their true feelings. They may wage quiet wars of gossip and character assassination, working underground to decrease a leader's credibility. This is guerilla warfare in the jungles of social circles. It is difficult to win and hard to determine who is friend or foe.

Sometimes people just float away, seeking another church or worse, none at all. Tension is quite high in many churches because we have not learned how to handle our anger well or because we somehow feel it is unholy to disagree. And appearances are deceiving: Just because people are not in disagreement does not mean they are in agreement. When people are apathetic, ambivalent, or confused, they will often give the impression that the improvement is fine. Then when leadership seeks support, whether it is in finances or time, they are disappointed. Some of the most dysfunctional families have very little overt conflict. The same is true of church families.

Myth 2: *Conflict is bad/unhealthy.* Conflict need not be feared. It is the typical and even healthy element in any innovation process, which often means saying good-bye to something familiar and working through the acceptance of something new. Conflict is quite common in any adoption process. Going back to the marriage counseling example, counselors know that when both spouses come in wearing their boxing gloves, it's a more positive sign than when they have given up arguing altogether. Conflict is a sign that people are engaged in the process of change, one way or the other. Conflict allows people to work through processes, develop communication patterns, and accept losses and additions. It raises problems or perceived problems that need to be addressed. Conflict enhances the possibility of making the improvement a reality. Therefore, savvy leaders welcome a certain degree of conflict as an ally.

Because we all like to be loved and accepted, leaders often exaggerate the degree to which conflict is negative. Weak egos need not apply for improvement processes, because they often can't handle the threat conflict creates. Remember, some conflict is nearly always necessary for a significant transition to take place. The key is how you deal with the conflict. When we run from conflict and try to brush it under the carpet, it has the tendency to intensify and produce toxic results down the road.

For example, let's say that in Jumpin' for Joy Church, Group A opposes plans to begin a more contemporary and relevant worship service. Group B favors this improvement idea. Even though these people disagree with each other, they have decided to work through the issues by talking and treating one another with love and respect. Because of the conversations, new ideas emerge. Group A realizes it may have acted negative and controlling. Group B concedes that it has been a bit insensitive and pushy toward the change. They negotiate a plan that seems to work for both groups.

Across the street at Power Chapel, they are undergoing similar struggles but experiencing far less benefit. Group C opposes the improvement plan that Group D promotes. But instead of talking to each other and hearing each other's fears, frustrations, and ideas, they decide to build emotional bunkers. They begin seeking allies among the congregation with whom they talk long and hard.

From outward appearances, Jumpin' for Joy seems like the most torn congregation because its differences are openly discussed. In reality, Power Chapel is more conflicted because interest groups have chosen to build silent silos of interest and avoid talking to other groups. If the Chapel continues, its situation will be ripe for a minor or major church split.

Myth 3: *I need not be concerned about conflict, because loving Christians will eventually get over their differences.* Perhaps this sounds naïve, but many well-intentioned people believe this in spite of countless testimonials reflecting the danger of unresolved conflict. As humans we think in terms of what is right for us. We also tend to justify our rightness and place it in spiritual terms with biblical justifications. While Jesus never compromised on the fundamentals or his obedience to the Father, he invested a lot of his efforts in bucking the current methods and traditions of his time. Aside from God's will, that's what got him crucified.

No fireman minimizes the risk of a single spark, especially when the fire hazard is high. Throughout the Southwest, you will see road signs that warn you of the fire hazard of the local forest. When it is low, the moisture content is sufficient to ward off most small fires. When the hazard is high, the parched vegetation is prime for catching fire. Savvy leaders know that every congregation has a different fire hazard rating based on its current situation. When momentum is strong and productivity high, a congregation is very resilient to individual disagreements and minor group conflicts. But when momentum is neutral or negative and relationships are fractured, the same amount of conflict and disagreement can create a blazing fire. More important than the size of the conflict is the fire hazard rating of the congregation.

TRUST AND THE LACK THEREOF

A major influence of the fire hazard rating is the trust or mistrust factor. Leadership can significantly reduce negative conflict when it understands the relationship of trust to improvement plans. When people trust a leader, they will go with him through difficult times, even when they initially disagree with an improvement idea. Conversely, they can threaten an improvement plan that they endorse when they mistrust leaders. Sometimes leaders bring on their own problems by subtly creating mistrust. Some examples include:

- When leaders say one thing and do another.
- When they make agreements they fail to keep.
- When they say one thing to one person and something else to another person.

- When they try to discredit people and assassinate character behind their backs.
- When they make excuses for mistakes and try to shed the blame.
- When they play politics to get what they want.
- When they develop groups of people and pit them against each other.
- When they look out for their own interests without personal sacrifice.
- When they employ manipulative tactics with people.
- When they spring surprises on others, especially staff and leaders.
- When they ignore input from others.
- When they do not take sufficient time to explain their dreams, plans, and motives.
- When they make autocratic decisions affecting others without their input.[3]

When we fail to effectively resolve conflict and avoid creating it when possible, we steal valuable energy from the improvement plan itself. Leaders can build trust by doing the inverse of some of the mistrust producers above. These include:

- Listening and conveying understanding.
- Following through on agreements.
- Keeping people informed instead of springing new ideas suddenly or changing course with little notice.
- Giving others credit when it is due them.
- Taking responsibility for mistakes.
- Avoiding actions that create mistrust (gossip, blaming).
- Keeping confidential information confidential.
- Seeking win-win outcomes.
- Saying what they mean and meaning what they say.
- Focusing on the problem, not the person.

SIGNS OF OVERT OR COVERT RESISTANCE

Sometimes we are not certain why people resist a new idea. Unfortunately, asking them will not always glean a clear answer. Any specific act of resistance may represent multiple reasons. When someone is experiencing negative circumstances such as marriage problems or financial setbacks, he might express his frustration somewhere besides home or the office. He might unleash his anger in a church setting instead.

One of the most important things leadership can do in analyzing conflict is to avoid assuming that the emotions expressed are all related to the specific improvement action. An individual's response is less important than trends. When several people articulate a common theme, pay attention. When the conflict appears to be random and/or sporadic, chances are that it stems from a source more complex than the change initiative.

Overt resistance can be seen in criticism, blaming, accusing, blocking ministry or finances, finger pointing, distorting facts, arguing, starting rumors, appealing to fear, selective truth telling, sabotaging, and intimidating or threatening. Covert resistance can be seen when a person agrees verbally but does not follow through, fails to implement an improvement, is absent a lot, acts uninformed when he or she isn't, withholds information, or stands by and allows an improvement to fail.[4]

Secure leaders understand the difference between resistance and the normal grieving process. Whenever people mourn, they typically go through a sequence of emotions that includes anger and depression. When we see people going through the anger phase of saying good-bye to a familiar style or ministry event, we can easily assume this is conflict and rebellion. Insecure leaders tend to jump to the negative conclusion. Instead of wrapping loving arms around the person, we keep them at arm's length, treating them like potential enemies. When a person is in the mild depression phase, insecure leaders assume the person is passively resisting the new idea or has lost confidence in the leader. Because these look so similar, we sometimes respond inappropriately to the person, thus alienating him when we need to be nurturing.

9A
Process of Acceptance

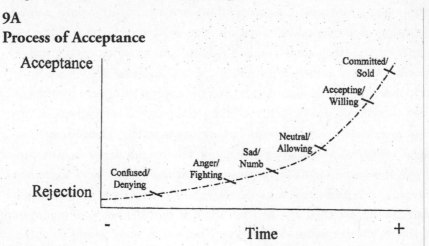

The previous graph depicts the course of a resistor over time.

On the left, when time is short, initial emotional responses to change include confusion and denial. We are either unsure about what is happening and what impact it will have, or we pretend that nothing has changed or will change. Oversensitive leaders may perceive this as resistance or personal rejection. As time passes, the change is clarified and confronted, resulting in an anger response, just as a grieving person discovers the reality of the loss. This is normal and healthy, as long as people do not get too fixed in this passage and cause damage within the church. As time goes on, the anger is replaced with a sadness and even a numb feeling. Losses hurt, leaving an emotional void where something once filled a place. Numbness is our emotions' version of an anesthesia, deadening the pain. As more time passes, the sadness is replaced by a neutrality and allowance for the improvement. A little later, acceptance and even a willingness become the norm. By this time, a healthy person has accepted reality and adapted. Over time, this acceptance becomes a commitment, such that when this new item changes, a person defends it like an enduring friend and the cycle continues.

The best way to ascertain a person's motivation is to look at his history and simply talk to him. When someone has been a negative problem-person periodically in the past, there is a good chance he or she will do it again when he or she disagrees with an improvement issue. If a person has been very positive and constructive in the past but appears to be angry or sad about the new idea, it is safer to assume he or she is going through a natural grieving process. Time reveals the character and temperament of a person, helping the leadership team to react appropriately.

Inappropriate response of leaders and improvement team members toward conflict is one of the most detrimental problems in a transition plan. When leaders underrespond, they allow conflict to fester and grow, creating a negative momentum that diminishes effectiveness and is difficult to stop. When leaders overrespond, they run the risk of damaging the improvement plan by offending resistors as well as alienating change allies who become sympathetic to their resistant friends. The empathy factor in faith communities can be huge.

Savvy leaders know that when they respond unlovingly to even a minority of naysayers, they can lose valuable support from loving Progressives and Builders. When improvement issues become primarily personal instead of organizational, we decrease the potential and increase the risk factor. That is why a biblical approach to conflict resolution is key to making the most of resistors.

Following is a graph depicting varying levels of conflict with appropriate Christian leadership responses. The left side reflects minor resistance and the right side, significant resistance. Above the line are the conflict characteristics. Below the line are leadership's appropriate responses. A leader who responds to a Level 1 resistance with a Level 5 response is like a person who drops a bomb to kill a fly. Conversely, a leader who treats a Level 4 or 5 resistance with a Level 1 response is a doctor who puts a Band-Aid on a broken leg. The outcome will be detrimental and costly.

9B
Appropriate Conflict Response Continuum

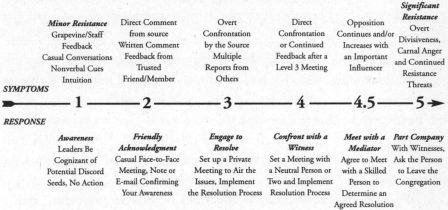

Minor Resistance	Direct Comment	Overt	Direct	Opposition	*Significant Resistance*
Grapevine/Staff Feedback Casual Conversations Nonverbal Cues Intuition	from source Written Comment Feedback from Trusted Friend/Member	Confrontation by the Source Multiple Reports from Others	Confrontation or Continued Feedback after a Level 3 Meeting	Continues and/or Increases with an Important Influencer	Overt Divisiveness, Carnal Anger and Continued Resistance Threats

SYMPTOMS

➤——— 1 ——— 2 ——— 3 ——— 4 ——— 4.5 ——— 5 ➤

RESPONSE

Awareness	*Friendly Acknowledgment*	*Engage to Resolve*	*Confront with a Witness*	*Meet with a Mediator*	*Part Company*
Leaders Be Cognizant of Potential Discord Seeds, No Action	Casual Face-to-Face Meeting, Note or E-mail Confirming Your Awareness	Set up a Private Meeting to Air the Issues, Implement the Resolution Process	Set a Meeting with a Neutral Person or Two and Implement Resolution Process	Agree to Meet with a Skilled Person to Determine an Agreed Resolution	With Witnesses, Ask the Person to Leave the Congregation

Conflict Level 1: *Awareness.* At this level, a member is irritated by a process or projected outcome. Although numerous minor irritations happen weekly in the life of local church ministry, these are rarely serious enough to address directly. The goal of the leader is simply to become aware of the conflict by listening to the grapevine—casual conversations, reading people's nonverbal communication, and using intuition. A member may seem a bit aloof, make a passing comment, or lack usual enthusiasm.

An overt response is not necessary at this point, but a leader who is unaware is liable to be caught off-guard if the resistance increases. Level 1 is akin to a minor cut on the hand, which you want to watch and make sure does not become infected. In larger churches, pastors are often intimate with only one to three social groups, which potentially creates awareness problems. Staff feedback is vital at this point. If you are not close to your people, it is difficult to be aware.

Conflict Level 2: *Friendly Acknowledgment.* Level 2 symptoms of conflict include direct comments from a person as to his/her frustration, a written comment, or a report from a trusted friend or staff member. To ignore resistance at Level 2, you run the risk of appearing out of touch, aloof, or uncaring. At this point, the leader needs to acknowledge the person's concern in a friendly, nonthreatening way. Your goal is to let the person know that you are aware of his/her frustration and will see what can be done to resolve it. You need to convey a caring attitude and perhaps better communicate the issues.

Many people want to be heard more than they need to have issues resolved. Tensions build when we avoid investing the time and energy to adequately listen. The meeting should take place privately and informally so as not to increase low-level tension or exaggerate the level of concern. Depending on the relationship, you may be able to accomplish this in a note, e-mail, or phone call, so long as rapport has been established beforehand. Keep the conversation friendly and caring.

Conflict Level 3: *Engage to Resolve.* Symptoms of conflict at this level include overt confrontation by the other person through something they say or write, or through reports of the person's unhappiness from several other people. Leaders and members in healthy relationships will take care of this in a private meeting initiated by the person who feels irritated; this is the biblical way. If this doesn't happen, leadership needs to set up the private meeting to lovingly confront the issue of contention.

A wise leader will strive to know something of the concerns beforehand so that he/she is not caught off-guard. Pastors with paid staffs can ask for weekly ministry reports that include any "heads up" feedback on potentially frayed relationships, keeping him or her informed of possible heat. Passing the buck is tempting but foolish when conflict reaches this level of intensity.

When people feel powerless or guilty or are ignorant of biblical principles, they are apt to tell people other than the person with whom they have conflict. They may masquerade this communication as "a prayer request" or "letting off steam," but it is often negative and potentially divisive. If you complain to a person who is not able to change the situation, you are being irresponsible and you are undermining the church community.

Sometimes leaders can circumvent the process. Recently, I (Alan) had a parent approach me about a frustration she had with our youth pastor. I graciously interrupted her and asked if she had shared this with the youth pastor. When she said she hadn't, I responded, "Well, the Bible says that if we have a beef with someone, we should go to him or her directly."

She answered, "I just thought as the pastor you would want to know about a problem I was having, like a manager wants to know about a dissatisfied customer."

I said, "I want to have this resolved, but the place to start is by talking to him. After you talk to him, if you feel that you did not resolve the situation, then come and talk to me. Then the three of us can talk it out." She never talked to me about it, and as far as I know, the situation was dealt with.

Sometimes adults can be like little kids, tattling to their friends and/or authority figures about a sibling's actions, instead of dealing directly with the sibling. Leaders need to use everyday opportunities to teach their people about biblical principles regarding relationships.

Conflict Level 4: *Confront with a Witness.* After meeting privately with another person, if you sense that the conflict is unresolved or renewed, it is a sign that you have a Level 4 conflict. The other party continues to talk to other people. You glean grapevine stories of his or her dissension. This person may have a track record of manipulating the facts and influencing people adversely, or you have a personality clash with him/her. Any of these circumstances may warrant a more involved response that includes bringing in other people, yet still in a private format.

The difference between Level 3 and Level 4 conflict resolution is that the latter involves a meeting with a third party as a witness. When a private meeting with an individual does not bring about the resolution desired, the Bible says to take another Christian and meet again. A neutral party may be most helpful, or each party may want to bring a listening team member. Sometimes we play games with people that are ways of avoiding truth telling and resolving differences. Games are more difficult to play with a third party involved. By including a third or fourth party in the process, we create greater accountability and increased chances for resolution. The extra party may just be a trusted friend. He or she could also be more of a professional arbitrator or counselor.

Note the biblical model for confrontation: Begin privately and gradually increase the number of people involved as things fail to be resolved. The typical church conflict begins publicly through gossip and grapevine, and only after significant stress do we turn to private reconciliation. Far too much hurt and pain are created when Christians fail to practice the biblical principles.

Conflict Level 4.5: *Meet with a Mediator.* Occasionally, when the parties in conflict are very valuable to a local congregation and there appears to be an impasse, bringing in a mediator to negotiate a treaty may be essential. The role of a mediator is to serve as a neutral party who can keep communication lines clear and move toward a mutual agreement. The goal of mediation is to keep both sides intact and to work out an agreeable settlement.

Professional mediators exist in the court systems, in insurance agencies, and within some counseling services. Other options are people within the local church who are respected by both parties in conflict and who have some basic negotiation skills or a neighboring church pastor or denominational official who understands your ministry context. A mediator should be brought in only after you have accomplished the resolution tasks of Levels 3 and 4.

Conflict Level 5: *Part Company.* Up to now, the goal of the conflict resolution is reconciliation. But when parties come to an impasse with significant resistance on the part of the church member/attendee, the latter should leave. Giving up a home church can be a very painful experience. You are often saying good-bye to friends, fond memories, ministry involvement, and numerous other emotional and tangible investments. That is why conflict can be so emotional.

But by now, both parties have probably lost hours of sleep and frittered away valuable productivity because of the pain. The bigger picture here is about what is best for God's kingdom. God is not glorified when his children duke it out. Imagine the pain he feels when his children are fighting and quarrelling. The respectable thing for a resistant person to do, after he or she has talked to the related parties through the biblical process, is to quietly leave the local flock.

To leave even when feeling innocent is something that only large-character people can do. It is much easier to stay and fight, to malign church leadership and resist at all costs. But those costs are nearly always too costly. They are toxic to the congregation and end up hurting individuals who are innocent bystanders and worse, pre-Christians who hear about the angry division at XYZ Church down the street.

This continuum is a helpful guide to show you what symptoms reflect what conflict level, and what appropriate response from leadership might be expected. When momentum is low and fire hazard is high, add a point to the level (treat a Level 2 like a Level 1). When momentum is high and fire hazard is low, subtract a point from the level (treat a Level 2 like a Level 1). When the conflict is with a person of significant influence, add a point value (treat a Level 1 like a Level 2). Thus, in a tension-filled church, when a person of influence has a simple irritation (Level 1) with the church, a shrewd leader would be smart to meet with that person to hear him out (Level 3 response).

Here is a graphic illustration of conflict resolution.

9D
Conflict Resolution

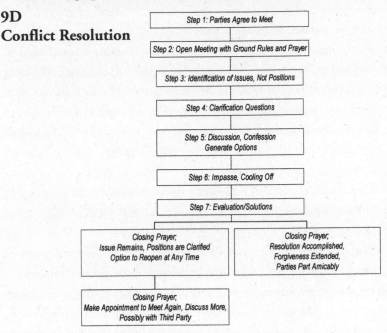

Step 1: Parties Agree to Meet

Step 2: Open Meeting with Ground Rules and Prayer

Step 3: Identification of Issues, Not Positions

Step 4: Clarification Questions

Step 5: Discussion, Confession
Generate Options

Step 6: Impasse, Cooling Off

Step 7: Evaluation/Solutions

Closing Prayer,
Issue Remains, Positions are Clarified
Option to Reopen at Any Time

Closing Prayer,
Resolution Accomplished,
Forgiveness Extended,
Parties Part Amicably

Closing Prayer,
Make Appointment to Meet Again, Discuss More,
Possibly with Third Party

Step 1: *Agree to Meet.* Communication is the first step to resolving hurt feelings and perceived conflict. We use the word *perceived* because often people think they disagree with each other only to find after talking that they have imagined their differences. The leader's responsibility is to initiate contact, even though he or she may not be the person who has the issue. Undercommunication increases conflict. Agreeing to discuss the issue is the threshold for modifying the perception of incompatible goals or interests.

Step 2: *Open the meeting.* When the meeting takes place, it is critical to establish a nonthreatening setting. Prayer is a useful tool to elevate the spiritual approach to resolution. Use prayer to seek God's wisdom, recognize the gifts and involvement of others, and express a desire to reach a resolution. Prayer lays the foundation for you to discuss the ground rules during the next steps:

- Speak cordially and with civility to each other.
- Be truthful and open.
- Focus on future actions rather than past occurrences.
- Be solution- rather than problem-oriented.

Step 3: *Identify Issues, Not Positions.* Each party has the opportunity to explain his or her side of the story without interruption. During the presentation, it is important to concentrate on the interests that surface, not the position he or she is taking on the subject. Interests provide the "whys" of the positions we take. Interest-oriented discussions pave the way for relational identity between the people involved. Our goal is not just to resolve a conflict, but to pursue resolution in a way that is esteeming and respectful to everyone involved.

James 1:19–20 says, "Take note of this: Everyone should be quick to listen, slow to speak and slow to become angry, for man's anger does not bring about the righteous life that God desires." When people are upset, angry, or afraid that they won't get what they want or need, they are more likely to talk "positions," which is adverse to what James recommends.

Step 4: *Clarification Questions.* Following statements by each party, each should ask questions about the issue. By better understanding each other's view, you move toward resolution.

Step 5: *Discussion/Confession/Generate Options:* To move from conflict to reconciliation requires an attitude change. Chances are that at this point you and the party have addressed some of the misperceptions about motives, talk, and actions that ignited the conflict. The goal is to establish mutual understanding, even if you agree to disagree. Discussion in Step 5 should move toward a primary and alternative solution. Brainstorm together about what options would work for both of you.

Making a choice means accepting responsibility, which is essential in reconciliation. For many people, the process of loving communication and being listened to are sufficient at this point. This is a good example of where the process is often more of a priority than the product. People want to know they are cared for and respected.

Step 6: *Impasse/Cooling Off:* At the same time, the people involved may realize that they have come to an impasse. This is where resolution does not seem feasible and you will need to deepen the communication. There are basically four types of impasses.

The *fact-based impasse* involves disagreements about truth, or judgments made on perceived reality. When people do not agree on the facts, they are apt to disagree on how they should respond to them as well. Does this condition exist? How can you substantiate and clarify the truth?

The *value-based impasse* involves disagreements about issues related to priorities, policies, and agendas. Because values establish uses of time, talent, and resources, we may end up disagreeing about results of values, which are more tangible.

The *interest-based impasse* involves disagreements over wants, power, privilege, rewards, and resources. Just as special interest groups lobby for the causes of their members, interest-based groups within a congregation do the same. Some of these are legitimate, like care for the widows in Acts 6:1. Others are more self-centered in nature.

The *nonsubstantive impasse* involves disagreements over issues that are not related to the actual matter at hand. These tend to be personal in nature and can be the result of an injured ego, nonchurch-related stress, and even spiritual warfare.

Establishing what kind of impasse you have is very helpful in moving toward resolution; misunderstanding it sends groups down rabbit trails and can even increase the tension involved. Some ideas for working through an impasse include brainstorming, separating the groups who in turn work with a neutral third party to create possible solutions and then share the ideas together, and even empowering a respected mediator/third party to determine a course of action.

If you have reached an impasse, don't get upset, and don't upset the injured party by giving up. Move to the next step.

Step 7: *Evaluations/Solutions.* Before concluding the meeting, go over what has been accomplished and where the parties are in the resolution process. If you need more time to develop agreeable solutions, establish a follow-up appointment. The goal is to enhance communication and to let the injured party know you care, whether or not you have resolved all the issues of contention. Celebrate accomplishments, good communication, forgiveness, and a willingness to meet. Close with a prayer of thanksgiving, acknowledging God's role in the process.

Basic training of people within your congregation on resolution processes can be very beneficial. The more people who are able to implement these skills, the less the pastor and leadership board have to take on.

APPLICATION TOOLBOX

Use the Appropriate Conflict Response Continuum (Figure 9B, page 243) to analyze past or current conflict issues. Make sure that the group using the tool is comfortable talking about the issues. You may want to begin by discussing hypothetical situations, past personal stories, or minor events. The tool can be very helpful as a discussion tool for staff members who are responsible for wisely walking through a conflict situation. Training improvement team and staff members with basic conflict resolution skills is a very proactive strategy.

Here are some questions to help you utilize the Appropriate Conflict Response Continuum:

- Think of a conflict condition and write out the details as to who is involved and what the issue is regarding.
- What are the perceived or obvious symptoms of conflict? How reliable are these perceptions? What level would you rate the conflict?
- What is the appropriate response to this level of conflict? Who should respond and what would be the most beneficial circumstances for the response?
- What are the potential benefits from appropriately responding to the conflict?
- What are the potential negative results if we underestimate the level of conflict or inappropriately respond?
- What positive or negative momentum issues have you factored into the calculations?
- What level of influence of the people in conflict have you factored into the calculations?

Americans are probably the most traveled people in history. Many of us venture thousands of miles annually, and we trek all over the world. But occasionally, you meet people who have never traveled more than a few miles from their place of birth. There were some American tourists visiting a tropical island. They had a native guide who was showing them the sights. They came to a big volcano that was spewing lava, smoke, and fire. One of the Americans said, "That looks just like hell." The native guide responded, "Wow, you Americans have been everywhere, haven't you?" Many church leaders think they know what hell feels like when they're in the fires of church conflict. Others relate more to Moses during the lesson on stoning, or Daniel in the lions' den. The more self-righteous among us identify more with Jesus on the cross. These sorts of feelings are quite common, because under the ordination frocks and behind the seminary certificate, we're all human.

Because we often unreasonably expect church to be conflict free and aren't sure how to handle our anger in groups, many of us get discouraged. Add to this the ongoing ministry stress and often scanty paychecks of clergy, and it is no wonder that a growing number of pastors are questioning if their careers are worth the effort. Lay leaders sensitive to well-intentioned pastors can make a big difference with encouragement and peer accountability.

Improvement teams also need to be encouraged. Many are volunteers, people who do battle daily in the corporate world but have little desire to turn church into a negative experience. Congregational members can increase the spiritual stamina of their churches by playing down the differences and playing up the values of Christlikeness and loving communication. Most of us have similar values that are based on the Scriptures. We tend to disagree the most on the strategic approaches to fulfilling these values. Emphasizing what we share in common is more important than focusing on how we differ.

In most improvement processes, a small minority make life difficult for improvement team members. While not ignoring these people, leaders need to be encouraged by the majority who are positive and hopeful about the future of their church. Sharing encouragement with each other is very important during times of stress and conflict.

"But encourage one another daily, as long as it is called Today, so that none of you may be hardened by sin's deceitfulness" (Heb. 3:13). "Let us hold unswervingly to the hope we profess, for he who promised is faithful. And let us consider how we may spur one another on toward love and good deeds" (Heb. 10:23–24).

Crash-and-Burn Story

It was a wonderful, strong, traditional church. I had been hired to oversee several staff pastors as well as to create a service that would connect with both the baby boomers as well as the unchurched in the community. I had pastored this kind of ministry previously and was confident that it could be created within the institutional structure of this large congregation. Adding to my confidence was the significant number of people who were hungry to experience the new style and to rekindle an excitement for reaching the lost through it.

The senior pastor was a very cautious man; he wanted to see the new ministry come to fruition without creating conflict or losing people along the way. So we invested a significant amount of time in surveying the congregation on their ideas, opinions, and expectations. We scheduled numerous meetings to discuss what kind of ministry or service would work best.

Eight of us were assigned to plan the new ministry, which would center around a Sunday morning worship service that was unique from the others. This group of eight did not include the senior pastor. Three of us were on staff and the other five were laypeople. We discussed the need to separate the service from the existing church for the purpose of giving it autonomy in the community, allowing it to distance itself from the massive church that had a reputation of traditionalism. The senior pastor did not like this idea, recommending that we keep it under the same roof in a fellowship hall adjoining the formal sanctuary.

In my mind, the watershed moment took place in a coffee shop, where our committee met to finalize the presentation of our plan. We all openly shared our concerns of whether the service would be authentically outreach oriented and contemporary under the leadership of the senior pastor. We agreed that someone else needed to be the main communicator, someone who would connect with a boomer or an irreligious person. One of the staff pastors said, "If we say this to the senior pastor, he's apt to feel threatened and get defensive."

I responded, "I'll tell him that we need him to be the senior pastor of the service and speak occasionally but we need someone else to do most of the preaching."

The staff pastor replied, "If you do, you might not be around very long. Right now, I need my job."

I leaned forward and said, "I don't need my job. If this service is going to have the integrity of an outreach event, the senior pastor cannot be the main communicator. He's a great guy, but he just does not relate to the unchurched culture."

Within the month, I had lost my job and the other staff member later was given my position. The senior pastor became the main speaker for the service, taking off his jacket as his approach to being relevant. The service never developed the edge to attract and hold the attention of the unchurched.

Crash-and-Burn Lessons:

- The one with the most power wins. If the senior pastor is not driving the improvement, it's apt to die. If the senior pastor is not able to connect with the pre-Christian culture and is unwilling to give up control of that ministry or service, it will languish. If the senior pastor is not willing to unleash others and empower them to do what he cannot, the change will die for lack of support.

Only through a radical shift in our thinking can we succeed in this new era. It calls for nothing but a complete break with tradition-bound ways.

—JOHN SCULLEY, Former CEO, Apple Computer, Inc.

COVENANT

The Bible refers many times to covenants—agreements that God makes with his people or that people make between themselves. Following is a sample of a covenant that those who are involved with improvement issues in your local church can write and agree upon.

Unlike a legal contract, this document is not designed for litigation or rights giving. Rather, it serves to clarify values and relationship priorities and communicate intentions. In spiritual terms, it's an example of giving up individual rights for the sake of the group and Christian example.

While this is a proactive tool, it can be useful even after conflict has arisen. We encourage you to consider documents like these as a team-building means to communicate love and affirmation prior to or during times of potential resistance.

We agree . . .

That the kingdom of God is bigger than any individual or group of people. We earnestly seek to do God's will for our congregation. We will work at setting aside personal agendas. If we see that differences of opinions arise, we agree to seek resolution in a God-honoring, biblical manner. This means going directly to the person(s) with whom we have a concern or disagreement instead of talking about the person behind his/her back.

We will esteem, love, and be respectful of others, even if we share differing ideas or priorities. Our goal is to unify, not divide. At the same time, we recognize that change and progress require us to think new thoughts and consider new methods, just as the Bible says that new wine needs new wineskins.

We recognize that change and improvement issues are subjective, involving varying methods and stylistic tastes. We will strive to be open to new ideas and sincerely weigh the pluses and minuses, not limiting God by our lack imagination. We want to become the best we can be at fulfilling our church's mission within our community. We will seek to do this with faith, hope, and obedience to God. If he takes us down new roads, we will trust him. If he calls us to enable others to do what we are not able to do, we will do that. God's work must progress. We will diligently pray and seek his wisdom to know how far and how fast to go, and what this means for us as individuals and as an entire congregation.

We agree to make this a concentrated effort. If we are not able to resolve our differences through face-to-face communication or even with the help of a third person, we agree to part ways without casting blame, pulling others away, or being generally divisive to our local congregation. We will strive to reflect the attitude of Christ, to be blameless and pure. Our goal is not to win individually, but to use our gifts and abilities to help our local church win as a whole.

We commit ourselves to this covenant, on _____
(date)

Signature(s)

> Our moral responsibility is not to stop the future, but to shape it . . . to channel our destiny in humane directions and to ease the trauma of transition.
>
> —Alvin Toffler

QUESTIONS AND ANSWERS

Q: We have not launched our improvement plan yet, but I'm scared to death about this whole area of conflict and resistance. Can you encourage me?

A: As we said earlier, churches are structured organizationally but tend to emote like family. Name one family you know well that never has heated discussions, disagreements, or conflict. Ever packed two or three kids into the family car and tried to decide on a restaurant? And congregations are just families of families. Improvement plans, by their very nature, often pit generations against generations and spouses against each other, not to mention friends against friends.

To stick our heads in the sand and pretend that conflict does not exist in even the healthiest of families and organizations is not going to benefit anyone. Be encouraged that if you've done your homework, you will be able to survive the channel of change. Keep encouraging each other on the improvement team and gather some prayer partners who are also mature, discerning, and full of mercy. God will use them to sustain you during those moments when you temporarily question your decision.

Q: There are some horrendous stories around about churches that have split over change issues. How do we keep these from tainting our leaders?

A: There are also some incredible stories of churches that have implemented improvement plans and are experiencing revival and the most joy in their history. There is a saying: "If you always do what you've always done, you'll always get what you've always gotten." The saying supports the idea that you cannot hope for new and better fruit by using the same old methods.

Every change involves risks. If you try to overcompensate for the fears and act like a major church change is a no-brainer, slam-dunk, guaranteed success, you'll have people jumping ship at the first wave or rock of the boat. A few negative experiences are part of change. At the same time, the best way to raise your chances of enjoying the fruit of improvement is to do your homework, which you are doing now, and to model after patterns of success.

You must admit the risks, but be confident that you've worked the process enough to move forward. If you're looking for reasons to be fearful and resistant, you'll find them. If you want to find reasons to move forward and take the calculated risks, you'll find those. As an improvement team, don't pretend the negative stories are fairy tales, but intentionally share the stories of success and let them become your models for patterning your improvement plans.

Q: What if we lose people? How can we justify that to others when they ask about so-and-so leaving?

A: You're apt to lose more people that you could have gained if you do not implement the improvement plan. We don't yet know the people who will come to our church if we make it more relevant and inviting. But these people have faces, souls, and talents and are potential friends and church leaders. Who is going to represent them? The goal of any improvement plan ultimately is to gain more people than we lose, and that is usually the case when the plan is well developed and deployed. Our goal is to pursue growth as a quality, not just a quantity.

While it is very tempting at times to wash our hands of those who are leaving, either to defend our self-esteem or to ridicule resistors for leaving, there is a better response. When someone asks why people are leaving, a good answer might be something like this: "God has given all of us free will. We all make decisions every day that affect our lives and the lives of those we know. The leadership of this church is doing what it believes is the best thing out of obedience to God and based on the biblical values we have discussed. Everyone is different. We eat at different restaurants, drive different cars, wear different clothes, and have different hobbies and interests. One size does not fit all. Sometimes, people need space to find a place of worship that fits them or their families better. We love them and need to pray for them as they consider a new church home. But all of us will be held accountable to do what we believe God's will is for us. We will miss them."

Although this response is certainly generic, it portrays the attitude leadership needs to have in explaining the absence of people who have left. Notice that it does not focus on particulars, specific names, or even perceptions. The goal is to remain blameless. There is the real possibility of doing further damage when you get into personal details, opinions, and perceptions. When we talk about people in their absence, the tendency is to be more negative than positive. Take the high road. You will gain more support as a leader as well as esteem those who choose to leave.

Q: In addition to working through the improvement and transition plan details, what else can we do to avoid the conflict of Levels 4 through 5 on the Appropriate Conflict Response Continuum?

A: No matter how well you know your people, there will be surprises down the road. The beautiful thing about organizational life in the church is that you can teach as you go. Creating sermons, Sunday school, and small-group lessons around body-life issues, themes of attitudes, handling differences, and biblical principles for resolution are wonderful assets for a church.

The downside of that is when pastors use podiums as whipping posts and go over the line in terms of targeting messages to specific people or groups. Because they're human, leaders run into the temptation to preach angrily about church problems. While attendees do not have that option, they tend to counter through their communication tool, the grapevine. Loving discipleship on unity amidst diversity can go a long way toward holding people accountable during teachable moments in the life of a congregation. Pretending that everything is fine when it is not will create a sense that the leader is running from reality or is oblivious.

While this book and its exercises are not a guarantee against significant conflict, most congregations will avoid traumatic resistance if they understand and implement the principles of organizational change. Creating a worst-case scenario is a helpful tool when developing a transition plan. In the worst case, how would you respond to a group set on dividing your church? Do you have mediators on hand to address the matters? Have you thought about what you will and will not stop doing if the resistance becomes intense? Creating a conflict action plan is akin to a community having a disaster plan waiting in the wings, hopefully never to be used.

> Beginnings are always messy.
>
> —JOHN GALSWORTHY

Discussion Starters

1. Why do you think that people in the church have such a difficult time dealing constructively with anger?
2. Can you think of an example where Christians did not resolve their conflict constructively? Explain the situation.
3. Can you think of an example where Christians did resolve their conflict constructively? Explain the situation.
4. What were the differences in how these people dealt with their disagreement?
5. What are the symptoms of divisive disagreement? When does a conflict turn from a harmless disagreement into a divisive one?
6. If it is appropriate, discuss past or current conflicts according to the appropriate responses.
7. What current teaching could be done to vaccinate the congregation from negative conflict?
8. How might you train people with conflict resolution skills?
9. If you have not yet rolled out your improvement plan, consider what areas might create conflict among the people in your church. How can you prepare to deal with this constructively?

> The winners of tomorrow will deal proactively with chaos, will look at the chaos per se as the source of market advantage, not as a problem to be got around.
>
> —TOM PETERS[5]

Contemplation

Anyone who claims to be in the light but hates his brother is still in the darkness. Whoever loves his brother lives in the light, and there is nothing in him to make him stumble. But whoever hates his brother is in the darkness and walks around in the darkness; he does not know where he is going, because the darkness has blinded him.

—1 John 2:9–11

Scripture

Read 1 Corinthians 13.

DEVOTIONAL THOUGHT

Being part of a family means that our connection is not based on preferences, styles, or temperaments. Being part of a family means that we share something deeper in common: our parents' gift of life. When God said that we are to love each other, he meant that our shared heritage should transcend individual differences. In other words, love becomes top priority, because it is the dominant trait of our Father.

Yet when conflict arises, peace at all costs is not the solution, because this atmosphere often harbors ministry dysfunction and eventual death of the congregation. Illness must be confronted. Some of the most loyal, loving, committed congregates are at times perceived to be just the opposite, because they raise concerns regarding irrelevance and ineffectiveness. The answer is to love in spite of differences and to honor God's kingdom. When Christians collide, the solution is not to either love or disagree, but rather to love even if you disagree. At times, conflict is the only true test as to whether we have God's love or a merely human replica. Love need not be a victim of differing views.

Why do so many faith communities allow things other than love to dominate their actions and attitudes? Why do individuals elevate personal tastes over the unity of the body and the reflection of God's character to love regardless of such issues? How can you become more loving during times of stress and even ministry disagreements?

Prayer

God, today give me the strength to love and esteem those who disagree with me about what is best for our faith community. Help me to never compromise on your command to love my fellow brothers and sisters. May the words I speak be edifying. Let my motives be pure and my actions blameless. Help me to keep the big picture in perspective and not be derailed by petty discrepancies. While they seem huge right now, they are minor in the scope of eternity. God, let me be like Jesus in how I face those with whom I disagree. Amen.

CHAPTER 10
Three Steps Forward, Two Steps Back: Persevering

Those who honestly mean to be true contradict themselves more rarely than those who try to be consistent.

—OLIVER WENDELL HOLMES JR.

My wife and I (Alan) had the opportunity as young pastors to be mentored by Ray and Anne Ortlund, authors and former pastors of Lake Avenue Congregational Church in Pasadena. They taught us that nearly any significant life task has "zones." The A Zone represents the dream phase of a goal, when you get excited about the vision, the possibilities, and when hope is high and actual problems seem manageable. Stress is low because you have not actually engaged challenges at this time. This is courtship: dreaming about a church plant, brainstorming a church turnaround, or experiencing a growth conference that catalyzes enthusiasm in you and your team.

Many people get so excited in the A Zone that they actually launch their idea. Not far into the process, they enter the B Zone. This is when your back is against the Red Sea and people are thirsty and begin murmuring about "the good ol' days." In almost every significant life event—marriage, work, ministry, parenting, or personal growth—you'll have B Zones. These represent our wilderness experiences. You feel like giving up. The giants are intimidating— you seem "like a grasshopper in their eyes." You begin to ask, "Why did we ever do this? What am I going to do? How did we ever get ourselves into this situation?" The B Zone represents the bottom of the S-curve we discussed earlier in the book. It is the stressful, problem-facing, low-momentum phase when retreat is a strong temptation.

While in the B Zone, many people choose the Q Zone; they quit. They take the path of least resistance. They remember the ease of former days, even if it was slavery. They fantasize about getting rid of the problem. The easiest way to avoid a giant is to run. In the B Zone, our faith is tested. Those of us who are weary in well-doing and small in faith tend to retreat. We pull back from the front line and may give up on marriage, a dream, a new job, ministry, or a significant church change.

But if we quit, we run the risk of losing all that we could have obtained. We exchange the potential good we seek for quick relief, immediate satisfaction. The problem with adopting the Q Zone is that when you do it once, you develop a tendency to do it again. A path worn to the Q Zone tends to be used time after time, reflected in multiple churches, jobs, relationships, marriages, or goals. Confidence is broken. Fulfillment never matures. Joy for living is depleted.

This is not to say that we should never quit. There are times to cut bait and let go, when the costs of continuing are just too high or when we've overstepped God's will. But more often than not, we quit too early. Human nature leads us to the Q Zone when the going gets tough in the B Zone.

When we persevere in the B Zone, eventually we will enter the C Zone: victory. This is the land flowing with milk and honey, where we enjoy the fruit of our labors. We are so glad when we get to the C Zone. We quickly forget the pain of the B Zone because the rewards of the C Zone are so fulfilling. We did it! We persevered! We've made it! High fives, back slaps, and hugs of celebration are in order at this point. We crossed the wilderness and the Jordan and finally we are here. Whether it is weight loss, accomplishing a new skill, working through marital struggles, or seeing a church improvement plan implemented, the C Zone makes all the work and sacrifice seem worthwhile.

The thing to remember when you are in the B Zone is that there is almost always a C Zone down the road, around the corner, over the next hill. The triumphal entry of Christ represented an A Zone—excitement, elation, high hopes. The trial, crucifixion, and tomb were clearly B Zone elements. In Gethsemane, Jesus considered the Q Zone, but he persevered. After Jesus' death, his disciples thought it was over; hope was gone. But then came the resurrection (C Zone); hope reigned. When you're in the B Zone, remember that chances are a C Zone is in the making.

Improvement Story: Indian Creek Community Church, Olathe, Kansas

In 1985, Indian Creek Community Church began with about twenty-five adults. They were committed to starting a church that would reach the unchurched. While totally unaware of other models or similar efforts, the congregation purposed to invite only people who had never attended a church before. Unfortunately, their worship and programs mirrored their rather traditional heritage, and as a result, they exhausted their network of friends and contacts within six months, with little growth to show for their efforts.

At that point, the need for change was obvious. They began reaching beyond their friends to the surrounding community by advertising and creating a few public interest programs. By the end of their first year, the church averaged 125. Through outreach and a phone solicitation campaign, the congregation continued to grow, reaching the two-hundred mark by the third year.

Church leadership began to realize that the worship service needed to become more seeker friendly in order to attract and keep the nonchurched visitors. Several leaders attended a Willow Creek conference. They loved the philosophy and recognized a common purpose: to reach the lost. The leaders returned and excitedly introduced the idea of using a seeker-target approach on Sundays, but they failed to realize the radical change of direction that would be required.

Drama was introduced, and public prayer requests were dropped along with long announcements. The result was an identity crisis. There was a sense among many members that the church was "selling out" its heritage and uniqueness to embrace something shallow, contemporary, and pragmatic. The perception was that the church was either outreach oriented or existed solely for discipleship/worship. Many founding families left. Their absence, coupled with a congregation largely of seekers, resulted in a leadership crisis.

The church attempted to find itself for several years, while a tug of war over philosophy and programming raged. Amazingly, the church continued to grow at an annual rate of about 10 percent. Attendance ranged between three and four hundred by 1994. That year, the leadership determined that the priority to reach seekers was a scriptural mandate that could not be compromised. But just as important was the need to disciple believers into fully devoted followers. The leadership decided to send groups of leaders to the annual conferences at Willow Creek in order to glean ideas. Just as critical was the decision to chart a realistic course for change. The top priority was to agree on a common goal. Everyone agreed that the biblical mandate was to build a biblically functioning, Acts 2 church.

Lay leaders took ownership. They decided to keep a blend of worship and discipleship while adopting a seeker-friendly programming style. The sermons were planned on a topical series approach to aid programming. Seeker-targeted events were added to the monthly calendar: dinner theaters, friend days, Easter egg hunts, Christmas Eve services, and breakfasts with professional athletes were leveraged to reach unchurched friends. The church has since incorporated several seeker-targeted series a year that include multimedia elements and the arts.

The result? Momentum is building. Attendance is pushing one thousand with more than $2 million in annual revenues. The ship has turned and is headed in the right direction.

Improvement Lessons:

- Don't initiate change until you have a consensus of people behind the reason for it.
- Just because you say you want to win the lost doesn't mean you are equipped to do it. You need to understand relevant models and methods for today's society.
- People say they want to change but often buck it when they see what it will cost emotionally. Use conferences to cast vision and share common experiences.
- Change can be slow and intentional with very positive results. Count the cost. Pay the price. And don't look back.

CENTRAL CHRISTIAN CHURCH: OUR STORY

Traversing the B Zone

One of the hardest things for me during the B Zone was losing key leaders who chose not to navigate the change with us. The chairman of the elders who hired me is no longer in the church. There are others from that initial elder group who are gone. I knew I was running with this God-given dream and that people were helped as a result, yet not everyone could support the idea. Some felt betrayed, so they left. This is part of the angst of leading. It just hurts.

Sometimes you have those who stay in the church even though they are hurt—and they stay hurt. They occasionally shoot their arrows and make life really difficult. I have experienced a few power struggles along the way. But I figured that time was on my side, that if I persevered and led with diligence, I would outlive the detractors.

If you're trying to cross the B Zone, don't overreact and give too much energy to those causing you frustrations. Patience is a real attribute. If you have people who are obstacles in your church, remember that you have the power of the pulpit and high visibility. You are the key comforter, communicator, and care-giver. Using that stewardship wisely allows you to outlive the opponents.

CHANNEL OF CHAOS

Another way of looking at the B Zone—the getting-through stage—is as the Channel of Chaos.

> And all the people gave a great shout of praise to the LORD, because the foundation of the house of the LORD was laid. But many of the older priests and Levites and family heads, who had seen the former temple, wept aloud when they saw the foundation of this temple being laid, while many others shouted for joy. No one could distinguish the sound of the shouts of joy from the sound of weeping. (Ezra 3:11–13)

In Ezra 3, there are two groups of people; one is rejoicing over change and the other is mourning it. One group is ready to move forward and the other is ready to go backward. When you are in the Channel of Chaos, it is very tempting to give up. But in Ezra, Israel was blessed with a leader who discovered how to maneuver through this channel. He persevered and by Ezra 6, the people completed the temple and experienced one of the greatest celebrations in Israel's history. Thus began a new era of ministry for God's people.

I (Gene) frequently hear pastors say, "When I interviewed with the congregation, they told me they were ready to change. They were excited about change. They needed change. And everybody was on board—until we actually changed." What we think we want and what we really want are often two different things. In order to persevere through the Channel of Chaos, it is important to understand the parts of the process. Natural progress through change involves four Cs: conflict, confusion, courage ebbing, and crushed emotions.

1. *Conflict:* Although we invested an entire chapter to the subject of conflict, we want to mention the concept again in the context of persevering because it wears out church leaders. Years ago, a cigarette marketing campaign showed smokers with black eyes, confessing they'd rather "fight than switch." That's true of a lot of congregational members, so much so that leaders finally say, "I'd rather switch than fight."

Use the principles in the last chapter. Remember to guard against overreaction. Paul wrote:

> God's servant must not be argumentative, but a gentle listener and a teacher who keeps cool, working firmly but patiently with those who refuse to obey. You never know how or when God might sober them up with a change of heart and turning to the truth, enabling them to escape the Devil's trap, where they are caught and held captive, forced to run his errands. (2 Tim. 2:24–26, MSG)

The people you are in conflict with matter to God. There is a tendency to develop a self-righteous attitude: "They just don't have a heart for people like us Progressives. If they loved God like we did, they would not resist the improvement." Usually, these people love God just as much as you do, but they are having a hard time negotiating the change.

2. *Confusion:* When leaders begin to feel inundated with direct and indirect feedback regarding change frustrations, there comes a time when confusion sets in. They begin to wonder: *Did we make the right decision? Did we implement it right? Should we have waited longer? Did we assume too much? Should I have personally participated in this process?* Thoughts like these begin to seep into the psyche of even the best leaders.

In the Bible, several times you see Moses going to God in the midst of challenges, asking whether or not God really knew what he was doing (Exod. 5:22–23, 6:12). In the Psalms, out of his own confusion David often questioned the faithfulness of the Creator (Ps. 10:1, 22:1). In Gideon's win with three hundred soldiers, confusion was a basis for the battle victories of Israel—when the enemy tribes lost their bearings and killed each other (Judg. 7). The lesson we learn from these stories is that during confusing times, leaders need to pull back, pray, and think through the process. One of the major benefits of an improvement team is that each member provides a reality check during times of confusion. This pulls individuals back to the agreed-upon plan. As Ed Norton, the sewer worker on the old *Honeymooners* TV show used to say, "United we stand. Divided we sink."

3. *Courage Ebbing:* Perhaps the most debilitating by-product of confusion is the loss of courage. When you need courage and motivation most, they can ebb away. Returning to the confidence that started you on the journey is a must. Courage is not blind bullheadedness. You can be sensitive to doubters without buying into the doubts that diminish the improvement plan. When Nehemiah led the charge to rebuild the walls of Jerusalem, the builders began to run into resistance halfway through the process. Look at the situation Nehemiah faced:

> [Different enemies] plotted together to come and fight against Jerusalem and stir up trouble against it. . . .
>
> Meanwhile, the people in Judah said, "The strength of the laborers is giving out, and there is so much rubble that we cannot rebuild the wall."
>
> Also our enemies said, "Before they know it or see us, we will be right there among them and will kill them and put an end to the work."
>
> Then the Jews who lived near them came and told us ten times over, "Wherever you turn, they will attack us." (Neh. 4:8–12)

During times of discouragement, it is the leader's job to encourage the people while he is containing his own fears. Note Nehemiah's example: "After I looked things over, I stood up and said to the nobles, the officials and the rest of the people, 'Don't be afraid of them. Remember the Lord, who is great and awesome, and fight for your brothers, your sons and your daughters, your wives and your homes'" (Neh. 4:14). A leader needs to embolden his people to do the work before them.

People of faith are called to confront their fears and rely on their Creator.

> Strengthen the feeble hands,
> > steady the knees that give way;
> say to those with fearful hearts,
> > "Be strong, do not fear; your God will come." (Isa. 35:3–4)

> "Therefore, strengthen your feeble arms and weak knees." (Heb. 12:12)

4. *Crushed Emotions:* Sometimes the Channel of Chaos (B Zone) involves

both organizational and personal elements. I (Gene) know this all too well, because it happened to me. The year was 1989. Things seemed to be going well at Central Christian. God was doing such a good thing. The church was changing and people were growing. We added a significant building addition, tripling the size of our facilities, which I knew was going to be a tremendous tool for advancing our mission. I'll never forget the night of the dedication. The chairman of our elders stood and said some very nice things about me and the leadership I had provided. I went home that night feeling on top of the world. I was certain we were going to sail into a tremendous new era of ministry.

But within an hour, I went from one of the greatest mountaintop experiences of my life to my lowest valley. My wife informed me that she was in love with another man. She left the next morning and never returned. That was a Channel of Chaos full of crushed emotions.

As you study the lives of believers and especially leaders, you discover that one of the common themes is that of brokenness.[1] In the process of being broken, we become, through God's shaping, the people he longs for us to be. We often curse the circumstances that bring the breaking, but normalcy is rarely a growth catalyst. God is not just interested in establishing churches. He desires his people to grow in the process. Ironically, the process by which we seek to catalyze our churches to be more fruitful also prunes us as individuals to bear more fruit. Conflict, change, discouragement, problem solving, and persevering are all character-building elements. Instead of cursing them, we need to bless them.

> Consider it pure joy, my brothers, whenever you face trials of many kinds, because you know that the testing of your faith develops perseverance. Perseverance must finish its work so that you may be mature and complete, not lacking anything. If any of you lacks wisdom, he should ask God, who gives generously to all without finding fault, and it will be given to him. (James 1:2–5)

Crash-and-Burn Story

When I came to the church, it was traditionally styled and ran about 350 on Sunday mornings. The church was program based, and most of the congregation expressed a very low level of maturity.

I should have realized what I was getting into when I came for the interview process. I met with the board for seven hours, sharing my values and dreams. They invited me to come and be voted on by the congregation. One older man in the church, who taught the largest Sunday school class of older adults, heard that I was really into small-group ministry. He started a rumor that I would cancel their class and make everyone join a small group if I came. So then more than one-fifth of the people voted against me. I was amazed and just kind of laughed it off, assuming the job wasn't right for me. But the board and regional official talked me into accepting the majority vote, so I did. I came to realize later that this spirit was indicative of the church's resistance to change.

A few weeks after we came to the church, the staff member overseeing our worship attended a Willow Creek conference. He returned excited and we talked for eight hours the next day. He wanted to transform our service into one that was seeker sensitive. I was not opposed to that but felt the need to direct our service as well toward more authentic, meaningful worship. We agreed that we would try to do both: offer contemporary worship with seeker-sensitive elements. We brought the idea to the board and it voted unanimously to accept the plan.

We immediately began announcing that we would be making some changes, such as turning our choir into an ensemble, using an overhead projector, and including drama and more contemporary music. I had been at the church just over six months when we made the change in worship-service styles. After the first or second week of the changes, I was invited to the house of the man who had helped start the church. He and his wife told me how much they loved me and appreciated my ministry. But then he said, "We need to make a change and get rid of the music man. He's going to ruin the church."

I shared my own uneasiness about some of the new elements in the service, but I supported the worship pastor and suggested that we let the new service run for a while and watch it. I explained our attempt to reach people outside the church with these new components. I'll never forget the man's wife looking at me as she said, "You're such a wonderful pastor and you have such a nice family. It would be so terrible for you and your family to lose everything—even your ministry." I was stunned. I don't remember what I said next, but I graciously changed the subject and said good-bye.

This couple then sent a multipage letter to every member in our church, as well as to our state and national governance, that ridiculed and maligned me and our staff member. I was accused of being a dictator and a wolf in sheep's clothing and of not caring for people. The next Sunday, more than one hundred people had left. When I called a board meeting to discuss the matter, the board suggested that I stay put and help the church through the process of change. Because some of the board members had older family members who were a part of this division, I knew it was tearing up their families. Needless to say, the process was incredibly humbling. The church has never really come back from that bump.

Crash-and-Burn Lessons:

- Recognize who is the true power base of your church. We never had a problem on the board, but the power base was among those who used to be in formal leadership.
- Be willing to let your church change gradually. I'm reminded of the story about the pastor who wanted to move the piano from one side of the platform to the other. When the congregation said no, he left. A year or so later, the former pastor came back to visit and noticed the piano on the opposite side. He asked the current pastor, "How did you do it?" The pastor responded, "I moved it one inch per week."

LEADERS' EGO STRENGTH AND CHANGE

Sometimes pastors and improvement leaders feel like the two young entrepreneurs who went to Mexico to start a bungee-jumping business. They had great dreams and pooled their money, buying everything they needed: building materials for a tower, a bungee cord, and insurance. They chose an active downtown area for their location. As they constructed the tower, a crowd began to emerge to watch. The entrepreneurs were finally ready for a test jump. One took the plunge. When he sprang up to his partner, the observing partner noticed a few cuts and scratches on his friend, but he could not catch him. The jumper bounced again and this time came up bruised and bleeding. He bounced a third time and his friend noticed he was really hurting, bleeding, with noticeable broken bones. Fortunately, the partner was finally able to catch his friend and pull him to the platform. "What happened?" he asked. "Was the cord too long?"

The injured man replied, "No. The cord was fine. But what's a piñata?"

During any significant improvement process, leaders will have moments when they feel like a piñata. Church change is not for the easily intimidated. Leaders who are most apt to persevere with health and well-being are leaders who have ego strength. This is not the same as having a big ego. Big-ego pastors run the risk of alienating people by intimidating them or losing potential gain because people do not trust their motives. Pastors and leaders with small, weak egos tend to either be frightened off by the risks of change and never pursue them or give up too soon when the going gets tough. Following is a matrix that compares ego size with ego strength.

10A
Leader Ego (size and strength)

	Small (humble)	Big (pride)
Strong (healthy self-esteem)	**1.** Confident Foot Washers (Jesus) / Servant Leaders / Strong & Loving / Velvet-Covered Bricks / Bold but Gentle	**2.** Bold & Daring / Pushers / Limelight Seekers / Manipulators / Win at all Costs
Weak (low self-esteem)	**3.** Humble / Compliant / Fearful / Self-Conscious	**4.** Braggarts / Attention Seekers / People Pleasers

Ego Strength (vertical axis) — *Ego Size* (horizontal axis)

The horizontal line represents the size of an ego, varying from small (left) to large (right). The vertical line represents ego strength, from weak (bottom) to strong (top).

Box 1: People with small but strong egos are humble and able to think beyond themselves and wash feet like Jesus. They have a good sense of who they are in Christ and enjoy positive self-esteem. They are productive members of the body of Christ.

Box 2: People with big and strong egos are bold and daring. They can be dangerous leaders in that they are very self-driven and self-promoting. They can greatly benefit an organization, but you never get the feeling they have a true servant's heart. While these people often make good change agents, you're never quite sure of their motivations. These leaders seek the limelight and applause and tend to create enemies among those who go against them. They have a difficult time washing feet, unless of course it will serve their ultimate goal.

Box 3: People with small, weak egos lack confidence and suffer from a poor self-concept and low self-esteem. We in the church sometimes confuse low self-esteem with humility; these look alike at times but are inherently different from each other. Because we value humility and compliance in the church, we often perceive people in this quadrant to be holier than they are. These people are the compliant and easily intimidated people who lack confidence to dare new things. They are not stuck on themselves so they portray a servant's heart, but some of this perceived humility is disguised low self-esteem.

In the past, the church has debunked the concept of self-esteem, which is little more than a psychological term for recognizing the love God has for us. We were created in the image of God. When leaders fail to recognize their God-given value due to early conditioning, bad theology, or emotional baggage, they diminish their ability to make the difficult calls that improvement often requires.

Box 4: People with big but weak egos suffer from pride and demand attention. These are the braggarts, the "I'm better than you" leaders who are easily offended if they do not receive enough affirmation and applause. These people talk big but deliver little. They do not have sufficient ego strength to stand up to difficult situations or people.

The most effective improvement-driving leaders are like velvet-covered bricks, tough but tender, firm yet loving (Group 1). A leader with a small but strong ego can often be perceived to have a large ego, because he or she is not quickly intimidated and is willing to stand up to opposition, bullies, and divisive members. People assume wrong motives for some leaders who have very pure and proper motives but are not pushovers.

Strong-ego people usually win the respect of other strong people without creating the negative effects many big-ego people do. The best example of this was Jesus. A classic demonstration of strength and humility is found at the Last Supper: "Jesus knew that the Father had put all things under his power, and that he had come from God and was returning to God; so he got up from the meal, took off his outer clothing, and wrapped a towel around his waist. After that, he poured water into a basin and began to wash his disciples' feet, drying them with the towel that was wrapped around him" (John 13:3–5).

This passage tells us that Jesus knew who he was. He had a strong sense of identity. Because of this healthy self-esteem, he was able to give up the pretenses of power and manipulation and model servanthood to his disciples. As you remember, these were the same men who spent their pastimes arguing who was going to be first and greatest in the kingdom. Discipleship and maturity are all about learning how to serve.

Leading a church improvement, let alone leading a church, can be an intimidating process. People you perceive to be friends and loyal followers can rear their heads in disgust as they process a change item. Conflict, turmoil, and a falling out of former loyalists all take a toll on the self-image and ego of a leader. Most pastors are nurturers and therefore take this kind of resistance personally. Take some time to figure out what kind of ego you have and how that affects your leadership. Check your motives. Know that you must establish your identity in Christ. Otherwise you'll be tempted to back down or walk out on people when the going gets tough.

SPIRITUAL WARFARE

While neither of us as pastors is overly superstitious in terms of the spiritual realm, we recognize the reality of spiritual warfare. Some churches seem preoccupied with the notion of demons as the cause of nearly every trial and tribulation in the life of a believer. But most congregations are aloof to the times when the enemy really is at work to disrupt the progress of the kingdom. Here is what the Word says in this regard:

> Finally, be strong in the Lord and in his mighty power. Put on the full armor of God so that you can take your stand against the devil's schemes. For our struggle is not against flesh and blood, but against the rulers, against the authorities, against the powers of this dark world and against the spiritual forces of evil in the heavenly realms. Therefore put on the full armor of God, so that when the day of evil comes, you may be able to stand your ground, and after you have done everything, to stand. Stand firm then, with the belt of truth buckled around your waist, with the breastplate of righteousness in place, and with your feet fitted with the readiness that comes from the gospel of peace. In addition to all this, take up the shield of faith, with which you can extinguish all the flaming arrows of the evil one. (Eph. 6:10–16)

Be especially aware, prior to a significant improvement plan launch and immediately after the rollout, that you may experience a powerful sense of confusion and discouragement. One of the enemy's strategies is to create a series of little skirmishes around the perimeter of the camp, which draw our attention away from the main objective. The tactic of diversion is potentially powerful. If he can get us to look away from our goal due to squabbling over petty issues, he has, in essence, rendered us powerless.

Later in Jesus' ministry, he had to confront the very man on whom the church was said to be built, Peter.

> He then began to teach them that the Son of Man must suffer many things and be rejected by the elders, chief priests and teachers of the law, and that he must be killed and after three days rise again. He spoke plainly about this, and Peter took him aside and began to rebuke him.
>
> But when Jesus turned and looked at his disciples, he rebuked Peter. "Get behind me, Satan!" he said. "You do not have in mind the things of God, but the things of men." (Mark 8:31–33)

Leaders need to be organizationally savvy, change aware, and relationally astute, but the bottom line is that sometimes, church chaos is a result of spiritual warfare caused by none other than Satan. We can blame it on any number of obvious possibilities, but faith communities must remember that the basis of their existence is spiritual in nature. They cannot explain everything that occurs in terms of a logical, human reason.

Spiritual warfare is more likely to occur within congregations that are serious about catalyzing their faith, improving their fruit bearing, and doing what it takes to expand God's kingdom in their community. Idling and maintaining kinds of churches are little threat to the enemy. A foreign military is far less interested in knocking out a missile that is missing a warhead than it is an armed rocket. To intentionally improve the effectiveness of your church is a spiritual act of war. Do not be surprised if a sense of chaos arises that is difficult to explain. The basis could very well be more spiritual in substance than anything else.

The way you wage spiritual battle is with spiritual weapons. The spiritual arsenal we are given includes God's Word, faith, and prayer. Remember that people are not the enemy as much as they are victims and tools of the enemy. If you encounter spiritual resistance in your church in the forms of serious dissension, doubts on the part of the improvement team, a series of relationship conflicts, foreign "vibes" felt by those with gifts of discernment, or a string of circumstantial oddities, gear up. Focus on the enemy, not people or circumstances. Emphasize prayer and time alone with God as an improvement team. Gather the intercessors of the church together to seek God's wisdom and presence.

> I lift up my eyes to the hills—
> > where does my help come from?
> My help comes from the Lord,
> > the Maker of heaven and earth.
> He will not let your foot slip—
> > he who watches over you will not slumber;
> indeed, he who watches over Israel
> > will neither slumber nor sleep.
> The Lord watches over you—
> > the Lord is your shade at your right hand;
> the sun will not harm you by day,
> > nor the moon by night.
> The Lord will keep you from all harm—
> > he will watch over your life;
> the Lord will watch over your coming and going
> > both now and forevermore. (Ps. 121)

A THEOLOGY OF PERSEVERANCE

The Bible shows us that throughout history persevering has been a key element of faith. Faith that gives up quickly is not faith in the biblical sense. Few of us consider ourselves to be an Abraham, Moses, David, Elijah, Jonah, or Paul, but these people were not faithful because they were great; they were great because of their faith. The saying "God doesn't call us to be successful; he calls us to be faithful," can be a cop-out. On the other hand, it is true that faith does not guarantee achievement, but spiritual success requires faith. One of our favorite stories is about a boat that telegraphed an SOS message during a terrible storm at sea. The Coast Guard quickly acted. One of the rookie crew members said, "The weather is terrible. We might not come back." The crew chief responded, "We don't have to come back; but we have to go out." Obedience is what God seeks, while ultimately we must leave the results to him.

Relational distress is among the hardest to endure. If you want to be liked, you're normal. If you need to be liked, you'll have a difficult time persevering through times of resistance. I (Gene) remember when a man in our church sent a letter to me and our elders. He referred to me as "Little Hitler." I had to recognize that I was probably not going to please this guy anytime soon. In John 5:30, Jesus said his ambition was to please the one who sent him. If Jesus couldn't please everybody, why do we think we can?

It's okay not to please everyone. If the pastor thinks he works for the church, he will be perpetually divided between the divergent requests of the people. If he works for God and as an expression of that serves the people, he must ultimately take his commands from God himself. It is equivalent to a construction subcontractor taking his cues from the general contractor instead of the client. We need to remember for whom we work and to whom we must give an answer.

One of the most painful losses for me (Gene) personally came after the identity of our church had changed. There were about thirty people who had been around a long time, people who were good, loved God, and called me their friend. When they finally figured out that the transformation was not just a phase we were going through, they left. Of all the people we've lost over the years, this loss hurt me most. Many of these people had helped lead, and supported the ministry in former days. Many of these people had been pillars. There is no denying the fact that it's painful to lose these kinds of members. But anyone who studies change inside or outside the church will tell you, it's part of the Channel of Chaos. Release them to God. Realize it takes all kinds of churches to reach all kinds of people and you will not and cannot reach everyone in your community.

Check out these words from Scripture:

All these people [Abraham, Noah, Enoch, Abel] were still living by faith when they died. They did not receive the things promised; they only saw them and welcomed them from a distance. And they admitted that they were aliens and strangers on earth. People who say such things show that they are looking for a country of their own. If they had been thinking of the country they had left, they would have had opportunity to return. Instead, they were longing for a better country—a heavenly one. Therefore God is not ashamed to be called their God, for he has prepared a city for them. (Heb. 11:13–16)

While the context of this passage has to do with establishing a spiritual kingdom, not mere church improvement, the principles hold true that if God is leading us to change, we must be about seeking the new land, not staying in the old country.

In every significant improvement process, there are those moments when you feel like you cannot go an inch further. Discouragement may be the single biggest tool that the enemy has in his arsenal. If you have not run into that condition, chances are you are either delirious or have waited far too long to implement the new idea. Rotten fruit will eventually fall off the tree, but it's rarely good to eat. Here are some biblical principles to encourage you to persevere during the difficult times.

- There are souls at stake; don't give up.

> Do not neglect your gift, which was given you through a prophetic message when the body of elders laid their hands on you.
>
> Be diligent in these matters; give yourself wholly to them, so that everyone may see your progress. Watch your life and doctrine closely. Persevere in them, because if you do, you will save both yourself and your hearers. (1 Tim. 4:14–16)

- Live by faith, not circumstances.

> It is a dreadful thing to fall into the hands of the living God.

> Remember those earlier days after you had received the light, when you stood your ground in a great contest in the face of suffering. Sometimes you were publicly exposed to insult and persecution; at other times you stood side by side with those who were so treated. You sympathized with those in prison and joyfully accepted the confiscation of your property, because you knew that you yourselves had better and lasting possessions.
>
> So do not throw away your confidence; it will be richly rewarded. You need to persevere so that when you have done the will of God, you will receive what he has promised. For in just a very little while,

> "He who is coming will come
>   and will not delay.
> But my righteous one will live by faith.

And if he shrinks back,
    I will not be pleased with him."

But we are not of those who shrink back and are destroyed, but of those who believe and are saved.

Now faith is being sure of what we hope for and certain of what we do not see. (Heb. 10:37–11:1)

- God grows us through perseverance.

We also rejoice in our sufferings, because we know that suffering produces perseverance; perseverance, character; and character, hope. And hope does not disappoint us, because God has poured out his love into our hearts by the Holy Spirit, whom he has given us. (Rom. 5:3–5)

- Finish well.

But you, keep your head in all situations, endure hardship, do the work of an evangelist, discharge all the duties of your ministry.

For I am already being poured out like a drink offering, and the time has come for my departure. I have fought the good fight, I have finished the race, I have kept the faith. (2 Tim. 4:5–7)

- No pain, no gain.

Endure hardship with us like a good soldier of Christ Jesus. No one serving as a soldier gets involved in civilian affairs—he wants to please his commanding officer. Similarly, if anyone competes as an athlete, he does not receive the victor's crown unless he competes according to the rules. The hardworking farmer should be the first to receive a share of the crops. Reflect on what I am saying, for the Lord will give you insight into all this.

Remember Jesus Christ, raised from the dead, descended from David. This is my gospel, for which I am suffering even to the point of being chained like a criminal. But God's word is not chained. Therefore I endure everything for the sake of the elect, that they too may obtain the salvation that is in Christ Jesus, with eternal glory.

Here is a trustworthy saying:

If we died with him,
    we will also live with him;
if we endure,
    we will also reign with him.
If we disown him,
    he will also disown us;
if we are faithless,
    he will remain faithful,
    for he cannot disown himself.

Keep reminding them of these things. Warn them before God against quarreling about words; it is of no value, and only ruins those who listen. Do your best to present yourself to God as one approved, a workman who does not need to be ashamed and who correctly handles the word of truth. (2 Tim. 2:3–15)

- You're not alone; all great believers have had to persevere.

Therefore, since we are surrounded by such a great cloud of witnesses, let us throw off everything that hinders and the sin that so easily entangles, and let us run with perseverance the race marked out for us. Let us fix our eyes on Jesus, the author and perfecter of our faith, who for the joy set before him endured the cross, scorning its shame, and sat down at the right hand of the throne of God. Consider him who endured such opposition from sinful men, so that you will not grow weary and lose heart. (Heb. 12:1–3)

- Harvesttime is coming.

Let us not become weary in doing good, for at the proper time we will reap a harvest if we do not give up. (Gal. 6:9)

- Look to God for your refreshment.

  I will refresh the weary and satisfy the faint. (Jer. 31:25)

  Come to me, all you who are weary and burdened, and I will give you rest. (Matt. 11:28)

- Keep your eyes on God, not people.

  He gives strength to the weary
  > and increases the power of the weak.
  Even youths grow tired and weary,
  > and young men stumble and fall;
  but those who hope in the LORD
  > will renew their strength.
  They will soar on wings like eagles;
  > they will run and not grow weary,
  > they will walk and not be faint. (Isa. 40:29–31)

WHEN BAD THINGS HAPPEN TO GOOD IDEAS

Chances are, your improvement team will need to untangle some knots that show up after your launch. The benefit is that you will have been working together for a while by then and should be able to communicate well and work as unified problem solvers. The Price Waterhouse Change Integration Team gives us a list of reasons to help determine why good ideas can go awry, even in sometimes optimum settings.[2]

1. *Failure to deliver early, tangible results.* When people do not see some kind of progress early on, they are prone to lose the motivation to implement further change. If you do not see measurable results within six months of an innovation, you are apt to see diminishing support for it. While large improvement efforts can take years to adopt, you need to make sure there are ways to measure progress early.
2. *Drowning in details.* The downside of most books and church conferences is that you see the results of what others have done without experiencing the details. But when churches strive to implement similar innovations,

they can quickly become bogged down in the minutia of details, only to get stuck in the mud. The most effective improvement instructions tend to simplify processes and don't reflect the innate complexity involved. As well, too much management tends to complicate things. Strive to keep it simple, streamlined. Empower people to make the calls necessary to implement the improvement ideas.

3. *Everything is high priority.* As we mentioned earlier, seek out the 20 percent of the changes that have the chance of yielding 80 percent of the returns. You cannot prioritize it all. When you expect your paid and unpaid servants to make everything a front-burner item, you will create unnecessary frustration, conflict, and stress. Figure out what it is you want to achieve and focus on the few things that will maximize the possibility of doing them.

4. *Old performance measures block change.* If you want to see different behaviors in ministry, you need to measure and reward different actions. If we rely on the old way of measuring effectiveness, we will tend to get the old levels of productivity. Make sure you have adopted and explained new measurements to your staff and workers, so that they are motivated to do the things that are acknowledged as important.

5. *Failing to "connect the dots."* When we get too many divergent improvement ideas going at the same time without a strong connection between them, we run the risk of losing energy. People begin to pit ideas against each other, vying for limited time and resources to accomplish them. This can be especially true in larger churches, where staff members drive their own ministry silos and feel aloof to whole-church priorities. Make sure everyone sees the big picture and understands where his or her piece of the puzzle fits.

6. *The voice of the customer is absent.* Who are your ministry customers? Are you gathering feedback from them? Who is asking them? What are they telling you? Ministry improvement means detailing who it is we are striving to serve. Many of us plan events for people other than ourselves without considering what they want or how to communicate with them. Many of our ministry services and events are nonproductive because we have overlooked the direct input of the people we hope to reach through the event. It is akin to a parent planning a party for a teenager without any input from the teen. The results are bound to be less than satisfying.

7. *The participants are not heard.* When leadership overlooks input from the church people who are actually going to benefit from the improvement, they are apt to have buy-in and ownership problems. Because the actual ministry workers usually understand what the customers want and how the ministry can be improved, they need to be involved in planning, evaluating, and implementing. When a few church leaders dictate top-down methods, you are asking for problems. Have you included ministry teams in the process of planning and implementing the improvement?

8. *Senior management wants to help but doesn't know how.* In terms of local church ministry, this means that pastors and leaders who talk change and membership empowerment must let go of control. There is a natural temptation for those in charge to retain the power. Pastors often have a difficult time trusting laity and staff with ministry improvement. They are tempted to put their hands back on the reins even after they have let go. Widespread improvement cannot be relegated to a few people who try to run the entire church.

9. *"What's in it for me"* is unclear. While some of your people are more motivated to serve others than to be served, most of your people are still thinking in terms of what's in it for them and their families. This is not necessarily evil or carnal but is a part of spiritual and emotional growth and maturity. Therefore, if we are to include this large majority in our improvement process, we have to effectively answer that question. When people are not satisfied with why they are involved in the new idea, they are prone to pull back and lose commitment to it.

10. *Too much conventional wisdom.* New ideas require new means and new processes. Many churches fail to implement improvement ideas because they try to accomplish them via old attitudes and processes. For example, some pastors think that creating a contemporary, relevant worship service is as simple as taking off your tie and throwing the lyrics onto a video screen. Fresh, out-of-the box ideas require out-of-the-box means. When you attempt to apply innovations using existing tools, the chances are high you'll return to the old style of ministry.

11. *Same old horses, same old glue.* Nearly always, new ideas require new people to implement them. If you are working with the same leadership team you've had over the last few years, chances are you will feel pulled to the former way of thinking and ministering. Employing new people in the

process can be risky, but it is usually necessary. New people bring new perspectives, ideas, talents, experiences, gifts, and energy. For some existing folk, including others is the final way of letting go of the past and embracing the future.

APPLICATION TOOLBOX

Baseball is a game of statistics. While fringe people simply look at the total runs after each inning or the final score, true fans know that the box score gives a much truer sense of how the game is going or how it went. Improvement teams are interested not only in the final score; they need to look at the details. As your own consultants, you need to come up with great answers less than you need to ask the right questions.

After you've rolled out the improvement plan, you are going to need frequent review and analysis. Plan on setbacks, unexpected challenges, and unplanned opportunities. As we've said before, remember, this is an art, not a science. Consistent as well as spontaneous feedback from the team will be key to keeping things from logjamming. Here is a list of items that you can use as a base to develop your own checklist for these update meetings. One person may want to manage the list, or every member may want to come with his/her own set of issues based on his/her perspective. The goal of the list is to be constructive and solution oriented.

1. What are some of the positive results we are already observing (statistics, testimonials, etc.)?
2. What has been easier than expected?
3. What has been more difficult than expected?
4. What has gone faster than planned?
5. What has gone slower than planned?
6. What has happened, positive or other, that we didn't anticipate?
7. What are some of the challenges that have arisen (conflict, resource issues, lack of talent, insufficient staffing, etc.)?
   A. What have we learned about ourselves and the process?
   B. What is our plan of action for each of these?
   C. What are the potential benefits of these solutions?
   D. What are the possible costs of these solutions?

8. What have we possibly overlooked?
9. Who has surprised us by stepping forward and/or adapting well? Who has disappointed us by his or her response?
10. Who needs to be affirmed and congratulated? How do we plan to do this?

WHAT TO DO WHEN LEADERSHIP CHANGES

Transitions take a toll on leaders as well as parishioners. Even good changes create stress. It is a common phenomenon for pastors to leave their positions within two years after finishing a major building campaign. Church plants often suffer when the founding pastor leaves within the first ten years of starting the church, because the plethora of changes that go on within the first decade of a congregation's life make it difficult to adjust to the differences in the follow-up pastor. While the trend of longer pastorates is increasing, it is not uncommon for pastors to leave a church before a change initiative has stabilized within its culture. What should an improvement team do to make sure that improvement continues when a pastor or significant lay leader moves midstream?

Obviously a leader would be remiss to lead a congregation into a significant improvement plan without the intent of sticking around. As a general rule, a leader should not plan to lead a church into a large-scale transformation process unless he or she is willing to stay until it is firmly established (until it is part of the church's culture, which can take years) or indefinitely. This is, of course, unless the pastor is one who has just stepped in to minister in an interim or crisis situation. In these situations, the pastor isn't expected to be permanent and so the congregation doesn't necessarily learn to count on him or her.

We know of church leaders who were the proverbial sacrificial lamb. When churches are very difficult to change, occasionally their fearless leader will initiate ideas then get driven off because of his radicalness. The following leader has an easier time catalyzing change because the people feel badly about how they treated his predecessor or they truly see things differently because the trouble they have experienced has induced clarity.

Improvement teams need to know that there is always the risk of losing a pastor. They must be confident in God's leading as well as in their own team effort before they move forward with an improvement initiative. Pastors with the best intentions can make promises of commitment and longevity that they may not be able to keep. You should not base your decision to adopt an improvement plan solely on the basis of a pastor's promise to stick with you to the end. It may not happen. We're all human.

When a pastor leaves in the midst of a major improvement initiative, there are a few things to consider. Some of these may have to do with the structure of your local congregation, but most churches rely heavily on pastoral leadership for their ministry decisions.

How far has the improvement plan been implemented? If the plan is significant yet has just come out of the chute, you may be better off to postpone it for a while to see what the next leader will do. If the plan is not transformational in nature, then lay leaders and staff may be able to drive it forward.

Is there a strong climate for the improvement already in the church? If the atmosphere is ripe for change, you may not need to wait for a new leader. You don't want to lose momentum or let the conditions change for the worse. Conversely, if the improvement is a difficult sell, the best advice is to wait.

How involved was the pastor in the improvement process? Some change issues are strongly lay driven. The pastor may be more of a permission giver and encourager than an actual catalyzer for the improvement. If the pastor was not a driving force behind the improvement, then move forward. If he was key to the plan, then wait to see who fills his shoes.

How dependent was the improvement plan on the pastor's ministry talent? If the new idea is talent driven, such as a worship service requiring a certain style of preaching, then you may need to wait.

Is the change staff driven? Many church structures leave staff up in the air until the next pastor comes. If that is the case, then put the plan on hold.

What are the chances of finding a pastor who will carry the baton the next stretch of the race? While leadership transitions can be tenuous, there are some great stories where the predecessor kept up with the pace of church improvement. If there is a replacement candidate, you may keep the change going in hopes of acquiring his/her talent.

Who will find the next pastoral candidate? If the improvement team or progressive members are influential, chances are you can recruit a pastor who buys into the new vision. If less-change-oriented people are responsible for finding a replacement, the chances are strong that the next pastor will not be so improvement minded, thus rendering the new idea virtually powerless.

While being precarious, pastoral changes can also be good opportunities to move improvement plans ahead. If the former pastor was not a strong leader who allowed the improvement but didn't drive it, a new pastor can be recruited who has the gifting and mindset to move it forward, faster. Congregations desiring significant change or experiencing it in its early stages should be very certain that the next pastor understands and preferably has experience with the anticipated ministry outcome. The new surge of conferences and books seems to create pastors who can articulate relevant ministry but are not able to do it. Many hopeful congregations are disappointed when the pastor they hired is not capable of implementing the style of ministry he so well verbalized during the interview process. If at all possible, research the pastor to make sure he has a track record of doing what you want to see changed in your church.

Some pastors who are nearing retirement age begin to drive a major change effort with the idea of putting their mantle on a protégé. This is a very unselfish approach to leaving a legacy. The best leaders leave organizations able to outlive themselves. When an organization dies when its leader leaves, it does not speak highly of the leader's ability as a leader per se. It is true that God has always used individuals; an anointed ministry will never be the same without the gifts of a specific leader. At the same time, far too many pastors create ministries that are dependent on themselves. A strong leader works to create an organization that stands on its own, much like a parent who prepares a child to live on its own.

The best leaders prepare for their own departures. Older leaders, especially those with long tenure in a church, can create a receptive climate for someone who is better equipped to fill the new vision. An aged leader can cash in some of his years of credit in order to take the heat off of the new guy proposing changes, knowing that the new leader would not have the same credibility for several years.

THREE STEPS FORWARD; TWO STEPS BACK

Now that we've performed our do-diligence of encouraging you to persevere under potentially adverse conditions, we would be remiss if we did not discuss the option of pulling back when you feel that the improvement measures are too large and/or too fast. Sometimes, the best approach is to move three steps forward and two steps back. The idea is to introduce the improvement significantly and then step back almost to square one, so as not to let too much opposition or stress develop. If you blow up a balloon a time or two, it will expand the latex. A flexible balloon will grow larger after it has been stretched a time or two. If you blow up a balloon to full capacity the first time, it's liable to burst.

Here are a few things to consider when you are trying to decide whether to take steps back, not as a permanent retreat but as a temporary adjustment:

- Does the improvement team think we should move back some? Keeping this team in tact as a unified group is essential to long-term impact, so rely heavily on this group for wisdom.
- Are we liable to lose a critical mass of people who are stakeholders if we stay at three steps? If so, we may be compromising long-term results for short-term satisfaction.
- Is it possible that we don't need to move a full three steps (or whatever distance) forward? Why?
- Do the people need more time to adjust to the improvement idea?
- Do we have the opportunity to pull back a bit without losing significant potential? If so, then two steps back may not hurt us.
- Can we enhance the chances of long-term improvement by building trust in the minds of the resistors, so they understand we are concerned with their well-being?
- Are there egos involved that make us unwilling to step back, so that we are insensitive to those who are resisting? Keeping pride in check is vital for both sides of the improvement issue.
- If we take a step back, have we determined how far and for how long? Steps back without follow-up procedures may be equivalent to a retreat.

While backing up two steps can feel discouraging after you have gone forward three, the net gain is one step. You are now one step closer to being the kind of church you want to be than you were before. As in exercise, you give the muscles rest after a workout, and then push them again. Runners, weight trainers, and all sorts of athletes know that you condition a little bit at a time. Any weekend warrior past the age of thirty knows that a game of pick-up softball or basketball is enough to do you in for a while. Going too far, too fast will leave you with an aching back, pulled hamstring, or worse. If you are in your ministry for the long haul, be patient.

Imagine the intimidating idea of writing a 365-page novel. But if you wrote a single page every day, you would have your novel at the end of a year. See the progress you are making in single steps, even though you would like to go further faster.

KILLING THE REMEDY TO SAVE THE PATIENT

We all make mistakes. Excellent surgeons sometimes lose patients because they fail to realize how dire a person's condition is until he is on the operating table. While the goal of this book is to reduce the percentage of misdiagnoses, there are no guarantees. Sometimes, even after laborious effort, improvement plans need to be scrapped. Whether it is incompetent leadership, improper timing, the size of the change suggested, or a strong unwillingness within the congregation to adopt a change, there are times when the chemistry is just not right. Good leadership knows when the risks are too great for a church and willfully concede without losing face or diminishing the validity of the need for improvement.

After all is said and done, stewardship is key. Will the change do more harm or more good? When the ultimate honest answer is "more damage," then the only solution is to pull up stakes and put the improvement plan on the shelf. Pastors and congregational leaders who drive an improvement plan regardless of the cost will answer for it. When ego, stubbornness, or reckless behavior results in the demolition of a viable though nonproductive congregation, no one wins.

Before making a decision to kill the plan, the improvement team and leaders need to agree that it is the only true option. The concession may mean losing progressive members who desired and drove the improvement. It may mean losing the pastor who dreamed of a new vision for the church. The prescription may be a temporary hiatus until certain opinion leaders buy into the innovation or leave. The bottom line is that God does not call leaders to blow up congregations. There is no shame in pulling the plug on a possible improvement plan. Attempting a major improvement is a valiant effort, but deciding not to implement it when it would destroy a congregation is just as honorable.

If the improvement plan would end in a church split, pitting Christian against Christian in a virtual holy war where Christ's reputation in the community is marred, it is more noble to stop. Don't balk at the time and resources invested. Don't regret the decision. Hold your heads up. Know in your heart before God that it was the right decision and then move on. Perhaps nothing will change. The church may die in the coming years. Maybe the pastor or Progressives will move. And perhaps in weeks, months, or years to come, the church will be ready for change and will experience a great harvest because wise leaders knew when to hold off. If God guides you to stop, you can expect his guidance and blessing for doing so.

Unfortunately, we may never know why God seemed to lead us into the change process without seeing it fulfilled. Abraham did not see the dream of a mighty nation completed. Moses never entered Canaan. David didn't get to build the temple he envisioned. We all die with a bit of our music left in us.

IF YOU DON'T LAUGH, YOU'LL CRY

A big part of transition is really about translating ideas between two cultures. Anyone who has tried to accomplish cross-cultural communication understands how challenging, frustrating, and at times humorous that can be. Following are nominees for the Chevy Nova Award. This is given out in honor of the General Motors fiasco in trying to market this car in Central and South America. In Spanish, *No va* means "It doesn't go."

- Coors put its slogan "Turn It Loose" into Spanish, where it was read as "Suffer from Diarrhea."
- When Gerber started selling baby food in Africa, they used the same packaging as in America, with the smiling baby on the label. Later they learned that in Africa, companies routinely put pictures of what's inside on the labels, since many people can't read.
- An American T-shirt maker in Miami printed shirts for the Spanish market that promoted the Pope's visit. Instead of "I saw the Pope" *(el Papa)*, the shirts read, "I Saw the Potato" *(la papa)*.
- Pepsi's "Come Alive with the Pepsi Generation" translated into "Pepsi Brings Your Ancestors Back from the Grave" in Chinese.
- The Coca-Cola name in China was first read as *"Kekoukela,"* meaning, "Bite the wax tadpole" or "Female horse stuffed with wax," depending on the dialect. Coke then researched forty thousand characters to find a phonetic equivalent to *"kokou kole,"* which translated into "Happiness in the mouth."
- When American Airlines wanted to advertise its new leather first-class seats in the Mexican market, it translated its "Fly in Leather" campaign literally, which meant "Fly Naked" *(vuela en cuero)* in Spanish!

God has given us the gift of laughter to dissolve many of life's tensions. Far too many of us take ourselves too seriously and God not seriously enough. Sometimes we misunderstand the importance of laughter and levity. The latter means to rise, to elevate. Change and improvement tensions can get you down. Reminding ourselves that God is in control is all we need at times to chuckle at a communication piece gone bad, or to laugh at how poorly we pulled off an initial improvement idea, or to smile at the way we justify our own narrow views.

While laughter at others' expense is never a plus, laughing at ourselves and our attempts to do our best can give us great mileage. Defensive people tend to be easily offended if they think we are poking fun at them, so be careful about "us/them" jokes, but find mutual experiences where levity can lighten the load. Few things cut tension more than laughter and smiling. Jesus sprinkled his talks with comical hyperboles and word pictures. Most of us miss them because comedy tends to be cultural and we lose it in the translation. Imagine the laughter when the people imagined a proud man swallowing a camel!

You may want to consider introducing funny mistakes or oversights as part of your improvement team gatherings. Some of them may be suitable for congregational broadcast. Enjoy the process. Did you know that humor and humility are from the same root word? People who take themselves too seriously and who struggle with pride usually have a difficult time having fun and laughing at their own expense. No one is perfect. Enjoy your blunders. Since comedy is at times enough to get us through a difficult time during an improvement process, humor really is serious business.

> An adventure is only an inconvenience rightly understood. An inconvenience is only an adventure wrongly understood.
>
> —G. K. CHESTERTON

QUESTIONS AND ANSWERS

Q: Everything is going so smoothly as we roll out our improvement plan. What are we missing?

A: Yippee! Maybe nothing. There are times when the perfect combination—a receptive congregation, a primed leader, the hand of God, and the right improvement idea—come together to form a synergistic victory with little loss of blood. On the old *A-Team* TV show, Hannibal used to say at the conclusion, "I love it when a plan comes together."

While we hope your transition continues smoothly, we suggest that you not congratulate yourselves prematurely. Don't assume that the improvement has become a part of your culture just because the early results look good. Also—and no one wants to hear this, but please take this recommendation seriously—consider the possibility that you waited so long for the ripe environment for improvement that you wasted potential fruit, letting it rot on the vine. If you decide this is the case, and the reason for your ease now, think of how you might increase the harvest next time by pursuing changes before it is so easy.

Finally, be careful not to tell others how easy it is to "do" change. With so many bleeding leaders and improvement teams struggling with changes in their local congregations, there's a fine line between hope sharing and discouragement giving when their situation is not as fruitful.

Q: I'm a pastor and I cannot guarantee that I will stick with this church through the entire improvement process. What should I do?

A: Whew, that's a tough one. The bottom line is that you need to seek God's wisdom and do his will. While that may sound trite, you are responsible for God's will in your life as well as the overall guidance of your present congregation. The deeper questions have more to do with issues of timing and why. For example, is your spouse's employment a factor, or do you have retirement plans pending, or is a job opportunity headed your way in the next year or two? If you have a definite time line, you may need to be open with your leadership and congregation and limit your involvement. You can still help create an atmosphere receptive to change for the next person without committing to overseeing specific changes yourself.

If the issue isn't other opportunities, then you might want to examine why you cannot commit. Do you believe you lack the talents to fulfill the new vision? Do you feel overwhelmed with the task at hand? Do you have the wrong temperament for enduring the potential resistance to change?

There is certainly integrity in not promising more than you can deliver. You may intentionally design your improvement team to be lay driven so that you serve as the catalyst and permission giver but not the actual improvement leader. The less sure you are about your length of service in that church, the more you can empower others to do the job so that less is dependent on your presence.

Q: Our pastor has only a few years remaining until retirement. Even though he talks about the need to change, we don't think he is able or willing to pay the price for such an involved process. What do we do?

A: Lame-duck administrations tend to be status-quo oriented. When an individual's personal preference becomes the dominant motivator of what does and does not get accomplished in a job or ministry, the whole loses for the sake of the one. Although you need to be respectful of your pastor and his position, you need to convey to him your desire to move forward. If timing is right and resources are available, you might want to consider hiring a predecessor now who will inherit the position after the pastor retires. This staff member can begin to develop an improvement plan, partnering with the retiring minister.

Another option is to pay the retiring pastor to be pastor emeritus and change his job description, allowing the church to hire an official replacement who is change oriented.

If resources are not an option, then lovingly talking to the pastor may allow brainstorming on what should change down the road. An amiable pastor may seek a retirement type of church in which to spend his golden years. He may also allow lay leaders to drive an improvement plan. Honest, respectful communication is vital. If a pastor has bought into a retirement mindset and wants to linger, it can be next to impossible to catalyze significant improvement within a congregation. Progressive types may do best to find another church that is more responsive to their innovations.

Q: Gulp. We bit off more than we can chew. Do we spit it out or risk choking to death? When do you apply the Heimlich maneuver?

A: The thing that makes transition processes so challenging is that the subjective element in each one is very high. The bottom line is that leadership and improvement teams must determine what is best for the congregation. If there is an overall sense of chaos that results in paralysis or shock, you may want to bring in a consultant. A consultant might be a church-change agent, a respected denominational official, or a pastoral acquaintance who has gone through a church improvement process. Many congregations wait too long to do this. It is better to be proactive than reactive—the money is better spent.

If in doubt, slow down. As we learned in the change formula, time is a significant factor. When churches get into dire situations, it is often because the leadership competence and congregational readiness factors were misperceived. Stop. Call a spontaneous, overnight retreat. Pay the price of a short-term getaway to avoid a long-term mistake. When your team is gathered, consider together: What is going wrong? What is going right? On what or whom are we basing our perceptions that we are choking? Do we need to yell "uncle" or stick with it?

If necessary, gather the opinion leaders together and call a truce for the sake of seeking God's will as a team. Assuming that the choking feeling is created by relationship tensions, open and loving communication will take you a long way.

Creating a compromise may be sufficient to keep you from choking to death. Avoid reckless moves in hopes of gaining some ground before the movement grinds to a halt. Faith involves risk, but gambling is not a spiritual sport. Seek the wisdom of experienced practitioners as well as those with the gift of discernment regarding God's will.

> It doesn't work to leap a twenty-foot chasm in two ten-foot jumps.
>
> —American Proverb

Discussion Starters

1. Think of a challenging experience in your personal past and identify the ABC (Q) Zones.
2. Think of a challenging experience from your church life and identify the ABC (Q) Zones.
3. What elements from the Channel of Chaos, if any, is your church experiencing at this time?
4. What are the positive hopes and expectations that you can focus on during the tough times?
5. How would you assess your congregation's response to the improvement so far?
6. What is going well? What is not going well?
7. How is leadership handling resistance?
8. Who is a potential consultant you could engage in case the going gets tough?

Contemplation

He said to another man, "Follow me."

But the man replied, "Lord, first let me go and bury my father."

Jesus said to him, "Let the dead bury their own dead, but you go and proclaim the kingdom of God."

Still another said, "I will follow you, Lord; but first let me go back and say good-by to my family."

Jesus replied, "No one who puts his hand to the plow and looks back is fit for service in the kingdom of God."

Scripture

Read Matthew 4.

DEVOTIONAL THOUGHT

In Matthew 4, Jesus was led into the desert to confront the enemy, who encouraged him to defer to his comfort zones and rely on his own power, regardless of God's will. Jesus had to confront the temptation. Jesus then went into the community and called out men who would become his disciples. When he invited them, they left their jobs and followed him.

Before we follow Jesus, we have to leave something behind. We bet that when Jesus called some of those men, the fishing nets looked pretty good. They were proven, familiar, and far more sensible than an upstart preacher who'd just walked in from the desert. What kind of renegades were these twelve spontaneous, irresponsible men who jeopardized their livelihoods and therefore their families? Others did not choose to follow. They said they were willing, but they kept one hand on the plow and an eye in the rearview mirror.

Jesus has the gall to ask us to follow him into new ministries and experiences and to not look back. Maybe he knows that if we keep looking back when the plowing gets tough, we'll run away. Then we'll miss the harvest he has in store for us.

Prayer

Dear God, I know you told me to follow you, to leave my comfort zones and proven strategies of the past, but I can't help but want to look back. I need you to give me courage to keep my gaze forward, not in the rearview mirror. Life was meant to be a forward process. Keep my focus on you. Show me today how my stubbornness and fear are hindering the establishment of your kingdom. I really want to do your will. Amen.

CHAPTER 11

The Golden Years: Celebrating Victories and Cutting Losses

Change has a bad reputation in our society. But it isn't all bad, not by any means. In fact, change is necessary in life, to keep us moving . . . to keep us growing . . . to keep us interested. Imagine life without change. It would be static . . . boring . . . dull.

—DENNIS O'GRADY

My second wife, Barbara, and I (Gene) have had quite a ride. We were married at our midweek worship service on January 13, 1993. The night was unforgettable. The attendees didn't know they were coming to a wedding. We had our service's usual worship time and baptisms. Then one of my best friends got up for the teaching time and said, "I know I'm supposed to teach right now, but I'm not going to. Instead, I have two major announcements. Number one, Gene Appel and Barbara Cowan are engaged. [Everyone applauded enthusiastically.] And number two, you're at their wedding." There were gasps and shock. Everybody thought he was kidding until family members who had flown in from all over the country started a procession down the aisle. We had a celebration. It was a mountaintop experience with this church family who had walked with me through some dark valleys.

My life is filled to capacity with countless blessings that have come as a result of going through various Channels of Chaos and emerging the better because of God's grace and involvement. For most of us who emerge from the transition of change, the other side is so rich.

Anything worth pursuing is at times challenging, painful, and costly. Whether it's following Christ, raising a family, or starting a new business venture, hardly anything significant in life is easy. While browsing in a monastery bookstore once, I (Alan) saw a sticker that said, "No Pain—No Gain." I chuckled to myself, because it was one of those slogans you'd presume would hang in a sweaty workout gym, not in a place of solitude and spiritual growth. But when I thought about it, what better place to explain the process of soul growth?

Every farmer knows that after the backbreaking, risk-taking seasons of planting and cultivating comes the abundant time of harvest. Some of the most rewarding, fulfilling, and life-changing results can come out of improvement strategies when they are effectively deployed. As someone said, "You don't pay the price; you enjoy the price."

If you have a strong sense of what needs to happen, we have said, an effective transition plan will help you obtain the desired fruit. Then you will have something to celebrate: You will have stories of abundance to tell because your church will be revitalized for the next level of ministry. Growth requires us to continue changing to allow for more and different effectiveness, so don't think you're done just because you've made one major transition. The fun part of ministry comes when you see lives changed and the enthusiasm in the eyes and words of those who have experienced the touch of God in their lives. As Gene and others who have undergone significant church improvement projects testify, the joys on the other side of the change process are well worth the pain of getting there. Ministry fulfillment is at its deepest level when the flow of the Holy Spirit is strongest. Visit nearly any vibrant congregation and you can simply feel the positive energy and excitement as you walk in the doors. This attracts more people as well as heats up lukewarm believers. The result is stories to be told.

POSTCARD FROM THE PROMISED LAND

Dear Uncle Ezekiel:

Greetings! I hope you are doing well. I'm so sorry that you were not able to leave Egypt with us, but we understand your desire to take care of your aging mother, God rest her soul. It has been a long time since my last letter. So much has happened since Moses led us out of our past. There have been so many incredible changes. Many people have died and left, but we are now inhabiting the Land of Promise. The giants have been here, to battle and challenge. But we've confronted our fears and the fruit has been worth every bit of the hassle. I can't tell you how thrilling it is!

As we estimated, Canaan flows with milk and honey. We are conquering strongholds, seeing God at work in our midst, and having the time of our lives in the process. Oh, Uncle, I wish you could experience what we're experiencing. My heart goes out to you in that land we once called home. We'll try to keep in touch.

Your loving nephew,
Caleb

THE POWER OF STORY

As you begin to make progress with your ministry improvement plan, the most powerful way to address the doubts of those who question the innovation is to tell stories of lives positively affected by the ideas implemented. Direct confrontation can create conflict and drain energy. When we miscommunicate during a conflict, we can lose ground. But nothing creates a positive attitude in a church culture more than the testimony of a changed life. Harvesting early feedback as you progress is important, because momentum takes time. While people can get caught up into varying opinions about style, methods, timing, resources, and structure, who can argue with a personal witness? More than any single transition element, good storytelling has the power to advance a cause.

When you think about it, the Bible is primarily a storybook of changed lives, showing what happens when people respond, with obedience or disobedience, to the sovereign God. One of the most overlooked tools in the church is that of storytelling. We tend to grossly underestimate stories' impact on those who hear them.

Stories impact listeners because they touch the emotional center of each person—the heart. By nature, we are primarily emotional beings. No matter how logical and intellectual we perceive ourselves to be, we make a lot of minor and major decisions in life based on emotion. One of the best ways to see this is how people respond to change. Conflict and resistance are rarely intellectual objections but nearly always emotional. Therefore when we want to initiate change, we need to do so via the heart and emotions, which good stories touch.

Every pastor knows how people pay attention when he tells a good story. Drowsy countenances wake up when the sermon concept gets an illustration.

Nothing beats a word picture because we think in pictures, not principles. We need illustrations to best understand concepts. When innovation doubters hear testimonials from people they can see, meet, and run into at the store, the impact goes straight to the heart.

Stories are also powerful because it's hard to argue with a testimony. In post-modern times, when truth with a capital T is rare, individual truth based on personal experience has greater impact than ever. People are very slow to reject individual experiences. How can you deny what I have witnessed? Who are you to invalidate my perceptions? Thus, legitimate life-change stories put to rest many naysayers who buck a new idea.

Stories are somewhat tangible results of conceptual truth. For years as a child, I (Alan) loved the game of baseball and watched it on television. It was not until I became an adult that I got to attend my first major-league game. The firsthand experience was so different from the broadcast version. The sights, smells, and crowd noise all added to the experience. Attending the game took baseball from concept and fantasy to reality. In the same way, while we talk a lot about faith, hope, and love, we realize how messy and theoretical these ideas can be. But when a person gives testimony to how these and other concepts have trans-formed his life, we all celebrate to know that they really work. Putting flesh to our faith is a significant accomplishment.

The church culture is certainly rich with stories. We value the role of story, because most of us have at least one ourselves. Our faith over the centuries has consisted of stories of saints, sacrifice, failure, repentance, love, challenge, hope, and of course, love. Most of us remember testimony meetings where people ran-domly stood and told about recent God-sightings in their lives. At baptismal services, we hear life events.

We need to understand that most of the people in our churches really do have good change intentions. They want to help people. They want people to make a life-changing connection with God. In short, they have good hearts. When we start telling stories of those who have made a God-connection via the ministry improvement, even the strongest naysayer will have a hard time saying a change is not worth the effort. When we do not provide the stories, it is much easier for doubters to object, pointing out the lack of evident fruit.

Success stories create excitement. You have to be a pretty stodgy person not to be moved by a story of a transformed life, whether it be salvation, a bad mar-riage salvaged, or a miracle of employment or health. We all like to see progress.

Life is so challenging that when a peer has a breakthrough, it musters hope in the rest of us. When the touch of a church improves lives by the power of God, we want to celebrate. And celebrations small and large generate excitement and enthusiasm.

Jesus knew the momentum that testimonials can create, which ironically is why he sometimes told people not to tell others what he had done for them.

> A man with leprosy came to him and begged him on his knees, "If you are willing, you can make me clean."
>
> Filled with compassion, Jesus reached out his hand and touched the man. "I am willing," he said. "Be clean!" Immediately the leprosy left him and he was cured.
>
> Jesus sent him away at once with a strong warning: "See that you don't tell this to anyone. But go, show yourself to the priest and offer the sacrifices that Moses commanded for your cleansing, as a testimony to them." Instead he went out and began to talk freely, spreading the news. As a result, Jesus could no longer enter a town openly but stayed outside in lonely places. Yet the people still came to him from everywhere. (Mark 1:40–45)

You might think that since Jesus came to establish God's kingdom, he would want everyone to tell all about their experiences with the Messiah. But Jesus knew the power of story. He realized that when people told their friends about their life transformation, the crowds would keep him from doing God's will. People were forever pressuring him to be their political king. Jesus frequently pushed back from the frenzied crowds who wanted to promote their agenda, not the Father's. They did not understand.

We can use stories, this same energy-generating method, to create positive momentum for accepting improvement.

HOW TO TELL A GOOD STORY

Most of us are not naturally exciting storytellers, but there are methods we can learn.

First, *use the right format.* Even the most interesting story can lose credibility if it is poorly told. Every story is different and should be told in a way that best fits the situation. Very few people can get up in front of a congregation and effectively give their testimony in a way that keeps interest and gets to the point. If you find such gifted people, let them loose with a little bit of coaching. Make sure the pastor or host stays nearby, just in case a person needs help concluding.

Many people do well via an interview format, where a host asks questions to which the person can respond. If you decide to try this, find a good interviewer to assist. Don't assume the pastor should do the job.

Technology provides some wonderful possibilities through different types of media. Creating a video of testimonies using music and graphics can inspire a media-savvy congregation. The extra sizzle enhances the professionalism of the testimony as well.

Written testimonies with photos can be passed around and shared with friends—opinion leaders can be very productive with this tool. Audiocassettes with stories from a church that successfully adopted a change are a great possibility for commuters.

Second, before you use any story, *validate it and get permission for its use.* If you tell the story of a person who is living a double life or who fabricated a testimony out of guilt or a desire for attention, it could backfire. The grapevine has a way of proving or disproving a person's word. The church at large has been guilty of putting sensational conversion stories on the front page before the convert has had an opportunity to be conformed in his or her new faith. We need to make sure we don't ask people to say more than is legitimately true in hopes of creating a story line that is more dramatic. I (Alan) blew it once by telling a person's story in a newsletter without obtaining her specific permission. She took offense and left the church because I had not communicated my intent.

Third, *sell God, not the church.* The best stories turn the attention to God, not to a person in the church or even a ministry innovation. If the latter is the main focus, people will begin to think the storyteller has been coached or planted to promote the innovation; the story will sour. Rather, let people mention how their lives were changed via another believer or a ministry improvement, but make sure the primary emphasis is on what God has done. Your goal, after all, is to elevate the awareness of God's power to transform lives through relevant ministry methods. Even if a direct connection is not made, people will tie in the testimonial with the ministry innovation. The subtle approach is usually best.

Use stories often. Make them a regular part of your worship services. Let people get used to them in different formats and varying lengths and angles. Most churches would do well to tell as many stories as they can harvest. In order to avoid monotony, employ a variety of methods to communicate. Use video clips, live interviews, written testimonials, small-group storytelling, and your own creative means. Storytelling used to be one of the primary ways people conveyed the gospel. Today, though, we rely heavily upon preaching, teaching, and impersonal illustrations. Some of the best illustrations are sitting in the congregation, especially those people who have been positively touched by an improved ministry.

APPLICATION TOOLBOX

Knowing what to tell and what to skip in a testimonial is important. You don't want to leave the good stuff on the editing floor, but you also want to get the most "bang for your buck." Here is an investigative reporter's outline for examining a story line.

- Who is the person whose story you are telling? Why was he/she selected?
- How long have you or someone in the church known this person?
- How did he/she find out about the church?
- What about the improved ministry that attracted this person?
- What was it specifically that created a desire for change in the person's life?
- What has changed in this person's life?
- Is there a way to validate this change (friends, referring person, fellow ministry team members)? Have others noticed a change in the person's life?
- What excites the person about his/her relationship with God? This church? The ministry improvement?
- Would the person be best at giving a live interview, giving a videotaped interview, or having a story written about his/her life?

CELEBRATE AND REWARD VICTORIES

Telling stories is just one way to celebrate victories and reward growth. The improvement team is responsible, when progress is made toward the improvement objectives, for making sure that adequate celebrations take place within ministries and the whole church. Throughout the Bible, God tells his people to celebrate various holy days, festivals, and victories. For some reason, modern churches have all but forgotten about celebrating God's work in our midst.

While corporations throw huge parties when they are promoting a new product line, celebrating a major accomplishment, or casting vision in a creative way, our charitable, nonprofit mentality often views these as wasteful and secular. What more important accomplishments can we revel in than those for the kingdom?

> I tell you, there is rejoicing in the presence of the angels of God over one sinner who repents. (Luke 15:10)

> But the father said to his servants, "Quick! Bring the best robe and put it on him. Put a ring on his finger and sandals on his feet. Bring the fattened calf and kill it. Let's have a feast and celebrate. For this son of mine was dead and is alive again; he was lost and is found." So they began to celebrate. (Luke 15:22–24)

> Suppose one of you has a hundred sheep and loses one of them. Does he not leave the ninety-nine in the open country and go after the lost sheep until he finds it? And when he finds it, he joyfully puts it on his shoulders and goes home. Then he calls his friends and neighbors together and says, "Rejoice with me; I have found my lost sheep." I tell you that in the same way there will be more rejoicing in heaven over one sinner who repents than over ninety-nine righteous persons who do not need to repent. (Luke 15:4–7)

> They will tell of the power of your awesome works,
>   and I will proclaim your great deeds.
> They will celebrate your abundant goodness
>   and joyfully sing of your righteousness. (Ps. 145:6–7)

HOW TO REWARD PEOPLE SKILLFULLY

Besides putting to death the myth that Christianity is boring and stoic, celebrating engages people to highlight what is important in kingdom work. Our friends at Leadership Training Network, a lay-ministry-equipping arm of Leadership Network, teach about motivating and rewarding people according to what temperament they reflect. There are Relators, Promoters, Analyzers, and Directors.[1] These correspond with the popular version of the four personality temperaments.

If you are familiar with these, you can quickly adapt different rewards to the appropriate temperaments, thus making them more meaningful to the receivers.

Relators enjoy approval and value getting along with others. Reward these people with personal and heartfelt affirmations, acknowledging that you're glad they're on the team and recognizing their part in the process. Progressive appreciation, as opposed to one big celebration, goes a long way with these people.

Promoters enjoy attention and value being appreciated. They like to have fun and are the people who celebrate publicly. Share some rays from the limelight. Balloons, plaques, inspiring compliments, and confetti tell Promoters they are appreciated.

Analyzers specialize in details and value getting things right. The best way to celebrate an Analyzer's ministry is to pay attention to the details, take time to dialogue, recognize the genius of order and structure, and genuinely acknowledge their role. Too much up-front hype and hoopla may backfire when esteeming this kind of person.

Directors enjoy being in charge and they value accomplishments. These people often sacrifice a lot and are self-starters. You show appreciation for them by unleashing projects under their control and then recognizing the fruit of their accomplishments. Another respected leader esteeming the Director in front of the team is perceived very positively.

Knowing the varying temperaments and how they perceive recognition is key to effective celebrations. Make sure as a team that the person who designs the celebrations considers the differences and does not think solely from his or her point of view.

Churches can employ an array of celebratory ideas that do not need to cost significant money. Thank-you items such as flowers, gift certificates, plaques, articles in the church newsletter, and parties are all tangible ways of recognizing hard work. The primary objective is to add fun to your ministry efforts. You can applaud people's enduring the stress of changes in creative ways. Hopefully, our primary motivation is to submit to each other out of reverence for Christ. At the same time, effective leaders know that people enjoy celebrating accomplishments and appreciate heartfelt thanks. For most of us, it doesn't take much to make us feel good about what we've done.

THE LIFE SPAN OF A CHURCH

I (Alan) grew up on a farm in southwest Iowa. The rural communities there and throughout the Midwest have suffered significantly in the last two decades. Traveling back to these once viable, small villages, I remember a sign that says, "Will the last one out of town please turn off the lights?"

There are people in every organization, churches included, who are called to turn off the lights. Not every church is healthy enough or has the resources or potential to undergo transformational change—nor is it God's will for every congregation to do that. While it seems almost sacrilegious for those of us with a church-growth, church-health mindset to suggest that some churches ought not change, it is true.

Every church has a life span. Outside of the return of Christ, all churches we know of today will eventually come to an end, including Central Christian and Scottsdale Family Church. The Willow Creeks, Saddlebacks, Ginghamsburgs, Community of Joys, and other teaching and model ministries that now attract so much attention due to their health and vibrancy will someday pass away. We just don't know the time, place, or cause of death.

Just as people are born, live, and die, organizations go through birth, life, and death as well. While we understand that humans have only so many years of earthly life, we assume that organizations should be able to go on forever. The only organizations that survive for more than a generation or two in our current culture are those that consistently renew themselves. When technology, politics, economics, or any number of factors disallow an organization to change, it eventually dies. The same is true of local churches.

Just as it is quite silly to see older people behaving like adolescents, it is silly and sad to watch congregations whose days are over clutch fearfully to the hope of turning things around when that potential has passed. We must learn how to go out with dignity, honorably closing our doors when our time has come. By clinging desperately to our hopeless future, we do a disservice to our people and to other viable ministries that could benefit from redistributed church assets.

While the focus of this book has been on church change, we must face the fact that many of our churches will not change and thus will ebb. Instead of fearing the end or neurotically avoiding the inevitable, we can spend the golden years of a church's life with joy.

One-seventh of all churches represent more than 50 percent of church attendance in America. Of the three hundred thousand congregations in the United States, approximately one-third are barely surviving.[2] Thousands of congregations across the country are on life-support systems. Dozens are joining them weekly. When is it right to pull the plug, remove the artificial life support, and let a local body meet a peaceful, respectful eternity? This is a very difficult question, because there are always people who are finding some sort of emotional, physical, or spiritual benefit from even a wilting congregation. Defenders of the declining church justify its existence with a number of defenses:

- Some people do not fit into the larger church.
- Some people do not feel comfortable in the contemporary church that offers a different style of worship.
- These people have invested so much time, energy, and resources into their church that they deserve to see it to the end.
- There is still potential ministry that can be done in the community.
- Maybe God will bring about a revival. If we pull the plug, we are taking away that chance. Christ raised Lazarus from the dead, didn't he?
- We need the facility for our day care, after-school program, and community meetings.
- We count each congregation statistically, and if we closed all the churches that are not making it, the numerical decline would make our district/conference look bad.
- We have a few older people in the church who started the church. Who are we to say their time is over? I'm not going to be the one who tells them that.

While all of these arguments are potentially viable, they reflect the resistance of people within the churches and the governing agencies outside the congregations to call it quits. As in physical life, we tend to be much better at celebrating our entrance into the world than we are our exit from it. Before church leaders continue to pour valuable assets into a congregation that is on its way out, we need to consider the big picture.

The key question to wrestle with is, *Are we being good stewards?* Stewardship is a primary biblical principle. God is shrewd at business, expecting a healthy return on his investment. As managers of his assets, both individually and corporately, we have to consider the investment-versus-return ratio. The size of attendance and income are not necessarily signs of life and vitality. Huge corporations that employ thousands of people and process millions of dollars can still be very unprofitable. We should not base church viability solely on how many are attending and how much money we are raising. The bigger question is, *What are we doing with what God has given us?*

When a church fritters away its resources, spending savings accounts, selling off assets, and conducting major fundraisers just to survive, it is likely wasting a valuable opportunity to minister through another congregation. When we invest every last dollar in mere survival, we lose the opportunity to extend our life to a new congregation or to invest it in an existing church that is doing well.

Most states allow and encourage citizens to carry donor cards, signifying that upon their death, their organs can be harvested to help other persons live. In this way, our physical body can, in a sense, go on living for many more years. Congregations can do the same by admitting when their effectiveness has ended and seeing that their resources are spread to those who can use them.

There comes a point of diminishing return in all organizations, when turn-around is far from likely and the existing resources could be reinvested in areas that are yielding fruit. Every church is different. Determining that point is a matter of measuring:

- Viable leadership: Are there leader gifts in the church to provide hope for change or a future?
- Community depreciation: If we hold onto our assets, will there be anything worth selling in order to reinvest in a few years?
- Potential ministry investment opportunities: Is there a viable ministry we know of that could greatly benefit from what we might pass on to it?
- Distribution of people into nearby faith communities: Are we the only ones left in ministry in our area or are there other churches that could care for the needs of our existing flock?
- God's will: Have we sought the face of God and asked him for wisdom regarding our future?

The fact is, what we perceive to be an ending is sometimes a beginning. Jesus told us that "unless a kernel of wheat falls to the ground and dies, it remains only a single seed. But if it dies, it produces many seeds" (John 12:24). In other words, what we view as the end of a church can also be a time of new birth for a church plant or for a struggling ministry with great potential.

Obviously, merely throwing money at a church never makes it viable. Church governance must research places to invest the ministry assets from one congregation to another. Far too many denominational agencies have divided money among several struggling congregations, which is wasteful, instead of taking the larger amount and investing it in one viable church that is reaching its community. We foolishly withhold resources from new churches that appear to be doing well, assuming they do not need the funds, keeping them from even greater fruitfulness.

Don't kill the golden goose. Business and professional sports have taught us that investing in good coaches and players makes a marked difference in outcome. Spreading money among a lot of mediocre players is not going to produce a winning season. Thus stewardship means putting our resources where they are most likely to produce a profit.

WHEN THE PAIN OF CHANGE MIGHT NOT BE WORTH IT

Just because a church isn't ready for change doesn't mean that it is on its deathbed. But in these days of rapid change, such a church is headed there much faster than one that confronts its need to improve on a continual basis. If there were such a thing as the Fountain of Youth, the church equivalent would be a readiness for continual improvement and change. Some congregations are not ready for change and therefore are actively or passively on their way to their own end. Here are some ways to evaluate whether a church should go through the potential stress and pain of change. Don't attempt innovation:

- *When the community makeup doesn't justify the change* (ethnikitis). Because most ministries are culturally sensitive, they are not prone to relate to more than one or two subcultures. When the critical mass of people within a ministry target leave an area, the chances are slim that kind of church will exist for long.

- *When the leadership is not willing to confront the dysfunction.* Whether it is a pastoral or lay-leader issue, church leadership that is unwilling to investigate and deal with ministry dysfunctions has pretty much doomed a congregation to failure. This does not mean that death is near. Many dysfunctional congregations last for years because of their resources. But for all practical purposes, they are not good candidates for change.

- *When a majority of influencers are against the change.* A pastor has to wonder whether or not it is God's will to bring about significant change in a church where a critical mass of opinion leaders are against the improvement idea. This does not mean that a pastor or other progressive leaders cannot intentionally prepare the congregation through education and inspiration, but to knowingly pursue improvement that will inevitably divide a congregation is rarely the will of God. Leaders who pick such fights would seem to be either bullies or sufferers from a martyr complex.

- *When a split would mar the future or defame Christ in a community.* Even people who never enter our church doors hear about our congregations. They watch our members on the little league fields, in restaurants and stores, and at school functions. When the grapevine spreads more about how inner fighting is tearing up our church than about what wonderful things God is doing, the kingdom is not advanced. Giving Christianity another black eye by pitting member against member is not God's will.

- *When the church structure does not allow the change agent to lead.* When the change agent is a staff member or a pastor who is called merely to teach and manage, or a lay leader who does not have the authority to bring about change, then improvement has been bridled. Some organizations are designed to maintain so strongly that they reject any person or idea that bucks the status quo. While inoculation against foreign bodies at times preserves the organism, it also kills the organism by attacking friendly entities not yet accepted.

Churches that have these or similar characteristics have all but signed their congregation's death certificate. The issue is now a matter of when, where, and who.

CONGREGATIONAL HOSPICE

Throughout the book, we have said that the changes don't affect us as much as the transitions. Death is a transition, so in reality, declining churches *are* changing—they are dying. As believers, most of us do not fear the afterlife; it's the transition that worries us a bit. Heaven is a wonderful place, but how we get there can be frightening. What do you do when the doctor says you have terminal cancer? You go through the grieving process, but once through the stages, it is possible to get to a point of peace and tranquility for the life you have lived.

There are several things a congregation can do when it knows its best days are behind it and it is unlikely it will ever turn the corner of significant improvement.

- *Consider helping plant a new congregation.* Let a new church use your facilities. Fund the new congregation and/or provide resources as a mentor might. This is one way of living beyond yourselves without significantly moving from your current status. Even if your church is small, you can partner with others who in turn help new churches get started.

- *Set criteria for pulling the plug.* Since the chances are strong that your congregation will never get better, you need to establish some tangible levels of money, attendance, and general ministry health that once reached, mean you will close your doors. Putting time and quantity into retirement plans shows that you are responsible about the decision not to change.

- *Turn over resources to more viable ministries.* You may loan money, staff, office space, expertise, contacts, and other items to a ministry partner that is prospering.

- *Develop a plan for the staff.* At times, congregations and denominational agencies feel obliged to take care of staff to the detriment of church resources. Establishing a plan that addresses timing, salary, and retirement and/or relocation benefits for existing staff during a retirement transition allows the church to do what is best for itself. A church should not exist to fund staff salaries/positions.

- *Develop a will and testament.* Leadership can write a formal charter explaining when the church should close and how the remaining assets should be divided. (This document may be influenced by legal and denominational parameters.) The time to agree on a final will is before life-support systems need to be implemented. Progressive and gifted leaders often leave a church before it closes, so getting these items in place prior to their leaving makes the last days more productive.

RETIRING A CHURCH

An acquaintance of ours, Tom Chambers, is a former NBA star. Not long ago, the Phoenix Suns retired his number during a ceremony at America West Arena in Phoenix, lifting his jersey to the rafters. No one on the Phoenix Suns will wear his number again, celebrating Tom's unique contribution to the sport.

The idea of closing a church seems so final, so sad, so negative. The reason for the inordinate amount of difficulty we have in closing dying churches is how we perceive them. When we think of closing as a death, we fail to consider the enduring ministry created by past influence. Over the life span of a typical church, many, many people are transformed by the gospel of Christ. When a church closes its doors, it is not finished. The impact of its ministry lingers long in the lives of those who have heard the Scriptures, prayed to God, taught a child in Sunday school, held the hand of a grieving member, and lived together in a faith community. Retirement is a transition. When a church retires, its influence does not cease. It continues, decentralized through the lives of the people it has impacted over the years.

To some people, this may sound like a lot of mushy talk that distracts from the painful reality of shutting down a faith community. But the only time we truly "shut down" a faith community is when it no longer influences people. This being the case, many existing churches shut down years ago. Like the bumper sticker says, "Elvis is dead. Deal with it." Many of our churches have died, and we need to deal with it. But the death of a church at the end of its life span is really more of a retirement, because the influence of the church continues through the lives of people who have moved, died, or now attend other faith communities.

Chances are, nearly every Christian who begins attending your church was influenced by some other church. Countless great church leaders attended churches that are now either nonexistent or mere remnants of what they used to be. It is very shortsighted to say that a church's impact fades at the church's retirement. We're all portable, temporary, passing. "Now listen, you who say, 'Today or tomorrow we will go to this or that city, spend a year there, carry on business and make money.' Why, you do not even know what will happen tomorrow. What is your life? You are a mist that appears for a little while and then vanishes" (James 4:13–14).

Before a church dwindles to nothing, it is best to celebrate its life with a respectful retirement celebration. A retirement party is a celebratory event that pays homage to previous leaders, significant accomplishments of the church in the past, and major players throughout the years. Wouldn't it be great if there was a ministry designed to throw these parties with media, sizzle, and fanfare, financially endowed so that even the most humble faith community could be heralded as a place where lives were changed eternally? Well, there is such a ministry. It is called heaven. But until we gather there, we can do our part to bring a slice of heaven to earth as we turn what appears to be a defeat into a victory.

Look at what your church has accomplished over the years in the lives of the people who have been a direct and indirect part of its influence. A retirement event is the opportunity to sing the praises of major milestones. Zig Ziglar is noted for telling audiences that he and his wife are celebrating their fiftieth anniversary. People always applaud. "I didn't say we've been married for fifty years," Ziglar admits. "But I heard that these anniversaries are so special, we decided to celebrate ours early." Perhaps you'll want to throw a retirement bash before everyone is gone. If there is no one present to attend the celebration, you have waited too long.

Make the effort to create a pictorial walk down memory lane. Invite former pastors to participate in the rally. Hire special singers, city officials, and local residents to hear eulogies of what God has done through this local faith community. You can create gifts that celebrate the church's impact, whether they are bookmarks, plaques, or even bricks of the building. Bring glory to God. Let people taste the good things he has done through this local parish over the years. Invite testimonials.

As pastors, we have performed a number of memorial services. Most clergy will tell you that the funeral for a Christian is a hopeful, celebratory event. In the same way, there is little room for tears and sadness at a church retirement ceremony. From outward appearances, we may be tempted to whisper, "Oh how sad, this church is a fraction of the congregation I knew. What happened to it? Too bad it ended like this."

That's not honorable. When the Phoenix Suns retired Tom Chambers's jersey number, no one said, "Poor Tom. He just doesn't have it anymore. What happened to him? What went wrong?" Everyone knew that every athlete has a season of top vitality. The same is true of churches. Every congregation has its life span. Some die of old age, some "prematurely," but nearly all have positive impacts over the course of their lives. Count the blessings. Let go of the losses. Plan a "Yeah, God" event.

The goal of this service is to bring a conclusion to a church with a noble history. Finish well. Go out with dignity. Let the community see God's people in a joyful, celebratory mood. Too many churches go out with a whimper instead of a victory chant. Make people glad they saw the finale. Don't let the talk of the community be, "Wow, they're closed down. I wonder what happened?" Pull out the stops. Take out an ad in the paper, thanking everyone for years of ministry receptivity. Explain how the assets will be used in the future. There is no need to hang your head in shame. You've fought the good fight; you've kept the faith. Sing it. Shout it. Let the people know that God has been yours throughout the decades. Be proud of your church's heritage. Don't let anyone malign the name of your congregation as it pursues retirement with dignity, a God-given right for every believer.

> We are chameleons, and our partialities and prejudices change place with an easy and blessed facility, and we are soon wonted to the change and happy in it.
>
> —MARK TWAIN

QUESTIONS AND ANSWERS

Q: What if we see few benefits from our change/improvement plans and so have few stories to tell?

A: Transitioning well does not guarantee that the changes you've incorporated are the ones that were needed or that you are able to implement them well. Many organizations make transitions that do not yield the results they sought. This can be very disappointing. There will always be naysayers on the sidelines who are waiting for a new idea to fail so they can whisper, "I told you so."

The fact is, stories are not only tools for advancing and even sealing the transition, they are signs that the improvement was effective. If you are not able to harvest legitimate stories of life change, then you have to question whether or not the innovation itself was effective.

But be encouraged: To have attempted a positive idea and failed is much better than to never have tried at all. The big issue is that if you have done what is necessary to make the transition phase as effective as possible, you will significantly diminish the negative fallout if the improvement plan is not what was needed.

Q: How do we avoid making people feel like they were insensitive, old-fashioned sticks-in-the-mud when we selectively pick stories that reflect the benefits of the improvement?

A: We all know that you can say the same thing in different ways and convey different messages. The key is context. If we publicize testimonials as a way of rubbing Builders' and Foundationals' noses in the mud, no one really benefits, certainly not God's kingdom. An attitude of humility and blamelessness goes a long way when telling the stories of those who have benefited from a recent church improvement plan. There are many ways to tell stories. Don't overstress how the new idea has made *the* big difference. Let testimonials from people who have benefited make the statement subtly.

At the same time, don't hold back. Share the good news. No one has access to as many church-life praises and thanksgivings as pastoral staff. Incorporate story sharing as a part of improvement team and church staff meetings, so that you can follow up on them and choose which stories to share with the congregation. Your stories can also include formerly reticent people who have had a change in attitude toward the improvement idea. This is a way of honoring the new by elevating long-term members who have earned the right to speak due to their years of commitment to the church.

Q: Are you saying that if we do not choose to change, we are deciding to die (retire)?

A: This book is about avoiding the death or unnecessary retirement of congregations that fail to pursue improvement ideas. When congregations choose not to change in environments of steadily changing society, they will become dinosaurs. The literature in both the corporate and the church world attests to that fact. The question is a matter of degree and timing.

Therefore we believe it is true: If you don't adapt to your culture (change when needed), your vibrancy and effectiveness to draw in the world will cease.

> There is a certain relief in change, even though it be from bad to worse; as I have found in traveling in a stagecoach, that it is often a comfort to shift one's position and be bruised in a new place.
>
> —Washington Irving

1. Tell your story of how you came to know Christ personally.
2. Tell the story of how someone you know became a Christian (include influential people, events, dates, and benefits).
3. Who are people with a story to tell in your congregation at this time?
4. How could you communicate this story in your local church?
5. Can you think of a church that waited too long to close its doors? What happened?

6. Do you need to retire your church? What are the stewardship factors that help you think about how you are doing?
7. Has your church experienced its best days? Why or why not?
8. How can you go out in a blaze of glory, instead of fading into the horizon?

> Only the wisest and stupidest of men never change.
>
> —CONFUCIUS

Contemplation

When the time drew near for David to die, he gave a charge to Solomon his son.

"I am about to go the way of all the earth," he said. "So be strong, show yourself a man, and observe what the Lord your God requires: Walk in his ways, and keep his decrees and commands, his laws and requirements, as written in the Law of Moses, so that you may prosper in all you do and wherever you go, and that the Lord may keep his promise to me: 'If your descendants watch how they live, and if they walk faithfully before me with all their heart and soul, you will never fail to have a man on the throne of Israel.'"

—1 Kings 2:1–4

Scripture

Read Ecclesiastes 3.

DEVOTIONAL THOUGHT

King David lived a grand life. He led Israel in great victories of faith during times of peace and times of war. Yet David also made mistakes. He died with unfinished dreams: The temple was yet to be built, and the political structure of Israel was not stable even though he anointed Solomon as his successor before he died. There was so much left to be done. But it was David's time, and so he "rested with his fathers."

As we've mentioned, a philosopher has said, "Most people die with their music still in them." It's true—when you think about it, we *all* die with music left in us, especially when we live vibrantly up to the end. There will always be unfinished business. There will always be one more book to write, one more deal to make, one more relationship to enhance. The same is true of churches. There will always be unfinished ministry, community needs, and people who are interrupted in their spiritual growth. That does not mean that the congregation should go on indefinitely. It may mean that the mantle of ministry should move to another person and/or congregation. There will never be a time when everything is accomplished and you can retire with the loose ends tied neatly in a bow. The cycle of life and death just seems to work that way.

What do you feel you need to accomplish personally before your life on earth is over? What does your church need to accomplish corporately before leaving the ministry community?

Prayer

God, help me to live my life to its fullest, while I have life to live. Help me to think of life more as a moving river than a static reservoir. And help me make the most of today, knowing that tomorrow may not come. Give me the boldness to pursue today what you've called me to do and to not procrastinate when times get better. Amen.

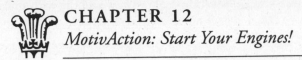

CHAPTER 12
MotivAction: Start Your Engines!

Culture does not change because we desire to change it. Culture changes when the organization is transformed: the culture reflects the realities of people working together every day.

—FRANCIS HESSELBEIN

While the chapters up to now have explained processes and practical tools, we want to close on a more inspirational note. We titled the chapter with a term we coined, *motivaction*. We created this term because churches are notorious for motivating their people but seeing little subsequent behavior change. Motivation that results in changed behavior is productive. Motivation that does not result in changed behavior is often deceptive in that it makes us feel we are doing something when we are not. Feeling the urge and acting on it are not the same. The spelling difference between motivation and motivaction is one letter, *c*. The *c* of course stands for *change*. When intention and activity mesh, motivaction occurs.

One philosopher said, "To motivate without seeing action is the equivalent of walking up a down escalator." Inspiration by itself is at times even counterproductive. We become jaded by one more conference, one more book, and one more guru promoting one more fad diet, church-growth plan, or managerial miracle. This is not a reason to avoid inspirational tools, but rather is a call to attach action to our motivational experiences. We trust that the following sections will be like our tossing a log on the fire, encouraging you to burn hotter and brighter.

CENTRAL CHRISTIAN CHURCH: OUR STORY

Accepting the Ongoing Responsibility

Though Central Christian is now the largest church in Nevada, change is still part of our daily vocabulary. The world is still rapidly changing. I don't think we've begun to grasp how Internet communication is going to affect ministry opportunities and social impact. We will have to continue to adapt to our changing society as a local church, answering questions such as: *How do we maintain high relationship values with so much technology around us? How can we touch people's lives and pray for and listen to them with such a high demand on our time?*

With some successful change under our belt, we now have the responsibility to use what we've received. What does God want to do beyond Central? We feel the burden of greater responsibility now. We want to help other churches navigate change and plant new congregations.

I have had to change as a leader as well. I've been here for fifteen years and these people have heard every sermon I have. I must be mentored, challenged, and instructed in order to stay fresh and to pass on old truths in fresh ways. It would be a terrible thing to think that I've arrived in any way. Once you've survived a change and thrived because of it, a seductive feeling tells you that you deserve a rest, but you can't afford to do that. The ever-evolving world we live in will not allow it.

> What is to give light, must endure burning.
>
> —Victor Frankl

A LETTER OF ENCOURAGEMENT TO PASTORS

For just a moment, put this book down and pick up your Bible. Read Hebrews 11:1–12:3, 12–15. Then consider: If the Scriptures were still being written, your name could very well be a part of this list. Throughout history, God has called men and women to specific ministry tasks that require faith.

We've said it before and we'll say it again: Don't institute change unless you are sure God has called you to it. Only vision-called people should take the risks of disrupting a faith community, which of course improvement and change do. If you are confident in your call from God, then use the ideas in this book and the wisdom of your improvement team and mentors to boldly lead your church into the future. The supply of willing leaders is far short of the demand. There is no time or room for those who would be timid. Too much is at stake. Too many lives are perishing. Too many congregations are languishing. God has not called you to please people, but to do his will in the context of your local ministry.

Remember Acts 5:29: "Peter and the other apostles replied: 'We must obey God rather than men!'" That's not an excuse for behaving like a bull in a china closet, but it is a license to confront those who seem to oppose your performing your duties as a leader in God's family.

Once you begin, continue with wisdom and perseverance. Nothing great was ever accomplished without significant struggle. The life of a leader is often lonely. Don't let anyone convince you differently. In those lonely times, you are fortunate if you have a friend, spouse, or lay leader who will support you. All of us have God to go to:

God has said,

"Never will I leave you;
never will I forsake you."

So we say with confidence,

"The Lord is my helper;
I will not be afraid.
What can man do to me?" (Heb. 13:5–6)

And when you experience conflict, don't feel strange or defective. Once you look behind the conference manuals, glossy brochures, and high-tech videos of even the best teaching churches, you'll find hair-pulling problems, staff challenges, and faith stoppers. Sometimes we do a disservice to each other when we herald fruit-bearing ministries without sharing the tough stories—the accounts of mind-boggling problems and resistance. Know that every church experiences these to some degree.

Hindsight really isn't twenty-twenty. We all tend to forget the pain when it is over. We exaggerate certain details, whether it be how difficult it was ("I used to walk a mile to school in the snow, with holes in my shoes"); how good we were ("The fish was this big"); or how well we responded to a challenge ("No big deal. I jumped on the ER table, put the paddles on my own chest, and jump-started my heart"). Bias, limited perspectives, and personal idiosyncracies taint our views. Letting us forget pain is God's way of helping us endure future challenges. If pain had a cumulative effect, our fear would render us paralyzed.

Marshall Shelley wrote a book years ago titled *Well Intentioned Dragons*. In it he contended that we all have sincere, earnest, spiritual people in our congregations who discourage, intimidate, and defeat us if we let them. No one can question their commitment or sincerity, but their criticisms to our face, power plays, and verbal barbs behind our backs undermine the ministry we are called to transform.[1] Read the life of nearly any biblical, historical, or contemporary leader, and you will find criticism in the process of progress. It's just as much a part of change as food is a part of eating, or air is a part of breathing. If you don't have it in your life, you have to ask the question, "What's wrong with this picture?"

> Don't grumble against each other, brothers, or you will be judged. The Judge is standing at the door!
>
> Brothers, as an example of patience in the face of suffering, take the prophets who spoke in the name of the Lord. As you know, we consider blessed those who have persevered. You have heard of Job's perseverance and have seen what the Lord finally brought about. The Lord is full of compassion and mercy. (James 5:9–11)

One of the best things a leader can do during times of stress and friction is to pray for those on his improvement team. You know that they are undergoing similar stress since they are as concerned as you are about the welfare of their church. The side effect is that prayer for others gets our attention off of our own pain. Praying for those who persecute us preserves our hearts from growing bitter. Praying for our teammates empowers them with God's presence. In John 17, Jesus prayed intensely for his improvement team, that they would stay strong and remain unified during times of stress and confusion. Good spiritual leaders lift their teammates to God as a part of their leading.

Sometimes the only thing that keeps you going as a leader during times of improvement transition is the consistent awareness of the needs around you, the faces of the people your church needs to reach for Christ. I (Gene) will never forget my first Christmas alone after my first wife left. After our candlelight Christmas Eve services, I intended to grab a quick dinner at a drive-through, take it home, do some laundry, and pack for an early morning flight back to the Midwest to spend Christmas day with my family.

I got away from the church about 9:30 P.M. and I was starving. All I had had to eat that day was a sandwich. I started driving around on this unusually cold and windy night and absolutely nothing was open. I thought, *I'll get something in the deli at the supermarket,* but it was closed. I'd never seen the "city that never sleeps" so quiet.

As I drove I began to picture everybody in their homes, celebrating Christmas Eve. All I could think was, *I'm hungry. I'm alone. It's Christmas Eve.* I finally drove out to Sam's Town, a country-western casino. To my surprise, the place was hopping. I walked into Mary's Diner, a fifties-style restaurant, and ordered the blue plate special. The scene was like a bad dream. I thought, *I can't believe it. I just spoke to more than two thousand people and here I am at Sam's Town on Christmas Eve, eating meatloaf and mashed potatoes and gravy, all by myself.* Just when things couldn't get worse, someone put a quarter in the jukebox and Elvis began singing, "Are you lonesome tonight?"

I started laughing to myself, maybe to keep from crying. For a few moments, I had some of the loneliest feelings in my life. But then the thought overwhelmed me, *Gene, here you are, one of the most blessed guys in the world. You have a church that loves you and more close friends than anyone should be legally allowed to have, and you're flying home in the morning to be with your family for Christmas. And if you, of all people, can experience these feelings of loneliness, imagine how tough life is for people who really have reasons to be lonely.* The Holy Spirit used that experience to mark me. As I walked through the casino on my way out, I looked at all the people playing the slot machines and video poker and table games and thought, *They're lonely tonight too. Why else would they be here on Christmas Eve?*

All around us are people who may seem put-together, successful, presentable, and savvy but are really empty and lonely. The world is full of people who need the good news of Christ, which we in the church have been given the responsibility to send. But we can't do it the way we used to, because the people today speak a different language. They do not assume the same values we do. They have not heard the Bible. They are depending on us to do whatever it takes to bring the message of salvation to them in words and pictures and media they understand. That is why you, a Christian leader, initiated change. That is why you are struggling today.

Maybe you wonder, *Gene, during those times when you thought there would be no tomorrow, how did you hang on? How did you get through?* What got me through was remembering that not only do I get to announce to other people that they matter to God, but I matter to God too. I remember the awful nights feeling all alone, feeling like I was a failure, and wondering if this dark season would ever end—much the way a leader feels when his church seems in unending conflict and change seems impossible. I often sang "Jesus Loves Me" quietly to myself to help me remember the love that I'd experienced. That's the love I'm committed to communicating for the rest of my life to anyone who will listen. And when that kind of love is hanging in the balance for a lost world, what else can a leader do but lead through the tough times? We must transition our churches

- because that's where the better fishing is.
- because heaven and hell are hanging in the balance.
- because God has called us to reach the lost around us.
- because the world needs to know Jesus loves them too.

"Whether it is favorable or unfavorable, we will obey the LORD our God" (Jer. 42:6).

A LETTER OF ENCOURAGEMENT TO IMPROVEMENT-TEAM MEMBERS

You are the Joshuas and Calebs of your church. What a privilege to be touched on the shoulder to develop a plan for going into the next promised land of your church. Many of you are staff and lay leaders, people with a heart for improvement who will work alongside your senior pastor or leader. Even though any leader worth his salt will encourage, develop, and motivate his team, as a team member, know that a part of your ministry is to encourage, support, and pray for your leader. Leading can be a lonely venture at times, and self-doubt can plague even the most confident of leaders. So never underestimate the power behind a note of encouragement, an e-mail saying, "We're behind you, Pastor. We must keep going forward. You're doing great." If a pastor/leader senses that you are aloof, disinterested, or at times resistant, it will gnaw away at his spirit.

Every strategic change requires people working together. There are at least six reasons for doing improvement by team:

1. *The power of encouragement.* Everyone goes through times of discouragement. Many church leaders, and perhaps even pastors, are unpaid servants who work other jobs, manage families, and squeeze chunks of time out of their schedules to minister. When we sacrifice our energy with limited,

tangible rewards, it can be doubly hard to stay motivated when stress increases. Be consciously aware of the need to praise, compliment, and encourage each other. We're all good at looking good and keeping a stiff upper lip in public. But have you ever not enjoyed a good word? Make sure team building is a part of every improvement team meeting and do more between official meetings.

2. *The power of accountability.* Your job is to make sure a rogue leader doesn't get out of hand and each team member properly fulfills his or her duties. Without significant levels of loving accountability, we all resort to our old habits, to what is familiar. People working as a team are able to fight that far better than individuals. Whether we call it peer pressure, socialization, or group psychology, the ability to help each other be responsible is a benefit of teams.

3. *The power of broad influence.* Every person has a sphere of influence—social circles in which he or she has impact. The best of us can be influential in only two to four social groups, even though we can participate in more than that. When you work together as a team, you significantly increase the number of social circles impacted by the team members. The cumulative result is far greater influence than one or two individuals can generate, regardless of their influence ability.

4. *The power of creativity.* My (Alan's) grade-school principal used to say, "Two heads are better than one, even if one is a cabbage head." I never understood that silly saying until later in life, when I read study results that showed that groups always outperform individuals in the area of creativity. People play off of each other. Ineffective improvement plans are often the result of one or two professional staffers who dictate how the new idea will be implemented in the old structure. Brainstorming quality ideas is nearly always a by-product of brainstorming a quantity of ideas. Different perspectives can significantly increase the acceptance of an improvement idea.

5. *The power of cumulative effort.*

> Two are better than one,
>> because they have a good return
>>> for their work:
> If one falls down,
>> his friend can help him up.

> But pity the man who falls
> > and has no one to help him up!
> Also, if two lie down together,
> > they will keep warm.
> But how can one keep warm alone?
> > Though one may be overpowered,
> two can defend themselves.
> > A cord of three strands is not quickly broken. (Eccl. 4:9–12)

Synergy arises from combinations of two or more, so there is more power in a group than in the cumulative efforts of the members by themselves.

6. *The power of community.* God does not call us to be Lone Ranger Christians. He calls us to community in part because that's where we grow the most. We receive grace as others use their gifts, and we grow others by using our gifts. In addition, we learn a lot about ourselves when we brush up against differing ideas, opposing opinions, and of course hot buttons. When you work as a team, you will get to know the strengths and weaknesses of other people as well as yourself if you are open-minded. There is such an incredible power that takes place within the community of God when believers work together toward a common goal.

The Bible tells us a wonderful story from the Book of Esther, where a beautiful, Jewish queen saved her people from slaughter. God had placed her in the right place at the right time. Throughout history, he has strategically placed his people to save lives, communicate the gospel, and advance his kingdom. At a crucial moment, Esther's uncle Mordecai told her: "Who knows but that you have come to royal position for such a time as this?" (Esther 4:14). Do not underestimate the uses of your life "for such a time as this." You are not a part of your church just to take up space. You are needed to advance God's work in your ministry through a church that is relevant, bold, and effective. Try hard not to get so consumed with the details that you forget the big picture. You have a calling just as real as your pastor's: "But you are a chosen people, a royal priesthood, a holy nation, a people belonging to God, that you may declare the praises of him who called you out of darkness into his wonderful light" (1 Pet. 2:9).

Periodically, God calls his church to reenlist and renew its commitment to him. Every time, there are those who are among the first to cross the line of going where God wants to go. They respond to Joshua's challenge: "But if serving the LORD seems undesirable to you, then choose for yourselves this day whom you will serve, whether the gods your forefathers served beyond the River, or the gods of the Amorites, in whose land you are living. But as for me and my household, we will serve the LORD" (Josh. 24:15). When God leads, there are usually those who receive that direction before the majority. If you are one of those people, keep the faith, hold your course, and be among those who step across the line.

As you consider the challenge and responsibility, also think about the blessing and opportunity of being on this team. You have a unique vantage point to see God at work in the midst of your church as a whole and in the lives of new and existing people individually. Enjoy your front-row seat. For years to come, people will benefit from your up-front and behind-the-scenes labor of love. You will give in ways that no one knows or acknowledges. You may be misunderstood, gossiped about, and associated with motives and actions that are not yours. Do not become discouraged. Consider it a part of life. All great events in life are typically surrounded with these kind of effects. Rise above them. Keep your attention on the big picture and let your motivation be to seek God's face during this time. The result is that your participation will do as much or more in you than you do in the lives of others. That's the way God grows his people whom he loves.

LETTER OF CHALLENGE TO CONGREGATIONAL MEMBERS

Did you know that the secret to church improvement and change is not in the leader? No. It lies in the hands and hearts of you and your peers. The power of leadership is not in the charisma, vision, or expertise of a few individuals. Where there are no followers, there are no leaders. In other words, if you choose not to go the way of improvement or change, your church will stay the same. Right or wrong, you and your associates will either hold your church back or help it forge ahead. Leaders have to have the support and participation of a critical mass. Even Moses, Joshua, and Caleb, no matter how well they cast the vision, could not force the people to go where they did not want to go. And so Israel wandered for an entire generation.

Most congregations do not have a generation to significantly improve. Most will be dead or on life-support systems if they do not change within the next two decades. Many are already there now. We do not have the leaders or resources necessary to plant enough new churches to reach our nation. We must have people like you, who will come alongside your pastor and lay leaders, to dream a new dream that existing churches will become relevant to the twenty-first century. Far too many kingdom resources are frittering away in so many local congregations that are unwilling to pay the price of significant improvement.

You have a choice. You can choose to stay where you are, enjoying things as they are in your faith community and allowing people around you to wander into eternities without God. Or you can partner with your pastor and progressive members and be a part of improving your church. When the pastor casts the vision of a new thing, you can fold your arms and criticize him or you can nod with approval. You can divide your church by bad-mouthing leadership, pitting people against each other, or you can work in unity, despite differing opinions. Just as your church leaders will be held accountable by God for how they lead your church, you will be held accountable by God for how you respond to them. "Obey your leaders and submit to their authority. They keep watch over you as men who must give an account. Obey them so that their work will be a joy, not a burden, for that would be of no advantage to you" (Heb. 13:17).

Your leaders will not do everything right. They may not communicate well or figure out everything needed for a thorough strategic plan, but you can either be a part of the solution or a part of the problem. There are so many opportunities for you to convey your faith, hope, and love in how you respond to suggested improvement ideas. If you do not like those proposed, volunteer your own. If you do not have the courage to speak up directly with the leadership of your church, you do not have the right to work against them.

Recently, I (Alan) went with my family to the Phoenix Zoo. A stop at the warthog exhibit caught my attention. The sign read, "The female warthog will typically give birth to 4–8 babies, but only 4 will live. The female only has 4 nipples and the young do not share." That last phrase echoed in my thoughts: "The young do not share." The spiritually and emotionally immature (young in development) do not share either. God has spoken to this issue: "Do nothing out of selfish ambition or vain conceit, but in humility consider others better than yourselves. Each of you should look not only to your own interests, but also to the interests of others. Your attitude should be the same as that of Christ Jesus" (Phil. 2:3–5).

No one can deny the personal desire to have his needs met. But there comes a time in the growth of a soul when our growth process takes us away from having our needs met and toward meeting the needs of others. The rest of the passage mentioned above reads:

> [Christ Jesus] who, being in very nature God,
>> did not consider equality with God
>>> something to be grasped,
>> but made himself nothing,
>>> taking the very nature of a servant,
>>> being made in human likeness.
>> And being found in appearance as a man,
>>> he humbled himself
>>> and became obedient to death—
>>>> even death on a cross!
>> Therefore God exalted him
>>> to the highest place
>>> and gave him the name
>>>> that is above every name. (Phil. 2:6–9)

God exalts those who submit their rights to care for the needs of others. For some of you, it may mean swallowing the pride of thinking that the way you're doing ministry now is the best and that you can't learn anything better. For others it may mean studying and experiencing what seems to be working in reaching our culture for Christ. Diverse needs require a variety of methods, aimed at the same goal, to connect people with God. Obviously God is working through different means these days, as you can see in the local congregations that are experiencing incredible fruitfulness. If God is blessing something, who are we to fight it?

> "We are witnesses of these things, and so is the Holy Spirit, whom God has given to those who obey him."
> When [those in the Sanhedrin] heard this, they were furious and wanted to put them to death. But a Pharisee named Gamaliel, a teacher of the law, who was honored by all the people, stood up in the Sanhedrin and ordered that the men be put outside for a little while. Then he addressed them: "Men of Israel, consider carefully what you intend to do to these men. Some time ago Theudas appeared, claiming to be somebody, and about four hundred

men rallied to him. He was killed, all his followers were dispersed, and it all came to nothing. After him, Judas the Galilean appeared in the days of the census and led a band of people in revolt. He too was killed, and all his followers were scattered. Therefore, in the present case I advise you: Leave these men alone! Let them go! For if their purpose or activity is of human origin, it will fail. But if it is from God, you will not be able to stop these men; you will only find yourselves fighting against God." (Acts 5:32–39)

For a few of us, being unified for the kingdom may mean leaving our church home of years rather than being divisive and disrespectful of leadership. This may be one of the most important decisions you've made in your life. You may not like it. You may not understand what the leaders of your church are advocating, but you don't want to be held responsible for bucking God's Spirit if he is moving your church in a certain direction. Perhaps you will not need to leave your church but merely to remain silent, waiting to see how God works his way in your local congregation. Jesus said, "If a kingdom is divided against itself, that kingdom cannot stand. If a house is divided against itself, that house cannot stand" (Mark 3:24–25).

The power that comes from a unified congregation linked arm in arm, and pushing forward to find the lost, is a powerful word picture for change. We give up our schedules, our agendas, to work as a team to find the missing. God has called you to be a part of a group of people, as family and friends, to do what it takes to reach the lost.

Perhaps no one individual has done more to reach the lost in terms of total outreach than Bill Bright. I (Alan) have had opportunities to sit and talk with Dr. Bright on occasion. His humble zeal is infectious. As I write this chapter, I have just finished hearing him speak. He said, "If the gospel is properly presented by Spirit-filled people, half of the people around you will respond to Christ." In addition to the term *Spirit-filled,* the key idea of his statement is *properly.* That means being sensitive to those who are lost, striving to speak their language, and doing our best to help them find Christ wherever they are in their spiritual pilgrimage.

You may be active in your congregation and excited about the great possibilities that people are starting to talk about. But you're wondering, *What can I do? I'm just a layperson; what difference can I make?* All through history, God has used people who seemed powerless but who accomplished significant things because they were employed by God. Remember that Moses had his Aaron and Hur, who held up his arms, allowing Joshua and Israel to win the war (Exod. 17:11–12). If nothing else, you can hold up the arms of the improvement-weary leaders in your midst. Your subtle but active support can make a big difference as you share your faith opinion with an anxious traditionalist, or reach out to your pre-Christian neighbor, or verbalize your excitement about a new idea during formal and informal conversations. Never underestimate the power of your constructive involvement.

Right now, I (Alan) am flying back from a trip to the Midwest. As I was tapping out these words on my laptop, a person handed me some airline snacks. I looked up to see who it was. My server was a man wearing a golf shirt, shorts, and loafers without socks. He's not dressed in the uniform of the airline flight attendants. Who is this rogue servant? Is he a fellow passenger who got recruited? Is he a substitute who did not have his uniform on hand? Regardless, I take the snacks. That's all that matters. You do not need a uniform to serve. If you are a church member who lacks any "official" title, ordination, or role, you are like the flight attendant without a uniform. You're still on the staff. You still have a job to fulfill. You're not a passenger. Get up. There are people who need to be served. The kingdom must progress. It may be the flight of your life!

GOOD-BYE, GOOD BUY

An advertising campaign used the slogan "Good-bye, good buy" to entice shoppers to come in because the sale would not last forever. Every improvement opportunity has a window. If you miss it, you often cannot regain what you could have had. Such is life. By this time, you have either begun the improvement process in your church by working through this book as a team or you have read this book as a way of boning up as a leader. Learn, read, and prepare. But don't let the preparation portion of your improvement process become a reason for missing your window of opportunity. There comes a time when every baby bird must be pushed out of the nest and test its wings. Your improvement plan must take flight. Cover your bases, but move forward.

We hope and pray that the concepts you have learned from this book and the conversations they have generated have been constructive to your ministry. We are excited to see how God will use your improvement team to bring about renewal and revival in your church. For many of you, your finest days are yet to be. God has new things prepared for you. We believe in you and what God has called you to do in his kingdom.

We offer this prayer of blessing for you:

> God, thank you for the pastor, staff, or improvement team member who has read this book. Encourage him or her to do what needs to be done to bring new wine to this church. Help him or her to have the faith to see the invisible and to believe in the milk and honey that lies in the new land.
>
> Help us to realize the calling we have to advance your kingdom. We have changed with the times to share the unchanging message of the gospel of Jesus Christ in a way that is relevant and connects with a culture that is always on the move. We have had the courage to say, "Let's do church in a different way, because if we don't, large numbers of people who are cynical and disinterested in Christianity are never going to know how much God loves them." We have had the foresight to say, "Let's use music that rings with God's truth but is presented in a style that is relevant to the culture." We've had the creativity to say, "Let's incorporate drama and video and creative communication in church services to help people see themselves and understand the significance of the Bible to the issues of their lives." We've had the maturity to say, "We understand that church is not only about us, but it's also about people outside these walls who need to know that they are valuable to God."
>
> And now, we pray that you will give us the wisdom you promise, so that we might know how we should implement these ideas in our church. Give us the grace to be patient with those who are fearful and the courage to move forward in spite of our own insecurities. We are here to serve you, so may your will be done in our faith community. We commit ourselves to you now, regardless of the costs. It is the least we can do for you, considering all you've done for us. In Jesus' name. Amen.

The world we created today has problems which cannot be solved by thinking the way we thought when we created them.

—Albert Einstein

Discussion Starters

1. What part of this book has meant the most to you personally?
2. What ideas in the book have been the most beneficial to your improvement team?
3. What questions do you still have regarding the improvement/change process in your ministry context?
4. How has your church's improvement plan impacted your spirituality thus far?
5. How has your church's improvement plan affected the relationships in your congregation thus far?
6. What surprises have emerged that you did not consider before the process began?
7. How have certain people disappointed you? How have certain people impressed you with their positive response? What have you learned about people in the process?
8. If you have begun to implement the improvement ideas, what benefits have you seen so far?
9. What do you anticipate for the future of your congregation?

APPENDIX A
Recommended Resources

RECOMMENDED RESOURCES

This is certainly not an exhaustive list of the good books on change. At press time, these stand out in our minds as the most significant. Usually the best organizational books appear in business sections first; the competitive demands for better service and profit motivate businesses to find solutions faster than those of us in kingdom work. Hopefully this tide will turn as more church leaders become organizationally savvy and kingdom passionate.

BOOKS ON CHANGE

Kotter, John. *Leading Change.* Boston: Harvard Business School Press, 1996.

Quinn, Robert. *Deep Change.* San Francisco: Jossey-Bass, 1996.

The Price Waterhouse Change Integration Team. *Better Change.* New York: McGraw Hill, 1995.

Bridges, William. *Managing Transitions.* Reading, Mass.: Perseus Books, 1991.

O'Toole, James. *Leading Change.* San Francisco: Jossey-Bass, 1995.

Robbins, Harvey, and Michael Finley. *Why Change Doesn't Work.* Princeton: Peterson's, 1996.

Rogers, Everett. *The Diffusion of Innovation,* 4th ed. New York: The Free Press, 1995.

Conner, Daryl. *Managing at the Speed of Change.* New York: Villard Books, 1992.

Smith, Rolf. *The 7 Levels of Change.* Arlington, Tex.: The Summit Publishing Group, 1997.

Waterman Jr., Robert. *Adhocracy.* New York: W. W. Norton & Co., 1990.

Hultman, Ken. *Making Change Irresistible.* Palo Alto: Davies-Black Publishers, 1998.

Galpin, Timothy. *The Human Side of Change.* San Francisco: Jossey-Bass, 1996.

RESOURCES FOR EVALUATING MINISTRY EFFECTIVENESS

Nelson, Alan, and Stan Toler, *The Five Star Church.* Ventura, Calif.: Regal, 1999.

Spiritual Growth Assessment, published by *Christianity Today, Inc.,* Carol Stream, IL (release date pending).

Barna, George. *Habits of Highly Effective Churches.* Ventura, Calif.: Issachar Resources, 1998.

RESOURCES FOR LEADERS

You can sign up to receive free biweekly leader lessons by Alan Nelson from LeadingIdeas at www.LeadingIdeas.org.

Bennis, Warren, and Burt Nanus. *Leaders.* New York: Harper & Row, 1985. They coined the phrase "Managers do things right. Leaders do the right thing." Great all-around book emphasizing what leaders do and how they think. Read anything Bennis and Nanus write.

Kotter, John. *A Force for Change.* New York: Free Press, 1990. Kotter explains how managers and leaders are different from each other. Read everything Kotter writes.

Nelson, Alan. *Leading Your Ministry.* Nashville: Abingon, 1996.
Hey, I wouldn't have written it if I couldn't recommend it! This book looks at leadership applied to the local church and people skills and explains the differences between the new and old pastoral paradigms as well as the new and old leadership paradigms.

DePree, Max. *Leadership Jazz.* New York: Doubleday Currency, 1992.
Using jazz as a metaphor for contemporary leading, DePree communicates his sage version of strong, servant leadership in creative ways. Read everything DePree writes.

Barna, George, ed. *Leaders on Leadership.* Ventura, Calif.: Regal, 1997.
This anthology gives insights from several respected church leaders. George has a great grasp of the need for leadership in the church as he studies church effectiveness across America. Read everything Barna writes.

Kouzes, James, and Barry Posner. *Leadership Challenge.* San Francisco: Jossey-Bass, 1990.
This is a classic leadership book because of its ageless principles as well as its unique angles of considering leadership effectiveness.

Sanders, J. Oswald. *Spiritual Leadership*. Chicago: Moody Press, 1967.
Sanders has made a wonderful connection between being both spiritual and a leader. He knew his stuff.

Conger, Jay. *Learning to Lead*. San Francisco: Jossey-Bass, 1992.
Conger writes about the art of transforming managers into leaders. Read everything Conger writes.

Hickman, Craig. *Mind of a Manager, Soul of a Leader*. New York: Wiley, 1990.
This book esteems the importance of both leading and managing, careful to emphasize the balance of both in a healthy organization.

Blanchard, Ken, Patricia Zigarmi, and Drea Zigarmi. *Leadership and the One Minute Manager*. New York: William Morrow, 1985.
This reader-friendly book is a quick overview of situational leadership, very applicable for change-oriented leaders.

BOOKS FOR GETTING STARTED

Warren, Rick. *The Purpose Driven Church*. Grand Rapids: Zondervan, 1998.
Hybels, Bill. *Re-Discovering Church*. Grand Rapids: Zondervan, 1995.
Barna, George. *The Second Coming of the Church*. Nashville: Word, Inc., 1998.
Regele, Mike. *Death of the Church*. Grand Rapids: Zondervan, 1995.

RESOURCES ON VISION

Hybels, Bill, and John Maxwell. *Casting a Courageous Vision* (video). South Barrington, Ill.: Willow Creek Association, 1997.

Quigley, Joseph. *Vision*. New York: McGraw Hill, 1993.

Nanus, Burt. *Visionary Leadership*. San Francisco: Jossey-Bass, 1992.

Barna, George. *Without a Vision the People Perish*. (Book and video) Ventura, Calif.: Barna Research, 1991.

Barna, George. *Turning Vision into Action.* (Book and video) Ventura, Calif.: Regal, 1996.

Covey, Steven. *First Things First.* New York: Simon and Schuster, 1994.

Beckwith, Harvey. *Selling the Invisible.* New York: Warner Books, 1997.

CONTACT THE AUTHORS AT:

Alan Nelson, Ed.D.
www.LeadingIdeas.org
10247 E. San Salvador
Scottsdale, AZ 85258

Gene Appel
Central Christian Church
P.O. Box 12505
Las Vegas, NV 89112-2509

Jim Mellado
Willow Creek Association
P.O. Box 3188
Barrington, IL 60011

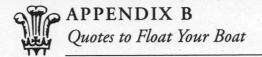

APPENDIX B
Quotes to Float Your Boat

In the writing of this book, our approach has been to synthesize the thoughts of a large number of thinkers and practitioners. We have done a good bit of research from a number of sources but have left multitudes of ideas, illustrations, and quotes on the proverbial editing floor. Sometimes, a pithy sentence or two can communicate an idea while standing alone. As if you haven't had enough by this time, here are a few snack quotes:

> Everybody resists chang—particularly the people who have to do the most changing. Potential leaders too frequently assume that others will recognize the potential benefits of their recommended changes and hence willingly adopt them by simple virtue of the fact that it's the right thing to do. Assuming that people will follow you because you are right is an error that trips up most potential leaders before they ever get out of the starting blocks.[1]

> No one becomes president of the United States (or leader of much of anything) without ambition. Even the saintlike Gandhi, when asked why he had gone to England, would answer, "Ambition!" That thoughtful scholar

of presidential leadership, James MacGregor Burns, reminds us that the real question is, "Ambition for what?" If we insist on perfection of character, we are unlikely to find many exemplary leaders, and our analysis will end in despair.[2]

Contrary to received wisdom, when leaders fail to bring about change, the fault seldom lies in a mistaken choice of how-to manuals. Leaders fail when they have an inappropriate attitude and philosophy about the relationship between themselves and their followers.[3]

Effective change builds on the existing culture. Anthropologists know that culture change occurs in one of two basic ways. The first is revolutionary. The second is evolutionary.[4]

Suppose you are an executive driving down the road with the corporate gas pedal floored, yet competitors are still passing you by. You are pushing your company toward change as hard as you can, but the car will not go more than 35 miles per hour. You bemoan the fact that your competitors are advancing with ease while you're running your vehicle into the ground just to keep up. Desperately, you look for answers. At the next gas station, you receive some good advice: "At twenty-five miles per hour, shift into second gear. You've done all you can in first gear."

So it is with managing change. First gear has served us well, but it now inhibits our performance. The way we used to approach change is no longer viable. As long as we maintain a first-gear mentality regarding change management, limited results are all we can expect. The secret to mastering greater levels of change is not to press harder on a pedal already floored. Traditional methods for managing change will not get us very far in today's world. The answer lies in shifting our perceptions toward change and how it is managed.[5]

Understand that commitment to a major change is always expensive, and that you either pay for achieving it or pay for not having it.[6]

The British Army first faced the Gatling gun (the ancestor of the modern machine gun) in battle. They were stunned by the enormous number of casualties that it inflicted. In the nineteenth century, the British troops still marched onto the battlefield in long lines to face the enemy. Their bright uniforms and antiquated tactics cost them five hundred men in a matter of minutes against the rapid-fire Gatling gun. The last battlefield communique from the field commander reveals the way preconceived notions can block our creative problem solving. The communique requested, "How are we going to get another five hundred men?" For the field commander, there was only one way to march into battle. Replacements were his only concern; alternative maneuvers were not considered.[7]

Whenever a discrepancy exists between the current culture and the objectives of your change, the culture always wins.[8]

The difficulty with perceiving a vision, is that too often the congregation is unable to discern between an authentic calling of Jesus Christ, and its abiding addictions to past ideals, forms, and procedures. Addiction is the right word. Just as an alcoholic, smoker, or drug abuser chronically denies the destructive impact of certain habitual behavior patterns, so also congregations simply cannot "see" that the demise of their congregational health is directly connected to their dogged and misplaced loyalty to the "sacred cows" of former ideals, forms, or procedures. Just as an addict dimly perceives the truth, but then rationalizes that a "gradual" change in the behavior pattern will "eventually" lead to freedom and health, so also many congregations only pretend to transform their church. They "play" with new mission statements, with restructuring the official board, or with experiments in worship, allowing these exercises in futility to deceive their constituency into thinking a genuinely authentic vision has replaced their destructive addictions. "We'll be really different—next year."[9]

In the thriving church system, the number of possible outreach ministries able to be undertaken simultaneously is without limit. Small or large, complex or simple, they all assume two basic principles:
1. Social service and sharing faith occur simultaneously and deliberately.
2. The practical and spiritual needs of the public are more important than the practical and spiritual needs of the church.
Evangelism is at the heart of all ministries, great and small.[10]

A system will produce exactly what it is designed to produce—and nothing else. This statement may seem obvious, but its truth is consistently ignored by countless declining churches. In the panic of church decline, these congregations lament falling worship attendance, reduced revenues, and aging membership—and at the same time they praise the close "family" bonds shared by the remaining members. They can't understand it! "How come people don't want to come to this family-oriented church?"

They blame everything except the one thing that is really wrong: the system!

The "church renewal" efforts of the last twenty years have largely been a failure, because these efforts merely tried to make the old system work better. Congregations sought to improve the organization through restructuring, believing that a more efficient hierarchy would enable the old system to regain vitality.[11]

In any serious change effort, it usually takes no more than several months for pure resistors to show their stripes. Once they do, you must get them out of the way, either through giving them different assignments or, if necessary, firing them. But for every pure resistor, one or more people are always ready to champion change from the outset. If you enlist them effectively, those people will make extraordinary efforts to advance new visions and possibilities.[12]

When the great management guru W. Edwards Deming met with a group of executives, he would often ask, "How many of you have dead wood on your staff?" Most or all the hands would go up. Deming would then shout at the group, "Did you hire them that way, or did you kill them?"[13]

As people in an organization become further removed from being able to influence changes that affect them, their understanding of, commitment to, and ownership of these changes decreases commensurately.[14]

Truly great companies understand the difference between what should never change and what should be open for change, between what is genuinely sacred and what is not. A well-conceived vision consists of two major components: core ideology and envisioned future.[15]

Incremental change is not enough for companies today. These companies do not need to improve themselves; they need to reinvent themselves. Reinvention is not changing what is, but creating what isn't. A butterfly is not more caterpillar or a better or improved caterpillar; a butterfly is a different creature.[16]

Consider this analogy. You inherit your grandmother's house. Unknown to you is one peculiarity: all the light fixtures have bulbs that give off blue rather than yellow light. You find that you don't like the feel of the rooms and spend a lot of time and money repainting walls, reupholstering furniture, and replacing carpets. You never seem to get it quite right, but nonetheless, you rationalize that at least it is improving with each thing you do. Then one day you notice the blue light bulbs and change them. Suddenly, all that you fixed is broken. Context is like the color of the light, not the objects in the room. Context colors everything in the corporation. More accurately, the context alters what we see, usually without our being aware of it.[17]

The CEO makes clear to everyone that the company is in crisis not because people have damaged it, but because good practices have outlasted their useful lives. No blame—that's crucial.[18]

It is better to be 80% correct and make the change happen than to be 100% correct after the opportunity has passed.[19]

Imagine that the change is a cue ball rolling across the surface of a pool table. What are the secondary changes that your change will probably cause? And what are the further changes that those secondary changes will cause?[20]

In one corporation that was relocating its headquarters, the "Transition News" kept everyone abreast of progress, squelched rumors, and featured articles on schools, health care, shopping, real estate, and other aspects of the new location.[21]

Leaders usually assume that all the feedback they will need will come up through regular channels and will be voiced at staff meetings in reply to the question "How are things going?" Such is seldom the case.[22]

GRASS: Guilt, Resentment, Anxiety, Self-Absorption, and Stress. These are the five real and measurable costs of not managing transition effectively.[23]

I define a team as an enthusiastic set of competent people who have clearly defined roles, are associated in a common activity, work cohesively in trusting relationships, and exercise personal discipline and make individual sacrifices for the good of the team. What I often encounter when working with top management "team" is individual self-interest, anger, insecurity, distrust, little cohesion, and continuous political posturing.[24]

Excellence is a form of deviance. If you perform beyond the norms, you disrupt all the existing control systems. You become excellent because you are doing things normal people do not want to do. You become excellent by choosing a path that is risky and painful, a path that is not appealing to others. The question is why would anyone ever want to do something painful? You have already answered this question. You do it because it's right.[25]

Few of us think about the pain suffered by those who dare to serve with both their heads and their hearts. Leadership is nothing like it appears to those who only follow. I suspect that such people have discovered that the pain of leadership is exceeded only by the pain of lost potential.[26]

Remember the elephant training parable. Trainers shackle young elephants with heavy chains to deeply embedded stakes. In that way the elephant learns to stay in its place. Older elephants never try to leave even though they have the strength to pull the stake and move beyond. Their conditioning limits their movements with only a small metal bracelet around their foot—attached to nothing. Like powerful elephants, many companies are bound by earlier conditioned constraints. "We've always done it this way" is as limiting to an organization as the unattached chain around the elephant's foot.[27]

Your new vision is new. That means something else has passed—namely the old vision. Empower the new vision by creating a passage ritual. Stress the good points of the past and optimism for the future. The English do it. At the funeral for a fallen monarch, the English chant, "The King is dead. Long live the King!" This ritual marks the passage of the old ruler—"The King is dead"—and the empowerment of the new ruler—"Long live the King!"[28]

I found that the entrepreneurial spirit producing innovation is associated with a particular way of approaching problems that I call "integrative": the willingness to move beyond received wisdom, to combine ideas from unconnected sources, to embrace change as an opportunity to test limits. To see problems integratively is to see them as wholes, related to larger wholes, and thus challenging established practices—rather than walling off a piece of experience and preventing it from being touched or affected by any new experiences.

Entrepreneurs—and entrepreneurial organizations—always operate at the edge of their competence, focusing more of their resources and attention on what they do not yet know, than on controlling what they already know. They measure themselves, not be standards of the past (how far they have come), but by visions of the future (how far they have yet to go).

The contrasting style of thought is anti-change-oriented and prevents innovation. I call it "segmentalism" because it is concerned with compartmentalizing actions, events, and problems and keeping each piece isolated from the others. Segmentalist approaches see problems as narrowly as possible, independently of their context, independently of their connections to any other problems.[29]

The 7 Levels of Change:
  Level 1: Doing the right things
  Level 2: Doing things right
  Level 3: Doing things better
  Level 4: Stopping doing things
  Level 5: Doing things other people are doing
  Level 6: Doing things no one else is doing
  Level 7: Doing things that can't be done.[30]

Sometimes innovation may just be a matter of getting rid of something.[31]

If change is the natural order of things in modern organizations, so, apparently, is resistance. Indeed, a study conducted by the Center for Creative

Leadership found that only 25 percent of employees embrace the change process. The rest try to actively stonewall it or "talk the talk" without really "walking the walk." One CEO ruefully explained that he had learned from bitter experience that logical arguments were not enough to convince skeptical employees they ought to change their way of doing things. "Logic is important," the CEO said, "but the most important thing is getting it into their hearts."[32]

In developing strong teams, understanding and valuing differences is essential. But in adapting to change, understanding and valuing commonalities is the key. We grow by focusing on how we are unique; we progress by focusing on how we are similar.[33]

If you take the pressure off, groups will revert to their old behaviors. Momentum is an amazing and wonderful force. Like a compass, it keeps you going in the same direction. If the direction you're going is the wrong one, however, momentum will kill you. Momentum, like a magnet, will pull you back in the old direction, the old way of doing things. Change is a temporary force that pulls you in a new direction; but it must be applied continuously until the new behaviors become the norm, the new north. If you take the pressure off too early in a change process, the group will revert to the old way of doing business, old relationships, old behaviors, old processes, old habits.[34]

Say the word "change" to any randomly selected group, and you will likely get three different types of responses. Some throw up their hands and say, "Not again." Others say, "Well, it's about time." The third group will simply throw up.[35]

The key challenge facing us every day: To keep taking the risk of change. . . . But unless you change, and take the risk of failure, you limit your opportunities for success. That's why questioning, probing, and reinventing are so important.[36]

Clergy who are financially and relationally dependent upon their congregation are naturally very sensitive to any voices of unhappiness that might threaten their security.[37]

It is not uncommon for congregations to want growth but not want change (not realizing that the two are inseparable) and to have to wrestle with their calling and self-understanding when growth happens.[38]

Two Jesuit priests both wanted a cigarette while they prayed. They decided to ask their bishop for permission. The first asked but was told no. A little while later he spotted his friend smoking. "Why did the bishop allow you to smoke and not me?" he asked. "Because you asked if you could smoke while you prayed and I asked if I could pray while I smoked!" the friend replied. (Principle: find the right way to get permission to change.)[39]

A mission statement has several key elements:
We are _____ (current role)
Who provide _____ (product or service)
For what reason _____ (purpose—why we do what we do)
To who _____ (customer)[40]

Change is inevitable. Except from a vending machine.

—Bumper Sticker

Life is either a daring adventure or nothing.

—Helen Keller

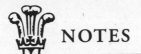

NOTES

Introduction

1. Charles Arn, *How to Start a New Service* (Grand Rapids: Baker Books, 1997), 16.
2. United States Census statistics for 1990 and 1999; *Yearbook of American & Canadian Churches 1990* (Nashville: Abingdon Press, 1990); *Yearbook of American & Canadian Churches 1999* (Nashville: Abingdon Press, 1999).
3. Barna Research Group, "American's Congregations: More Money but Fewer People," December 6, 1999.
4. Charles Arn, *How to Start a New Service*, 23.
5. Barna Research Group, "The State of the Church, 2000," March 21, 2000.
6. George Hunter, *Church for the Unchurched* (Nashville: Abingdon Press, 1996), 20.
7. Ibid., 179.
8. Bill Hybels and Mark Mittelberg, *Becoming a Contagious Christian* (Grand Rapids: Zondervan, 1996).
9. Barna Survey Analysis Report to WCA, from PastorPoll, conducted in October 1999, p. 21.
10. George H. Gallup and Timothy K. Jones, *The Saints Among Us* (Harrisburg, Penn.: Morehouse Publishing, 1992).

Chapter 1

1. Cited by staff at the Church of the Nazarene Conference on Evangelism, Kansas City, Missouri, January 1999.
2. George Barna, *Inward, Outward & Upward: Ministry That Transforms Lives* (Ventura, Calif.: Barna Research Group, Ltd., 1999), 5–6.
3. Ibid., 7.
4. George Barna, *The Second Coming of the Church* (Nashville: Word, Inc., 1998), 1.
5. Mike Regele, *Death of the Church* (Grand Rapids: Zondervan, 1995), 184–85.
6. Robert Quinn, *Deep Change* (San Francisco: Jossey-Bass, 1996), 103.

Chapter 2

1. From a speech given in San Bernadino, California, December 1998.
2. William Bridges, *Managing Transitions* (Reading, Mass.: Addison-Wesley Publishers, 1991), 77.
3. James Collins and Jerry Porras, *Built to Last* (New York: HarperCollins, 1994), 83.
4. James O'Toole, *Leading Change* (San Francisco: Jossey-Bass, 1995), 11.

Chapter 3

1. George Barna, *Second Coming of the Church*, 36.
2. Robert Quinn, *Deep Change*, 170.
3. Everett M. Rogers, *Diffusion of Innovations*, 4th Edition (New York: The Free Press, 1995), 392.
4. William Bridges, *Managing Transitions*, 60.
5. Ibid., 81–82.
6. Ibid., 43.
7. John Kotter, *Leading Change* (Boston: Harvard Business School Press, 1996), 4–14.
8. William Bridges, *Managing Transitions*, 3.

Chapter 4

1. Everett Rogers, *Diffusion of Innovation*, 324–25.
2. Harvey Robbins and Michael Finley, *Why Change Doesn't Work* (Princeton: Peterson's, 1996), 52.
3. Adapted from Everett Rogers, *Diffusion of Innovation*, 232.
4. Harvey Robbins and Michael Finley, *Why Change Doesn't Work*, 2.
5. Ibid., 67.
6. Ibid., 56.
7. Ibid., 56–58.
8. Ibid., 66.
9. William Bridges, *Managing Transitions*, 24–25.
10. Ibid., 24, 25.
11. Ibid., 37.
12. Harvey Robbins and Michael Finley, *Why Change Doesn't Work*, 2.

Chapter 5

1. Harvey Robbins and Michael Finley, *Why Change Doesn't Work*, 45.
2. Unpublished report from the Willow Creek Association performed by Barna Research, 1998.
3. James Belasco and Ralph Stayer, *Flight of the Buffalo* (New York: Warner, 1993).
4. James Collins and Jerry Porras, *Built to Last*.
5. Harvey Robbins and Michael Finley, *Why Change Doesn't Work*, 18–19.
6. Ibid.
7. Ken Blanchard and Drea and Patricia Zigarmi, *Leadership and the One Minute Manager* (New York: William Morrow, 1985).
8. Harvey Robbins and Michael Finley, *Why Change Doesn't Work*, 89.

Chapter 6

1. George Barna, *Without a Vision the People Perish* (Ventura, Calif.: Barna Research, 1991), 12.
2. Burt Nanus, *Visionary Leadership* (San Francisco: Jossey-Bass, 1992), 3.
3. Ibid., 8.

4. Theodore Levitt, *Marketing Imagination* (New York: Free Press, 1986), 166–67.

5. George Barna, *Without a Vision the People Perish*, 57.

6. Ibid., 110.

7. Joseph Quigley, *Vision* (New York: McGraw Hill, 1993), 116.

8. George Barna, *Without a Vision the People Perish*, 113.

9. Burt Nanus, *Visionary Leadership*, 121.

10. George Barna, *Without a Vision the People Perish*, 147.

Chapter 7

1. Price Waterhouse Change Integration Team, *Better Change* (New York: McGraw Hill, 1995), 7–8.

2. Ibid., 4.

3. Ibid., 4–6.

4. Ibid., 5.

Chapter 8

1. Harvey Robbins and Michael Finley, *Why Change Doesn't Work*, 79.

2. Robert Jacobs, *Real Time Strategic Change* (San Francisco: Berrett-Koehler, 1994), 123.

3. Michael Beer, Russell A. Eisenstat, and Bert Spector, "Why Change Programs Don't Produce Change," *Harvard Business Review* (November/December 1990): 92–95.

4. Ken Hultman, *Making Change Irresistible* (Palo Alto: Davies-Black Publishers, 1998), 5.

5. William Bridges, *Managing Transitions*, 15.

6. Ibid., 80.

7. Ibid., 30.

8. Ibid., 52.

9. Ibid., 32–33. I adapted these somewhat.

10. Price Waterhouse Change Integration Team, *Better Change*, 82–83.

11. Ibid., 30.

12. William Bridges, *Managing Transitions*, 52.

13. Ibid., 32.

14. Peter Senge, *The Fifth Discipline* (New York: Currency and Doubleday, 1990).
15. Peter Drucker, *Innovation and Entrepreneurship* (New York: HarperBusiness, 1985), 28.

Chapter 9

1. As cited in William Bridges, *Managing Transitions,* 81.
2. Ibid., 79.
3. Ken Hultman, *Making Change Irresistible* (Palo Alto: Davies-Black, 1998), 154–55.
4. Ibid., 102.
5. Tom Peters, *Thriving On Chaos* (New York: HarperCollins, 1987), 31.

Chapter 10

1. Alan Nelson, *Broken in the Right Place* (Nashville: Thomas Nelson, 1996).
2. Price Waterhouse Change Integration Team, *Better Change,* 17–21.

Chapter 11

1. *Leadership Training Network Level One Training Manual* (Dallas: Leadership Training Network, 1999), 10.
2. Conversation with Leadership Training Network staff member, 1999.

Chapter 12

1. Marshall Shelley, *Well Intentioned Dragons* (Minneapolis: Bethany House, 1994).

Appendix B

1. James O'Toole, *Leading Change* (San Francisco: Jossey-Bass, 1995), 13.
2. Ibid., 34.
3. Ibid., 37.
4. Ibid., 73.

5. Daryl Conner, *Managing at the Speed of Change* (New York: Villard Books, 1992), 42.

6. Ibid., 160.

7. Ibid., 166.

8. Ibid., 176.

9. Thomas Bandy, *Kicking Habits* (Nashville: Abingdon, 1997), 25.

10. Ibid, 85.

11. Ibid., 102.

12. Douglas Smith, *Taking Charge of Change* (Reading, Mass.: Addison Wesly, 1996), 47.

13. Rob Rebow and William Simon, *Lasting Change* (New York: Van Nostrand Reinhold, 1997), 51.

14. Robert Jacobs, *Real Time Strategic Change*, 17.

15. James Collins and Jerry Porras, *Built to Last*, 83.

16. Tracy Goss, Richard Pascale, and Anthony Athos, "The Reinvention Roller Coaster," *Harvard Business Review on Change* (Boston: Harvard Business School Press, 1998), 85.

17. Ibid., 88.

18. Roger Martin, "Changing the Mind of the Corporation," *Harvard Business Review on Change*, 126.

19. Norman Augustine, "Reshaping an Industry," *Harvard Business Review on Change*, 170.

20. William Bridges, *Managing Transitions*, 21.

21. Ibid., 41.

22. Ibid., 42.

23. Ibid., 125.

24. Robert Quinn, *Deep Change*, 161.

25. Ibid., 176.

26. Ibid., 177.

27. James Belasco, *Teaching the Elephant to Dance* (New York: Crown Publishing, 1990), 17.

28. Ibid., 203.

29. Rosabeth Moss Kanter, *The Change Masters* (New York: Simon & Schuster, 1983), 28–29.

30. Rolf Smith, *The 7 Levels of Change* (Arlington, Tex.: Summit Publishing Group, 1997), 13.

31. Ibid., 130.

32. Peter Brill and Richard Worth, *The Four Levers of Corporate Change* (New York: AMA, 1997), 50.

33. Harvey Robbins and Michael Finley, *Why Change Doesn't Work* , 56.

34. Ibid., 80.

35. Ibid., 83.

36. James Champy, *Reengineering Management* (New York: HarperBusiness, 1995), 38.

37. Gilbert Rendle, *Leading Change in the Congregation* (Bethesda, Md.: The Alban Institute, 1998), 13.

38. Ibid., 32.

39. Ibid., 133.

40. Dennis Jaffe and Cynthia Scott, *Getting Your Organization to Change* (Lanham, Md.: Crisp Publications, 1999), 210.